THE YEAST CONNECTION COOKBOOK

WILLIAM G. CROOK, M.D.

MARJORIE HURT JONES, R.N.

SQUAREONE
PUBLISHERS

The information in this book is intended to be helpful and educational. It is not intended to replace medical treatment or diagnosis. If the need be warranted, the reader should consult a medical or health professional.

Square One Publishers
115 Herricks Road
Garden City Park, NY 11040
(516) 535-2010 • (877) 900-BOOK
www.squareonepublishers.com

Library of Congress Cataloging-in-Publication Data
Crook, William Grant, 1917—
    The Yeast Connection Nutrition Guide and Cookbook

    Includes index.
    1. Candida Related Complex. 2. Candida diet—recipes.
    I. Jones, Marjorie Hurt, date.   II. Title.
    89-060269
ISBN 978-0-7570-0059-1

Printed in the United States of America

10   9   8   7   6   5   4   3   2   1

Contents

SECTION THREE   **Other Helpful Information**

This book is dedicated
with warm regards to

C. Orian Truss, M.D.
and
Sidney M. Baker, M.D.

Introduction

Yeast is not a household word, but it should be because it affects so many people. Our practice of taking antibiotics for colds and flu that are caused by viruses and not bacteria and our diets loaded with sugar and refined carbohydrates have made yeast a permanent resident in our bodies.

Having some yeast in our intestines is normal, but when antibiotics destroy the "good" bacteria that normally keep yeast in check, overgrowth begins. Yeast attack and poke holes in the intestinal lining leading to a condition called "leaky gut." Through those holes and into the bloodstream escape 180 different toxic yeast by-products as well as bacterial toxins, and incompletely digested food molecules. Sugar plays an insidious role in this process because it is yeast's favorite food and when it is present in the diet, it makes yeast grow out of control. *The Yeast Connection Cookbook* gives you tools to help get sugar out of your diet.

I didn't learn about yeast overgrowth until my naturopathic training in the early 1980's after I graduated from medical school. In medicine I was only taught that yeast was either a pesky vaginitis or a life-threatening blood infection in hospitalized patients on numerous IV antibiotics. Dr. William Crook was one of the pioneers in the field and in my naturopathic training I learned about his work and began treating yeast in the early 1980's.

In 1986, because I was known as the local expert on treating yeast, I had the honor of being a guest with Dr. Crook on a television talk show called "Speaking Out with Harry Brown" in Toronto. During our ninety-minute program the station's phone lines were flooded with calls. They tabulated 80,000 people trying to reach the show to ask about yeast. In the aftermath, the station received countless requests for transcripts from the public, doctors, and hospital clinics. Dr. Crook and his emphasis on yeast had really struck a chord.

I've even begun to call Dr. Crook's type of yeast Crook's Candidiasis to differentiate it from the medical definition of yeast as a vaginitis or a blood infection.

Crook's Candidiasis encompasses:

1. Yeast in the intestines that overgrow and change from a bud-
   ding state to an invasive state under the influence of antibiotics, birth control pills, cortisone, and a refined sugar diet
   causing intestinal inflammation and leaky gut syndrome
   including symptoms of IBS;

2. Allergic reactions to yeast that cause burning and itching
   of various parts of the body including nasal membranes,
   sinuses, skin, and vagina;

3. Multiple and sometimes severe reactions in the body to
   the almost 180 yeast toxic by-products and waste products,
   either by direct toxic reactions or allergic reactions to
   these yeast by-products as they pass into the bloodstream
   due to leaky gut.

4. Body-wide allergic reactions and toxic reactions to undigested food molecules, bacterial toxins, and parasitic toxins that pass into the bloodstream due to leaky gut.

I never forgot my meeting with Dr. Crook. His generosity and
caring were palpable and his legacy is contained in books such
as the *Yeast Connection Cookbook* and *The Yeast Connection Handbook* which are modern-day classics. The basis of treating yeast
and keeping it under control is diet. There is no drug nor will
there ever be a drug that eliminates yeast or that deals with the
massive toxic reactions that you see in Crook's Candidiasis.

The key to getting yeast under control is to follow a diet that
starves yeast by not feeding them sugar and other foods that they
crave. That's why this book is so important and vital to your success
with a yeast program. And if you repopulate your gut with benefi-
cial organisms called probiotics found in organic yogurt (with no
added sugar) or probiotic capsules you will do even better. You
can learn about the six-step yeast-fighting plan at www.yeastcon-
nection.com.

Since I began treating yeast there have been many breakthroughs
in diet and supplements that make your battle with yeast much
easier. In health-food stores and large supermarkets you can
find numerous wheat-free products; a natural sweetener called
Stevia; non-dairy milks—soy, almond, rice; chemical-free cleaning products and cosmetics. At yeastconnection.com there are
natural supplements that treat vaginitis and yeast overgrowth.
Yeastconnection.com also offers an invaluable series of telecon-

ferences on yeast and wellness that make it much easier for you to begin your yeast-fighting journey and to find support on your way.

I'm honored to be the medical advisor to <u>yeastconnection. com</u> and work with Dr. Crook's daughter, Elizabeth Crook, as we continue his valuable work.

Dr. Carolyn Dean

Foreword

As a health care team involved in diagnosing, treating and counseling people with candida-related health problems, we've helped many patients by changing their diets. Yet, accomplishing needed changes is a difficult task not only for the patient—but for the physician and nurse as well. Fortunately, this book by William Crook, M.D., and Marjorie Hurt Jones, R.N., helps to answer this difficult and perplexing question.

This book is clearly written, well organized and richly illustrated; it helps the person with candida-related health problems, including those with food sensitivities, answer the question "What foods can I eat and which ones must I avoid?"

In addition, Crook and Jones offer practical guidance on a wide variety of dietary issues through an easy-to-understand question-and-answer format. Although dietary advice is given in general terms, we feel this book also addresses the unique needs of individual patients with their own nutritional requirements and allergic profile. This is unfortunately not often the case with many diet cookbooks.

We personally feel this book also puts the anti-candida diet in proper perspective. In our experience, most patients with Candida-Related Complex also suffer from other sensitivities—often to other common foods or food additives. Patients often narrow their diet to avoid obvious food allergens, without properly diversifying their diet. This carries a threefold risk of poor nutrition, new food sensitization and boredom.

We think one of the most outstanding features of this book is the emphasis on *diversification* of foods. A wide variety of foods not only offers optimal nutrition, but lessens the likelihood of new food sensitivities from developing in the future.

Food diversification is emphasized through the extensive recipe section, which offers many recipes for the allergic patient in search of good nutritional hypoallergenic meals. Recipes that are offered are personally appetizing and interesting as well. Recipes are given for difficult situations such as breakfast planning. A particularly helpful section on food preparation is offered for those unaccustomed to selecting and preparing a wide variety of certain foods.

The book is also unique in that it goes one step beyond the usual diet-and-recipe cookbook format. It offers suggestions for a positive psychological perspective for those beginning their journey to wellness through proper diet and nutrition.

In summary, this book offers a rare combination of good reading *and* good eating—enjoy!

George F. Kroker, M.D., FACAI, FAAEM
Leslie Peickert-Kroker, B.S.N., M.S.
La Crosse, Wisconsin

Preface

In the early 1960s, C. Orian Truss, M.D. of Birmingham, Alabama stumbled on the relationship of a candida vaginal infection to fatigue, depression and symptoms in many different parts of the body. During the next fifteen years, Truss continued his observations on candida and reported them for the first time at a medical conference in Toronto in 1977. Although he published his findings in a Canadian health journal in 1978, 1980, 1981 and 1984 and in a book, *The Missing Diagnosis*, only a handful of physicians learned about them.

But, word spread to the public through the press and media and by "networking." During the early 1980s, people all over the world began to learn about the relationship of *Candida albicans* to many chronic health disorders. Countless people found relief using a special diet and prescription and non-prescription antifungal agents.

I learned about candida-related disorders from a patient and, subsequently, from Dr. Truss in 1979. This knowledge changed my life and enabled me to more effectively and appropriately treat many of my difficult patients. Subsequently, it led me to write *The Yeast Connection*, which was first published in December, 1983.

During the next five years, thousands of people from all over the world have written me. And on many occasions, I've been thrilled to hear, "Your book was all about me. Reading it and following your suggestions changed my life!"

Yet, others wrote asking for more information about nutrition. They wanted to know what they should and should not eat to overcome their candida-related health problems and enjoy good health.

Still others asked about food allergies and sensitivities, including how to identify and manage them. Finally, many wanted recipes and menus that would be tasty and which would suit everyone in the family.

To provide this information, I sought the help and consultation of Marjorie Hurt Jones, a professional cook, author and editor whose publications I'd long admired (these included *The Allergy Self-Help Cookbook* (Rodale Press) and a 16-page booklet, *Allergy*

Recipes, Baking with Amaranth,) and I said, "Marge, I need your help in preparing a book which will serve as an authentic, accurate, useful resource for people with candida-related health problems. Because of your experience in originating, combining and testing hundreds of recipes in your own kitchen, please take charge of the recipe section.

"I'm especially interested in providing our readers with recipes and menus which—

- Feature more complex carbohydrates and less protein and fat.
- Contain no sugar, honey, corn syrup, maple syrup or other simple "quick-acting" carbohydrates.
- Feature vegetables of all sorts, that most of our readers know little about. These include arugula, boniata, breadfruit, chayote, daikon, and celery root.
- Tell people how to use the grain alternatives, amaranth, quinoa and buckwheat.
- Help readers with candida-related disorders who have found they're allergic* to many common foods including yeast, dairy products, wheat, corn, eggs, legumes and other foods
- Provide kitchen and family tested recipes for breakfast— perhaps the most difficult meal of the day.
- Will help the food sensitive person rotate and diversify his or her diet."

Marge responded and said,

"I'd be delighted to serve as your collaborator and co-author. And because of the many questions I receive from the readers of my newsletter; I know a lot of people out there need help. So let's get the show on the road."

Four types of allergic reactions have been identified and classified. One of these (Type 1) is mediated through a blood fraction called, "IgE." Reactions of this type produce scratch tests in individuals sensitive to pollens and other inhalants, and much less commonly in individuals sensitive to food. However, many and perhaps most individuals who show the adverse food reactions discussed in this book will not show positive scratch or other immunologic tests.

Some of the mechanisms for these food reactions remain obscure. Since they may not involve antigen and antibody reactions, many physicians prefer to call these food reactions intolerances. hypersensitivities or adverse reactions.

Preface to the Second Edition

When I wrote Section I (Nutritional Information) of this book almost 10 years ago, I talked about many things including the growing chemical pollution of our food supply and I included suggestions to help you "lighten your chemical load."

I also discussed food allergies and the rotated diet and included detailed instructions to help you identify these allergies and lessen their impact on your health.

My advice in these two areas has not changed. Neither have my recommendations about candida-control diets which avoid sugar and other simple carbohydrates. I also continue to warn readers about the health problems which develop in people who eat foods which are high in fats, especially beef, pork, lamb and cow's milk.

I learned about the health problems which develop in people who feast on these foods from the late Nathan Pritikin. Based on his observations, during the last twenty-five years I've eaten less meat and more vegetables, fruits and whole grains. I've also recommended Pritikin-type diets to my family, friends, patients and readers of my books.

Yet, during the 1990s, I've read reports and heard lectures by physicians, nutritionists and other professionals who are concerned about health problems which are developing in people who have focused their attention on "low-fat" or "fat-free" diets. Here's what they say is happening in many of these people.

They're loading up on too many simple carbohydrates including not only sugary food, but breads, pasta and cereals. These foods cause problems of many types including yeast overgrowth.

In addition, a number of observers are saying that high carbohydrate diets cause the "Insulin Resistance Syndrome" which leads to obesity and other disorders.

Here's another problem with the low-fat, high-grain diets. They're often deficient in the essential fatty acids. Still another problem is that people who consume lots of grains may develop gluten intolerance and/or other types of food sensitivities.

Finally, some people may not take in enough of the protein

foods that their bodies need for immunity, stable blood sugar levels, proper hormonal functioning and tissue repair.

Although I continue to urge people to eat lots of vegetables, I agree with the professionals who do not like the government's new Food Pyramid. Here's one reason: it recommends six to eleven servings of grains per day. Accordingly, in the second edition of this book, I've rewritten my comments on proteins, fats and carbohydrates.

I've also replaced out-of-date material with new information and Marge Jones has reviewed and updated a number of her recipes. We hope you'll enjoy and be helped by this book and we'll appreciate your comments.

William G. Crook, M.D.
Marjorie H. Jones, R.N.

October, 1997

What This Book Is All About

This book provides you with the latest nutritional information about the foods you should eat and those you must avoid to control candida and regain your health. It is also designed to serve as a companion to the third expanded and updated paperback edition of The Yeast Connection *and to provide more information and help for individuals with food allergies and other sensitivities.*

It is also written for anyone interested in selecting, preparing and eating foods which promote optimal health.

In the Introduction, I review new information you need if you want to conquer your yeast-connected health problems. I especially comment on the importance of diets containing less fat and less protein and more complex carbohydrates, especially vegetables. I also discuss the importance of food sensitivities in causing symptoms in patients with candida-related disorders.

In the chapter entitled "Are Your Health Problems Yeast Connected?" you'll find an improved and more concise history questionnaire.

The history is important in indicating the possibility that your health problems are related to the common yeast *Candida albicans.* Yet, I stress that you should go to your physician for a review of your medical history, a careful physical examination and appropriate laboratory tests before assuming that yeasts are the main cause of your problems.

In my chapter on proteins, carbohydrates and fats, I point out that your body needs a variety of foods to fulfill your requirement for energy and to repair your body tissues. I included the comments of professionals who have become concerned about the "craze" over low-fat, high-carbohydrate diets.

There are also questions and answers about candida-related health problems. Included is information about *Candida albicans,* where it is found and how it is related to disorders in distant parts of the body. I also review the factors which promote the development of yeast-connected health problems, and summarize the steps you need to take to regain your health.

In "What to Eat and Drink—and What to Avoid," I discuss foods that are good for you and some that aren't. In this section I talk about vegetables, meats, grain alternatives, eggs, water, yeast-containing foods, fruits, nuts, seeds, coffee, teas, alcoholic beverages, diet drinks, dry cereals, grains and milk.

In the next chapter I talk even more about vegetables, milk, yogurt, bread, chicken and fish.

Many of today's foods are chemically contaminated. I discuss this subject in the chapter "The Chemical Problem." I list foods that are usually chemical contaminated, plus those which are less apt to contain chemicals. I also give you suggestions about what you can do to obtain safer foods, both for yourself and for others in your community.

In the chapter "Obtaining the Foods You'll Need," I suggest that you clean out your kitchen and get rid of nutritionally deficient foods. And I give you suggestions for selecting and purchasing better food.

Later, I discuss food allergies and rotated diets.

Then in the chapter entitled "Getting Started," I give you detailed instructions for carrying out a trial diet. In question-and-answer form I tell you how to eliminate foods you may be sensitive to (especially milk, wheat, corn, eggs and yeasts).

I also give you instructions for returning the eliminated food to your diet and noting which ones cause reactions. Menus and meal suggestions are included to tell you what you can eat while you're carrying out your elimination diet.

In the final chapter of the first section, "Moving Ahead," I provide you with easy-to-follow instructions for the weeks and months after you've completed your trial elimination diet.

Section 2 of this book was written by my collaborator and co-author, Marjorie Hurt Jones, R.N., a professional cook, author and nutrition counselor. In introducing this recipe section, Marge refers to her own candida- and allergy-related problems. And she said,

"I want to emphasize that my own recovery required more than a special diet."

Yet, she also says,

"If you really want to enjoy better health, planning and preparing nutritious meals is the place to start."

In discussing her special recipes, she acknowledged that many folks who look at the list of foods to avoid are apt to wail,

"What's left for me to eat?"

In responding, Marge points out that her recipes feature vegetables of all sorts, a variety of grains, plus the grain alternatives amaranth, quinoa and buckwheat. She designs her recipes so that they focus on foods most people can eat and enjoy.

The recipes are divided into the following groups: Breakfasts, Lunches, Breads, Soups, Salads, Dressings, Fish, Vegetables, Main Dishes, Desserts and "Etc." Marge introduces each section with helpful comments. Her detailed instructions for selecting and preparing foods will enable even the most inexperienced cook to obtain professional results.

In Section 3, "Other Helpful Information," you'll find information on techniques and ingredients. You'll also find detailed instructions for the person with severe and persistent yeast-related health problems, including those with multiple food sensitivities.

Included in these instructions are food lists and menu suggestions for a four-day rotating, diversified diet. Also included in Section 3 are a listing of food sources, a suggested reading list and references.

SECTION 1

Nutritional Information

Introduction

If you want to overcome a yeast-connected health problem, you must change your diet. Yet, deciding what to eat and what not to eat isn't easy. Here's why: Many professionals who have studied and written about yeast-connected health disorders give different answers to the question "What is the best diet?"

Candida pioneer C. Orian Truss, M.D., in his second paper, emphasized the importance of "avoidance" measures which are needed to control candidiasis. And although he recommended a low-carbohydrate diet, he also noted that . . .

"Many patients are allergic to cereal grains . . . (and) . . . carbohydrate restriction may eliminate . . . food allergens from the diet."

Following the lead of Dr. Truss, in the first edition of *The Yeast Connection* (published in December 1983), I included a low-carbohydrate diet with a total carbohydrate content of less than 100 grams per day. I listed the carbohydrate content of foods and suggested that my readers count carbohydrates.

Nevertheless, because the late Nathan Pritikin taught me that diets containing 350 grams (or more) of complex carbohydrates promoted good health, I didn't like to recommend *only* a low carbohydrate diet, especially for the long haul.

So I included a second diet, the candida-control diet. This diet restricted sugar, corn syrup, fructose, honey, white flour, white rice, raised breads, cheeses, dried fruits and other foods containing yeast and molds. But it did not limit complex carbohydrates.

During 1984, as I gained more experience in treating my own patients and learned from the experience of others, I modified my diet recommendations. And in the second edition of *The Yeast Connection* I said,

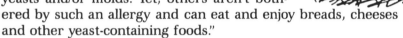

> "Limit fruits . . . especially during the early weeks."

Here's why: Fruits, in spite of their fiber content, are readily converted into simple sugars in the digestive tract, thereby encouraging the growth of *Candida albicans*.

During 1985 and early 1986, several consultants, including John Rippon, Ph.D., of the University of Chicago, commented,

> "Many people with candida-related health problems develop symptoms when they eat a yeast or mold containing food. Such symptoms are caused by an allergic reaction to yeasts and/or molds. Yet, others aren't bothered by such an allergy and can eat and enjoy breads, cheeses and other yeast-containing foods."

Based on this information, I again revised my dietary recommendations in the third, expanded, updated paperback edition of *The Yeast Connection*, which I completed in the summer of 1986.

During the late 1980s and all through the 1990s, I continued to receive hundreds of letters each month from people with candida-related health problems. Many asked for the names of doctors who would listen and help.* Others expressed gratitude. Still others wanted more information about diets.

Thirty-eight-year-old Sarah B. wrote,

> "I suffered for years with fatigue, depression, PMS, headache, digestive disturbances, bladder infections, irritability and the feeling of being 'spaced out'. I consulted many doctors and was given different medications. Yet, my symptoms continued to plague me and get worse. Because examinations failed to reveal the cause of my symptoms, I felt like a hypochondriac.

---

*In 2000, the International Health Foundation (IHF) completed the following new publications: A 36-page booklet for adults, *Information for You* which includes a list of health professionals who have expressed an interest in treating patients with yeast-related problems; and a 24-page booklet, *A Special Message for the Health Professional* which is designed for you to show your own health professional. To obtain these booklets, send a $25 donation to IHF, Box 3494, Jackson, Tennessee 38303. See also the IHF section on my website, *www.candida-yeast.com*.

"Today with the help of an interested physician and a knowledgeable, kind and compassionate nurse on his staff, I'm 90% well. I've been on a sugar-free, yeast-free diet, antifungal medication, linseed and primrose oils, vitamins, minerals and *Lactobacillus acidophilus*. Thank you for writing *The Yeast Connection*. It really helped me. Yet, I'd love more meat-free recipes."

To obtain more information about diets, in December 1986, I sent a questionnaire to physicians, nurses and patients. Here are the questions I asked:

1. Do potatoes, yams, peas, beans and other high-carbohydrate vegetables promote candida?
2. Do grains cause problems?
3. Do you feel the grams of carbohydrates should be counted?
4. Does everyone with a candida-related health problem need to avoid breads, mushrooms, cheeses, condiments, leftovers and other foods containing yeast?
5. Food allergies and/or sensitivities occur commonly in people with yeast-related health problems. In your experience, what foods cause the most sensitivity reactions?
6. Do food sensitivities improve following anti-candida treatment?
7. Most people like sweetened foods. In advising your patients, what do you recommend?
8. What diet instructions do you give your patients for the long haul after they have been on your treatment program for several months?

The responses I received were interesting and varied. The majority recommended:

1. Avoiding sugar and refined carbohydrates.
2. Eating more complex carbohydrates.
3. Eliminating fruits during the early weeks of the diet.

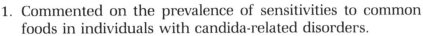

All respondents:

1. Commented on the prevalence of sensitivities to common foods in individuals with candida-related disorders.
2. Pointed out that while sensitivity to yeast-containing foods occurred in half their patients, the remaining half tolerated yeasty foods.

I read and reread these responses and dozens of others. I also visited by phone and in person with a number of my colleagues who generously shared their knowledge with me. I also read a number of excellent references on nutrition in the medical and lay literature.

Based on feedback from my consultants, and information I obtained from other sources, I again realized the importance of what I had learned from the late Nathan Pritikin: *High-protein and high-fat diets play an important role in causing many chronic health disorders, while high–complex-carbohydrate diets promote good health.*

In a January 1987 conference in San Diego, Sidney M. Baker, M.D., in discussing yeast-related illness in the gut and the importance of good bowel flora, said in effect,

> "If we're trying to promote good health, we should not be putting people on low-carbohydrate diets with the idea that we're 'starving the yeast.' Eating a diet rich in complex carbohydrates is the best way to promote normal bowel flora in the person who has some immune dysfunction."

Later in 1987, I became more and more aware of the horrendous chemical contamination of foods of all kinds, including chicken, fish, watermelon, strawberries and other foods most Americans had been led to believe promoted good health.

I also discussed candida-related health problems with Elmer Cranton, M.D., Harold Hedges, M.D., George Kroker, M.D. and Leslie Peickert-Kroker, R.N., and other knowledgeable professionals and I became even more convinced that *food sensitivities* play a major role in causing symptoms in patients with CRC (Candida-Related Complex).***

So it became obvious to me that readers of *The Yeast Connection* and other folks with CRC and other chronic health disorders, needed more and better information about foods they should and should not eat, to regain and maintain their health. I felt that they also needed more specific instructions on how to identify and avoid foods they were sensitive to, how to shop for chemically less contaminated foods and finally how to prepare them.

My co-author, Marjorie Jones, and I have worked to provide you with this information. We sincerely hope we have accomplished our goal and that this book will help you change your life and your health.

---

*The important role of food sensitivities was discussed by a number of speakers at the September 1988 Candida Update Conference in Memphis. Included among those who discussed CRC and food sensitivity were Robert Dockhorn, M.D., Sherry Rogers, M.D., Leo Galland, M.D. and John Crayton, M.D. (Professor of Psychiatry, Loyola Medical School, Chicago). In his presentation, Dr. Crayton said, "Reports have emerged which support adverse reactions to foods with the presence of an overgrowth of *Candida albicans*. The diagnosis is usually made on the basis of a clinical picture characterized by fatigue, weakness, depression and a variety of somatic problems which may involve every organ system—

—We studied a group of patients recruited for a research project addressing the relationship between food intolerance and brain dysfunction.—Antibody responses to *Candida albicans were determined for three antibody classes—Symptomatic subjects had significantly higher anti-candida antibodies of the IgG and IgA classes compared with controls—*

—The data suggests that food-intolerant-polysymptomatic subjects have higher antibody levels to candida antibodies than asymptomatic controls."

***The new name, CRC, or Candida-Related Complex,* was suggested by George Kroker, M.D., La Crosse, Wisconsin, to apply to individuals with candida-related health problems. Previously, many different names had been used to label these individuals, including: Chronic Candidiasis, Chronic Polysystemic Candidiasis, Candidiasis-Hypersensitivity Syndrome, the Yeast Syndrome and "Candida."

Are Your Health Problems Yeast Connected?

If you've read books which deal with yeast-related health problems, you need not fill out this questionnaire.

However, if this is a new concept for you, answering the questionnaire can be the first step in changing your life. If your score is high, you'll need to read my 1995 book, *The Yeast Connection and the Woman* and my 1997 book, *The Yeast Connection Handbook*.

This questionnaire is designed for adults who suspect their health problems may be yeast connected. If your answer is yes to any question, circle the number in the right-hand column. When you've completed the questionnaire, add up the points you circled. Your score will help you determine the possibility (or probability) that your health problems are candida related.

A. Have you taken repeated or prolonged courses of tetracyclines, sulfa drugs, Keflex, ampicillin, amoxicillin, Ceclor or other broad-spectrum antibiotic drugs?   **4**

ANTIBIOTICS

B. Are you bothered by recurrent vaginal, prostate or urinary infections?   **3**

C. Do you feel worse on damp days or in musty, moldy places?   **3**

D. Have you taken repeated or prolonged courses of prednisone, Decadron, cortisone or other steroids (including those administered by nebulizers such as Vanceril and Beconase)?   **2**

E. Are you bothered by fatigue? Are you so tired that you feel like 34-year-old Linda, who wrote, "I could even sleep on a bed of nails"?   **2**

F. Are you blue and depressed—so depressed you sometimes feel life isn't worth living?   **1**

G. Are you bothered by headaches, irritability, memory loss or a feeling of being "spaced out"? 1

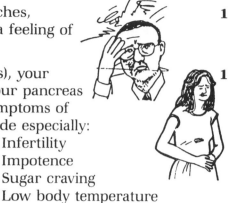

H. Are your ovaries (or testicles), your thyroid, your adrenals or your pancreas working as they should? Symptoms of hormone disturbances include especially: 1

PMS	Infertility
Menstrual irregularities	Impotence
Loss of sex interest	Sugar craving
Loss of orgasm	Low body temperature

I. Are you bothered by digestive problems, especially bloating, belching, rectal gas, constipation, diarrhea or abdominal pain? 1

J. Does your skin itch, tingle or burn? Is it unusually dry? Or are you bothered by hives, psoriasis or other rashes? 1

K. Do your muscles, bones or joints bother you? Aching? Weakness? Stiffness? Swelling? 1

L. Are you unusually sensitive to tobacco smoke, perfumes, colognes or fabric store odors? 1

M. Do some foods disagree with you—or trigger your symptoms? 1

N. Have you taken birth control pills? Did the pill provoke symptoms? 1

O. Have you been checked carefully by two or more physicians and given one (or more) of the following answers? 1

    a. "There is no organic explanation for your complaints."

    b. "You must have an emotional problem. You need to see a psychiatrist."

    c. "Most of your symptoms are due to stress."

    d. "I'll put you in the hospital again and repeat all of your tests."

Scoring for Women:

If your score is 8 or more, your health problems are *probably* yeast connected.

If your score is 12 or more, your health problems are almost *certainly* yeast connected.

Scoring for Men:

If your score is 6 or more, your health problems are *probably* yeast connected.

If your score is 10 or more, your health problems are almost *certainly* yeast connected.

Note:

Many of the symptoms listed in this questionnaire may be related to other causes. So, before concluding that your health problems are yeast connected, you should go to your physician for a careful physical examination and appropriate laboratory studies and/or other tests.

As pointed out by Ray C. Wunderlich, M.D., of St. Petersburg, Florida,

> "Desirable at all times is a balanced approach that holds a healthy respect of *Candida albicans*. . . . At the same time, one does not wish to overlook the many other health departures that invite the candida syndrome.
>
> "Those who suspect that they have symptoms due to candida overgrowth must not plunge headlong into a quest for a 'magic bullet.' Best and most long lasting health will be fostered by careful inquiry into yeast, but also, into psychological, nutritional, allergic, degenerative and toxic factors."

Comments About Proteins, Fats and Carbohydrates

 To fulfill your requirements for energy and to build, maintain, and repair your body tissues, you need to eat a variety of foods. Good foods promote good health and poor foods play an important role in causing disease.

To understand how your body works, let's compare it to an automobile. To "run" smoothly, your "motor" requires the right kind of fuel, and complex carbohydrates are essential ingredients. They provide calories for energy plus fiber, vitamins, minerals and other nutrients.

If you do not provide your car with the right fuel, it won't run.

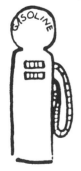

And it won't start again until you fill it up.

Your body—like your car, won't "run" as it should if it doesn't receive the proper fuel.

Your body's "motor" is made of millions of cells. A cell looks this:

The food you consume contains many different substances. These include carbohydrates, proteins, fats, fiber, vitamins and minerals. It is digested, broken down and separated into different nutrients, including glucose. Glucose is the main fuel that feeds your brain and all of the cells of your body.

Glucose is carried to millions of cells in your body by your bloodstream. Your heart pumps the fuel.

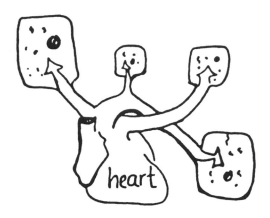

When you're healthy and your body receives a steady supply of fuel, it runs smoothly. You feel calm, alert, energetic and satisfied. These good feelings come when your blood glucose (sugar) is maintained within a normal range.

The foods you eat regulate your blood sugar.

Your brain, pancreas, liver and adrenal glands also play a part in regulating it.

Your Brain
(the "control tower")

Your Pancreas
(manufactures *insulin*)

Your Liver
(stores *glucose*)

Your Adrenal Glands
(manufacture many important hormones)

PROTEINS

During the last hundred years, more changes have taken place in our western civilization than during previous thousands of years. These changes have affected every part of our lives, including what we eat. Our agrarian forebears—even as recently as the early part of the twentieth century—ate more plant foods than animal foods. Yet, beginning after World War I, westerners—especially Americans—fell in love with meat, dairy products, eggs and "high protein" diets. We somehow came to feel that such diets were good for everybody.

Many people seemed to feel that they needed to consume high protein foods at every meal. And a typical menu for many families included ham and eggs for breakfast, a turkey sandwich for lunch and a hamburger or a chicken for supper. In addition, some people would drink a glass of milk with each meal and have a dish of ice cream at bedtime. Such diets, which featured high protein animal products, also were were also high in fat.

Excessively High Protein Diets Aren't Good for You

Beginning in the 1950s, medical reports were published which showed that heart disease, stroke and other blood vessel diseases were the number one cause of death and disability in Americans. Among these studies were autopsy reports of Caucasian and Oriental soldiers in their early '20s, who were killed in battle during the Korean War.

Here's a brief summary of these reports: All of the Caucasians showed deposits of cholesterol and other materials in their arteries and in some 25% of the soldiers, some of their small arteries were blocked. By contrast, the arteries of the Orientals showed none of these changes. They were clean and wide open.

Other studies of Orientals living in Asia showed that they rarely developed heart and blood vessel problems. Looking at these findings, some observers concluded that Orientals were genetically less apt to develop these diseases. Yet, still other studies showed that second and third generation Orientals who lived in America developed as much vascular disease as their Caucasian neighbors. The obvious explanation: Orientals living in Asia ate more vegetables and seafood while those living in America consumed the typical high-protein, high-fat American diet.

Nathan Pritikin, A Nutrition Pioneer

The increasing incidence of heart disease concerned many people, including Nathan Pritikin. This California businessman began urging people to change their diets. And in several best-selling books and on two programs on CBS: "60 Minutes" in the 1970s, Pritikin urged people to eat more vegetables, fruits, grains and fewer animal products.

He also founded the *Longevity Research Institute* in California. At this institute, people with disabling heart problems and other chronic diseases, were put on a one to two month exercise and diet program. The diets featured vegetables, fruits and grains and contained 10% protein, 10% fat and 80% complex carbohydrates.

Pritikin and his physician colleagues demonstrated that many individuals with serious vascular diseases regained their health without drugs or surgery. They also found that some 80% of people with adult-onset diabetes were able to throw away their insulin syringes and their pill bottles.

At a nutrition conference in Florida, I met and visited with Pritikin and I was impressed by what he said. We began to correspond and I became one of his "disciples." In the mid-1970s, Pritikin invited me to become a member of the advisory board of his institute, and I attended two of his conferences.

The presentations I heard and the people I talked to led me to recommend the Pritikin diet to all of my adult patients and to my friends and relatives. And, in the first edition of *The Yeast Connection* which was published in 1983, I told the stories of two of my friends whose lives were turned around when they followed Pritikin's program.

High Protein Diets May Contribute to Osteoporosis

According to a number of reports I've read, people who consume high protein diets put out more calcium in their urine. In discussing the mechanisms in his book, *Food For Life*, Neal Barnard, M.D., stated that in countries where people consume a lot of milk and other dairy products, there is actually *more* osteoporosis than in other countries.

In documenting his statement, Barnard cited studies of pre-menopausal women which showed that high calcium diets did *not* lead to stronger bones.

In his 1994 book, *Preventing and Reversing Osteoporosis*, nutrition authority, Alan R. Gaby, M.D., said,

> The American diet tends to contain too much, rather than too little, protein. Studies have shown that excessive dietary protein promote bone loss . . . the effect of dietary protein in osteoporosis, might be explained in part by the phosphorus content of many high protein foods.*

More Support for Lower Protein Diets

During the 1980s and 1990s, John McDougall, Sadja Greenwood, Dean Ornish and other physicians began to write and talk about the importance of diets containing less protein and fat and more complex carbohydrates.

In her 1992 book, *Menopause Naturally*, Greenwood, an assistant clinical professor at the University of California Medical Center in San Francisco, urged women to use meat as a flavoring agent, rather than as a centerpiece of the meal, and she said,

> You can eliminate milk, eggs and all animal proteins from your diet and still be healthy in your adult years. Complete vegetarians, known as vegans, get their calcium from broccoli, kale, collards and other plant foods (and all the protein they need in beans and whole grains.)

And in his best-selling 1997 book, *Eight Weeks to Optimum Health*, Andrew Weil said:

> The dietary changes recommended in the Eight Week-Program are intended to move you in the direction of eating less fat (especially less saturated fat), less animal protein and more complex carbohydrates including grains, fruits and vegetables.

---

*Gaby, A.R., *Preventing and Reversing Osteoporosis*, Primer Publishing, Rockland, CA; p. 15.

Some People May Not Take In Enough Protein

On commenting on protein requirements, nutrition authority, Beatrice Trum Hunter said,

> We need adequate amounts of quality protein for good health. The amounts may vary with age and digestive efficiency. The higher the quality of the protein, the less we need. The quality is measured by "protein efficiency rate," and protein from animal sources has better quality than protein from plant sources.

In commenting on soybeans as a source of protein, Hunter pointed out that soybeans should be used only in fermented forms such as tofu and tempeh because the highly processed forms (textured vegetable proteins) are low in quality.

Is There a Place for Animal Products in Your Diet?

The answer you get depends on whom you ask. In my opinion, which I've formed after reading many different articles and books and interviewing a number of different people—the answer is "yes." But choose the sources of the protein products you eat carefully. I have several concerns about animal foods.

- Most of them, especially beef, pork, lamb and whole cow's milk, are loaded with saturated fat. (You'll find further comments on animal foods on pages 57, 61, 63, 65-68 and 69-73.)
- They contain high levels of pesticide residues. (You'll find a discussion of the reasons on pages 79-80.)
- Animals are often injected with hormones and/or given antibiotics.

FATS—GOOD AND BAD

High fat diets aren't good for you

During the 1990s, America has jumped on the low-fat bandwagon. As you look at TV or read your newspapers and magazines, you'll see dozens of ads each week which state, "fat free," "low-fat," or "reduced fat."

Reducing your intake of luncheon meats, sausage, fat cuts of meat, butter and mayonnaise is a good idea. So is avoiding margarine and other foods which contain partially hydrogenated fats and oils. If you'll take a look at the labels of boxes and cans on the shelves of your supermarket or convenience store, you'll find that most contain partially hydrogenated oils. Here are a couple of examples: Triscuit baked whole wheat wafers contain partially hydrogenated soybean oil, and Zesta saltine crackers contain partially hydrogenated soybean and/or cottonseed oil.

Why do food processors hydrogenate fats and oils they put in these products? This process allows them to start with cheap, low-quality oils and turn them into products that will not spoil on the grocery shelf.

Why are these products bad for you? There are many reasons. Here are the comments of Udo Erasmus,

> Partial hydrogenation produces margarines, shortenings . . . and partially hydrogenated vegetable oils. These products contain large quantities of *trans*-fatty acids and other altered substances, some of which are known to be detrimental to health because they interfere with normal biochemical processes.*
>
> *Trans*-fatty acids have been shown to increase cholesterol, decrease beneficial high density lipoprotein (HDL), interfere with our liver's detoxification system and interfere with EFA function.

Here are other reasons why high-fat diets aren't good for you:

1. Most fats that people consume in quantity everyday contain no vitamins, minerals, fiber or essential fatty acids.
2. Fats are rich in calories (270 calories per ounce as compared to 120 calories per ounce for carbohydrates and proteins).
3. High-fat diets increase your chances of becoming overweight and of developing vascular diseases (including high blood pressure, heart disease, stroke, blocked arteries in the leg, diabetes and other degenerative diseases).
4. High-fat diets increase your risk of developing certain cancers, especially cancer of the colon, breasts, endometrium (lining of the uterus), ovaries, pancreas, lungs and probably also the prostate.
5. Chemical toxins, including DDT and other insecticide resi-

---

*Page 103, Erasmus, U., *Fats That Heal and Fats That Kill*, *Alive Books*, Edition, 1993)

dues, are concentrated and stored in the fat tissue of animals. So when you eat fat-containing bacon, steak, pork chops or chicken (with the skin on it), you're taking in more chemical toxins.*

Some Fats Are Good For You

You should not avoid all fats because (as is the case with carbohydrates) there are good fats and bad ones. The good ones are called essential fatty acids (EFAs), and you need them in order to enjoy good health.

These good fatty acids are found in plants and their seeds, including flaxseed (linseed), walnut, olive, sunflower, safflower, corn, canola and evening primrose. They're also found in the fat of cold-water fish, including salmon, mackerel, sardines, tuna and herring.

In a chapter of his 1997 book, *Detoxification and Healing: The Key to Optimal Health*, Sidney M. Baker, M.D., of Weston, Connecticut, pointed out that "too much of the wrong kind (of fat) is bad . . . but too little of the right kind is just as bad. In no other area of nutrition is the adage, 'You are what you eat' more true."

In his continuing discussion, Dr. Baker pointed out that our bodies are composed of billions of cells of various sizes, shapes and functions. And the good fats and oils (EFAs) provide a waterproof boundary for each cell and make these boundaries more flexible. This allows the cells to carry out their normal functions in preserving good health.

The good fats and oils (EFAs) also help your body store energy and provide the raw materials you need to make an important group of hormones, the *prostaglandins*. And as you may have read and heard, consuming more fish oils can help people with heart problems, arthritis, menstrual problems and other disorders.

The most important EFAs are divided into two groups (Omega-3 and Omega-6). These rather strange names are derived from their chemical configuration. Let me explain. EFAs are composed of a string of 18 to 20 or more carbon atoms. You might compare them to a string of pearls.

---

*See pages 71–80, for more information about the chemical contamination of foods.

Most of the pearls (carbon atoms) are connected by a single link. Yet, two to six of these atoms are linked by a double connection, or "double bond." The Omega-3 fatty acids have a double bond on the third carbon atom in the chain, and the Omega-6 fatty acids have a double bond on the sixth carbon.*

In discussing the importance of essential oils, Baker tells the story of Andrea, a nine-year-old girl who was referred to him because of unpredictable outbursts of rage. She was also troubled by painful, dry and cracked skin on her feet. In evaluating Andrea, Baker found that she was deficient in the Omega-3 fats, a major component of flaxseed oil. After taking a tablespoon of flaxseed oil daily for two weeks, her feet became "completely normal" and her outbursts of rage stopped within a month.

According to Baker, most people with fatty acid problems are deficient in Omega-3 oils. Here is a list of symptoms commonly seen in these people:

1. Cracking fingertips—worse in the winter.
2. Patchy dullness of the skin.
3. Mixed oily and dry skin—sometimes called "combination skin."
4. Chicken skin, characterized by rough bumps on the back of the arms.
5. Alligator skin, usually on the lower legs.
6. Stiff, dry, unmanageable brittle hair.
7. Dandruff and hair loss.
8. Soft or brittle fingernails.

More About Flaxseed, Flax or Linseed Oil

Seeds from the flax plant are crushed, yielding an oil. This oil is known by several different names—flaxseed, linseed and flax.

---

*You'll find more information about the essential fatty acids in *The Yeast Connection Handbook* (pages 99–100) and *Tired–So Tired! and the "yeast connection"* (pages 86–102). You'll find an even more comprehensive discussion of fats in the following books: *Fats That Heal and Fats That Kill*, by Udo Erasmus, (Alive Books, Canada, 1993), *Detoxification and Healing, the Key to Optimal Health*, by Sidney Baker, (Keats Publishing, 1997) and *Power Healing* by Leo Galland, (Random House, 1998).

Some people prefer one name, while others use a different one. And this can be confusing. You may also be confused (and concerned) because you've used linseed oil in your housepaint.

During the past several years Until recently I've used these names interchangeably. But, to lessen the chances that my patients (or readers) will get the wrong kind of oil, I recommend that you use only the nutritional flax-seed oil or flax oil.

In discussing flax oil, Udo Erasmus commented,

> Flax oil is our richest source of the valuable Omega-3 fatty acids . . . providing our bodies with adequate amounts of these miracle nutrients works wonders for our health. . . . Flax oil reverses conditions caused by a deficiency of alpha-linolenic acid. It is beneficial in treatment programs against all major degenerative conditions, including cancer, cardiovascular disease, diabetes, multiple sclerosis, arthritis, premenstrual syndrome, overweight, and many more. At 50-60% Omega-3s, flax oil contains almost twice as much of these miracle nutrients as fish oils, which go up to around 30% Omega-3s.

Improving the Quality of Fats in Your Diet

1. Cut down on the "bad fats." Avoid especially fat-laden meats including sausage, luncheon meats, marbleized steaks and bacon. Also avoid deep-fried foods and the hundreds of processed and packaged foods that contain coconut oil, palm oil and hydrogenated or partially hydrogenated vegetable oils. Limit butter, cream, sauces and fatty cheeses.

2. To get the calories you need plus the essential nutrients found in fats . . .

   a. Eat more cold-water fish, including salmon, mackerel, sardines, tuna and herring. Since some fish (like every food we consume) may be contaminated with mercury or other chemicals, obtain your fish and seafood from a variety of sources.* When you buy sardines, look for sardines packed in sardine oil.

   b. Choose olive oil or unrefined vegetable or seed oils for cooking and salad dressings. You can also use limited amounts of corn, sunflower and safflower oils.

   c. Take one tablespoon (more if you're underweight) of un-

---

*See pages 71–73, for a discussion of chemical contamination of fish and other seafoods.

refined flaxseed (flaxseed) oil each day. Mix it with lemon juice and use it as a salad dressing or mix it with a little butter for a soft spread. Or you can take it straight. You can also stir flaxseed oil into soup, stew or other liquid foods after they are removed from the store; or use it to season vegetables after cooking. I've even used flaxseed oil on my baked potato as a substitute for butter.

Here are suggestions for the purchase and use of flaxseed oil:
1. Always buy it in sealed, airtight bottles. Dark bottles are preferable.
2. Store the bottle in your refrigerator or freezer.
3. If the oil is purchased in quantities of one pint or less and used within a few months, it should not become rancid.
4. Buy only dated flaxseed oil and use it within 2–3 months.

CARBOHYDRATES: GOOD AND BAD

The good carbohydrates are called "complex carbohydrates" and they're found in vegetables, whole grains and fruits. Like simple carbohydrates, they contain glucose. However, the glucose molecules in these foods, especially in the vegetables and grains are tied together in long chains that are metabolized slowly providing you with a more even flow of energy.

In the mid and late 1990s (as you've seen and heard on TV), vegetables and fruits are "in." For example, on a winter 1996/1997 program on The Today Show, Dr. Art Ulene said, "If you want to enjoy optimal health, eat seven vegetables a day."

Good Carbohydrates

In her best-selling 1996 book, *Stop Aging Now,* nutrition authority, Jean Carper, in a chapter entitled, "Plate Full of Miracles," had this to say,

Eat all the various fruits and vegetables you can. There is nowhere, repeat nowhere, that you can get the injections of anti-

aging potions you get from eating fruits and vegetables . . . They possess countless known and unknown agents that transform your cells into fortresses against the free radical forces of aging. Much of what we call aging is really a fruit and vegetable deficiency!*

In her discussion, Carper cited the comments of many prominent nutrition researchers including Gladys Block, Ph.D., University of California at Berkeley, Dr. JoAnn Manson of Harvard Medical School, Paul Jacques of Tufts University and researchers from a number of other medical centers.

Why are fruits and vegetables so valuable? They include all sorts of nutrients in addition to vitamins and minerals. They are called "plant pharmaceuticals." They include the red pigment, lycopene, in tomatoes and watermelon, sulforaphane in broccoli, indole-3-Carbinol in cabbage, glutathione in grapefruit, quercetin in grapes, onions and tea, lutein in tomato juice and lycopene in tomatoes.

Carper cited a number of research studies which showed that women vegetarians seem to be spared cancers of the breasts and ovaries and are less apt to be troubled with adult-onset diabetes, gallstones, kidney stones, osteoporosis and arthritis.

*Carper, J., *Stop Aging Now,* Harper-Collins, New York, NY 1995. Pages 168–181.

Bad Carbohydrates

These include refined sugar, brown sugar, corn sugar (and syrup), white rice, white bread, white pastas and other white flour products. When you eat these simple carbohydrates, they're converted into glucose too rapidly.

Although you may get a quick "pick-up" and feel more energetic when you eat sweets,

this burst of energy doesn't last long. And before you know it, you become jittery

and suffer a let down.

Here's why: When you eat a lot of sugar-containing foods, your pancreas tends to overreact and you put out too much insulin. This causes your blood glucose to drop rapidly—often lower than it was before you ate anything.

When this happens, you're apt to feel nervous, tired and hungry.

| NERVOUS | TIRED | HUNGRY |

So the cycle continues and you're apt to crave sweets. As soon as you eat them, you're apt to feel better. But if you load up on these simple carbohydrates, you relieve your symptoms for only a short time and your blood sugar tends to go up and down like a yo-yo.

Concern About High-Carbohydrate Diets

During the 1990s, a number of professionals have expressed their concern about what's happening to many people on low-fat, high-carbohydrate diets. According to certified nutrition specialist, Anne Louise Gittleman, of Bozeman, Montana,

> The time has come to take the carbohydrate craze to task. I am very concerned about the carbohydrate-related health problems so many of my clients are complaining about. Carbohydrate overloading tends to displace protein foods that the body needs for immunity, even blood sugar levels, proper hormonal functioning and tissue repair.
>
> Plus the carbohydrates everyone is eating such as bread, pasta and potatoes are deficient in the essential fatty acids that control the cardiovascular reproductive and nervous systems.*

*Gittleman, A.L., Beyond Pritikin, 2nd edition, 1996, page 1.

I was especially impressed by what Gittleman had to say as for a number of years she worked as a nutritionist at the Pritikin Longevity Institute.

Other professionals who've expressed a similar concern are Kendall Gerdes, M.D., George Juetersonke, D.O., and Barry Sears, Ph.D. At the Boston meeting of the American Academy of Environmental Medicine in October 1996, they spoke about high carbohydrate, low-fat diets causing the *"Insulin-Resistance Syndrome"* which results in obesity and many other health problems.**

CONCLUDING COMMENTS

If you're confused about what you *should* or *should not* eat, you've got a lot of company, and finding the right answer isn't easy because many "authorities" disagree (sometimes violently) about the best diet for optimal health.

Here now is some (but not all) of the advice I give my patients, friends, and relatives.

1. Eat more vegetables of all kinds, the more the better.
2. Eat more fruits of all kinds (yet if you're troubled by yeast related problems—don't overdo).
3. Where possible, purchase vegetables in season from local growers and farmers, because they are less apt to be chemically contaminated.
4. Eat whole grains or grain alternatives. but don't overload.
5. Some animal products may be O.K., but you don't need them to be healthy. Especially avoid high fat meats.
6. Avoid processed and packaged foods which contain partially hydrogenated fats, food coloring, sugar and other hidden ingredients.

---

* According to the summer 1997 issue of *NOHA News*, Dr. Gerdes recommended *The Sugar Trap and How to Avoid It* by NOHA honorary member, Beatrice Trum Hunter. He and Dr. Juetersonke take their patients off all sugars and grains including all pastas and breads and all fruits. In the discussion, they said that some fruits are probably fine for the people who do not yet have the insulin resistance syndrome.

According to this report, these physicians have had great success with diets which emphasize green vegetables. They said that their patients lose their symptoms of fatigue and depression and gradually lose weight.

All three doctors talked about the new "food pyramid," which recommends six to eleven servings of grains per day as the base for all our diets. They called the pyramid "a prescription for a disaster." They mentioned the importance of exercising, adjusting the vitamins and minerals and other micronutrients and avoiding the deleterious effects on our cell membranes from *trans*-fatty acids such as those found in margarine.

This newsletter is published quarterly by the not-for-profit Nutritional Health Association, $8/year for non-members. Write Box 380, Winnetka, IL 60093.

7. Make sure you take in enough good oils.
8. Sharply limit your intake of sugar, corn syrup and other refined carbohydrates. This is especially important if your health problems are yeast connected.
9. Take a comprehensive multi-vitamin and mineral product and other nutritional supplements.

Questions and Answers About the Yeast Connection

Q: What is "the yeast connection"?

A: The yeast connection refers to the relationship of the common yeast, *Candida albicans,* to health problems that affect people of all ages and both sexes.

Q: Is *Candida albicans* the same yeast that is present in breads and other foods?

A: No, it's a different yeast. You might think of it as sort of a cousin to the food yeasts. When we study candida under a microscope, we see that it has different forms: a cellular form called *blastospores* and branching forms called *mycelia* (for a more detailed discussion, see *The Yeast Connection,* pages 320-323).

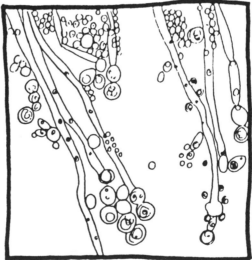

Q: Where is this yeast found?

A: *Candida albicans* normally live on the dark, warm interior membranes of your body in harmony with billions of friendly bacteria. It lives especially in the digestive tract and vagina.

Candida causes no problems when your immune system is strong and your intestinal membranes and gut flora are normal.

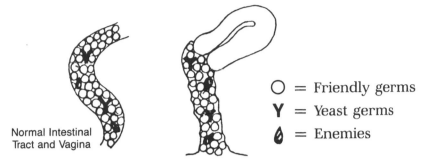

Normal Intestinal
Tract and Vagina

O = Friendly germs
Y = Yeast germs
◊ = Enemies

However, when antibiotics are used to kill harmful bacteria, good bacteria are killed as well. This allows candida to flourish.

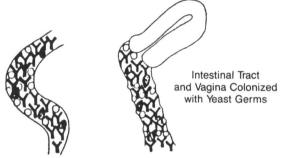

Intestinal Tract
and Vagina Colonized
with Yeast Germs

When this happens, vaginitis, mouth and throat infections (thrush), diarrhea, bloating, constipation, diaper rashes, jock itch and other problems may develop.

Surprisingly, candida can also be related to fatigue, depression, headache, irritability, memory loss, PMS, menstrual disorders, sexual dysfunction, infertility, recurrent infections and food and chemical intolerances.

In addition, many other severe chronic health disorders may, at times, be yeast connected, including asthma, psoriasis, multiple sclerosis, Crohn's disease, mitral valve prolapse, hyperactivity, learning disorders and autism.

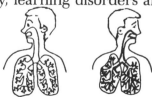

Q: How can candida be related to so many different problems in distant parts of the body?

A: In two ways. First a person can develop a candida allergy.* Such allergies have been clearly described by many physicians.

Second, and even more important, metabolic waste products or toxins are released from the candida organisms in the intestinal tract or vagina. These toxins are then carried by the blood or lymph channels to other parts of the body.

Moreover, research studies by Iwata in Japan and Witkin and associates at Cornell University show that candida infections can cause immunosuppression—meaning that you, the host, are more vulnerable to illness.

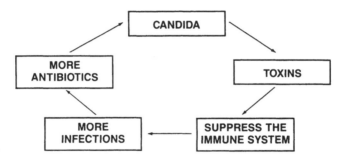

Q: Are there other observations or reports that support the role of candida in making people "sick all over"?

A: Yes, the clinical and laboratory studies of C. Orian Truss, M.D., of Birmingham, Alabama. Beginning in the early 1960s, this board-certified specialist in internal medicine noted that candida was related to fatigue, depression and a wide variety of other chronic disorders.

During the next fifteen years, Truss continued to make observations about the role of candida in making his patients sick. He first reported his findings at a meeting in Toronto in 1977. Subsequently, he published them in a series of four articles (1978, 1980, 1981, 1984) and in a book, *The Missing Diagnosis.*

---

*In the Foreword to the paperback edition of *The Yeast Connection*, James Brodsky, M.D., Diplomate, American Board of Internal Medicine and Instruction, Georgetown University School of Medicine, stated, "There is much evidence to suggest that *Candida albicans* is one of the most allergenic microbes." And he cited a number of scientific reports to support this statement.

In 1982, because he needed a laboratory basis for the diagnosis of patients with candida-related disorders, Truss initiated studies on 24 of his patients. The design of the study was to evaluate the protein, fat and carbohydrate metabolism in patients whose history suggested mold sensitivity and chronic yeast overgrowth.

Truss presented his preliminary findings at the Conference on Human Yeast Interaction (Birmingham, December 1983). He subsequently published a preliminary report in the Summer 1984 issue of *The Journal of Orthomolecular Psychiatry*. In this 27-page report, he reviewed many biochemical interrelationships and described the methods he used in studying both amino acids and fatty acids. He noted significant abnormalities in both of these important components.

Recently, George Kroker (a Fellow of the American College of Allergy and Immunology) and James M. Brodsky (a Diplomate of the American Board of Internal Medicine and an Instructor, Georgetown University School of Medicine) provided additional support for the Truss hypothesis. In a chapter entitled "Chronic Candidiasis and Allergy" (in the 1987 book *Food Allergy and Intolerance*), Dr. Kroker comprehensively discussed the role of candida in human illness. He also reviewed the medical literature and listed 104 references. And he said,

"The emphasis in this chapter . . . will be towards outlining the broader role for *Candida* species in causing chronic illness from tissue *sensitivity* to the organism and/or its by-products, rather than from direct tissue *invasion* by the organism itself."

Q: Why might a person develop a yeast-connected health problem?

A: Such a problem develops when the immune system isn't strong enough to keep candida under control. So anything that weakens your immune system will make you more apt to develop a candida-related health problem. The triggering agents especially include:

1. Repeated or prolonged courses of anti-biotics, which wipe out the friendly bacteria and promote the overgrowth of candida. Candida allergies may then develop. In addition, candida toxins are produced, further weakening the immune system.

2. Corticosteroids and birth control pills also promote the proliferation of candida.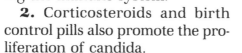

3. A poor diet, especially a diet loaded with sugar and junk food and lacking essential nutrients.

4. Exposure to harmful chemicals such as petrochemicals, formaldehyde, tobacco smoke, perfume, insecticides and weed killers.

5. Viral infections of all sorts, including infectious mononucleosis (and other Epstein Barr virus infections) and AIDS.

Q: I think I understand, but could you tell me how these different factors interact and cause problems?

A: Yes, here are two examples:

A teenager with acne takes tetracycline, a broad-spectrum antibiotic. This antibiotic wipes out friendly bacteria in the gut and encourages the growth of candida. Women who take tetracycline and other antibiotics are also apt to develop vaginal yeast infections.

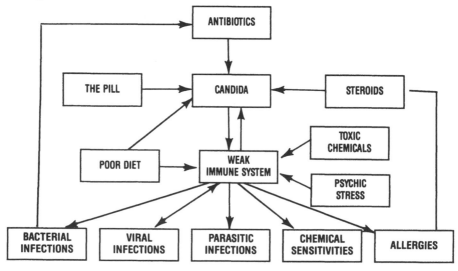

As noted by Iwata and Witkin, candida produces toxins which can cause immunosuppression. As a result, the teenager may develop other bacterial infections or become more susceptible to environmental chemicals and foods. In addition, latent viral infections may become activated and play a part in causing the Chronic Fatigue Syndrome (CFS).

Here's a second example: A factory or farm worker may be exposed to an overload of chemical toxins. These toxins weaken the immune system and lead to a variety of bacterial infections, including bronchitis and/or sinusitis. When these infections are treated with broad-spectrum antibiotics, overgrowth of candida results. Another vicious cycle is set up. So you can see that the Candida-Related Complex (CRC) can develop in many different ways.

Q: Why are most physicians skeptical? Why do they reject the role of candida in making people sick?

A: They haven't read the pioneer clinical observations and metabolic studies of C. Orian Truss. Nor have they seen the other reports in the medical literature which provide support for the Truss hypothesis and which explain how candida causes disturbances in distant parts of the body.

Instead, they have read the negative statement of the Committee on Scientific Affairs of the American Medical Association (September 1987). They've also been influenced by the statement of the Practice Standards Committee of the American Academy of Allergy and Immunology (AAAI), which was released in August 1985.

Here are excerpts from the AAAI critique:

"The Practice Standards Committee finds multiple problems with the Candidiasis Hypersensitivity Syndrome:
   The concept is speculative and uproven.
   a. The basic elements of the syndrome would apply to almost all sick patients at some time. The complaints are essentially universal; the broad treatment program would produce remission in most illnesses regardless of cause.
   b. There is no published proof the *Candida albicans* is responsible for the syndrome.
   c. There is no published proof that the treatment of *Candida*

albicans infection with specific antifungal agents benefits the syndrome.

This statement has been quoted, adapted and repeated in the medical and lay press on many occasions in the past four years. (For a further discussion of this subject, see "A Special Message to the Physician" in *The Yeast Connection and the Woman,* pages 6–14 and pages 650–654.)

Q: Are there tests to prove that I do or do not have a candida-related health problem?

A: Yes and no. First to explain the "yes" answer. Several laboratories carry out candida immunoglobulin and other antibody studies.* Individuals with a candida-related health problem tend to have higher levels than those who do not. However, as is the case with many laboratory tests, these tests do not make the diagnosis.

Accordingly, to tell if your health problems are candida related you should:

1. Have a knowledgeable physician carefully review your medical history and carry out examinations and tests so that other causes for your symptoms can be ruled out or identified and appropriately treated.

2. Review your own history using the questionnaire on page 26.

.MEDICAL HISTORY

* Repeated antibiotics during childhood
* Acne during teen years
* Recurrent urinary infections
* Frequent vaginitis
* Jock itch
* Sexual dysfunction
* Fatigue, depression, headache
* Visits to many different physicians
* Digestive symptoms
* Crave sweets
* Sick all over, etc., etc.

3. Follow a trial treatment program.

Q: How do I get started and what steps must I take?

A: The first important step: *Believe in yourself!* Say to yourself, "I can and will regain my health." The second step: *Take charge.* Say to yourself, "If it's going to be, it's up to me."

Read, study and learn. Be responsible. Although you'll need help from kind and caring health professionals, you must make the major decisions.

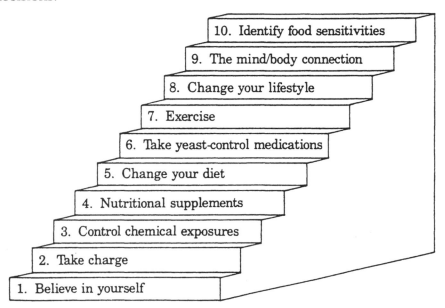

10. Identify food sensitivities
9. The mind/body connection
8. Change your lifestyle
7. Exercise
6. Take yeast-control medications
5. Change your diet
4. Nutritional supplements
3. Control chemical exposures
2. Take charge
1. Believe in yourself

Q: Where and how can I find a medical doctor or other health professional who will work with me?

A: I wish I had a simple answer to your question. Yet, at this time locating such a health professional is difficult. You'll find more information in the 2001 editions of *The Yeast Connection Handbook* and *Tired—So Tired! and the "yeast connection."*

Included will be information about the small, nonprofit International Health Foundation (IHF). In 2000, IHF completed the following new publications:

- A 36-page booklet for adults, *Information for You*, which includes a list of health professionals who have expressed an interest in yeast-related disorders.
- a 76-page booklet, *Children's Health Problems*, including ear problems, food allergies, ADHD, autism and yeast problems.
- A 24-page booklet, *A Special Message to the Health Professional.* This booklet is designed for you to show to your own physician. Included are summaries of reports in the mid and late

1990s which support the relationship of yeast infections to many chronic health disorders.

You'll find information about these booklets and about my telephone hotline on my website, www.candida-yeast.com. I answer questions on the hotline most Tuesdays between 12:45 and 2:15 p.m. Central time (731) 660-7090. Please send your questions by e-mail before calling.

Q: Is there other advice you'd like to give me?

A: Yes. If you're like most people with a candida-related health problem, you resemble an overburdened camel. To regain your health, you'll need to unload many "bundles" of straw. This will take months—even a year or two—but then your camel will be off and running.

What to Eat and Drink— and What to Avoid

Every food you eat contains calories. Protein, fats and carbohydrates (starches) provide these calories. When you obtain them from a variety of good foods, you'll also take in essential nutrients, including amino acids, essential fatty acids (EFAs), vitamins and minerals. You'll also get fiber—so important in maintaining the health of your digestive tract and of your entire body.

Vegetables

Vegetables are good for you! And the more vegetables you eat, the healthier you will be. (Especially if they haven't been doused with chemicals and insecticides.) Feature vegetables, especially vegetables you don't usually eat. If you'd like to read about a ten-day diet of vegetables that made some young men a lot healthier and stronger, read the first chapter of Daniel in the Bible.

Daniel and three of his friends were being trained to serve in Nebuchadnezzar's royal court and were offered the same food and wine as other members of the court. But Daniel and his friends didn't want to partake of the royal fare. So Daniel asked the chief steward to intercede:

"He asked the superintendent for permission to eat other things instead. . . . Daniel talked it over with the steward who was appointed by the superintendent . . . and suggested a ten-day diet of only vegetables and water.

"The steward finally agreed to the test. At the end of ten days, Daniel and his three friends looked healthier and better nourished than the youths who had been eating the food supplied by the king. After that, the steward fed them only vegetables* and water, without the rich foods and wines. . . . When the three-year training period was completed . . . in all matters requiring information and balanced judgment, the king found these young men's

*In the recipe section of the book, you'll find a comprehensive discussion of 54 different vegetables, including some you know about and others you may have never heard of.

advice ten times better than that of all the skilled magicians and wise astrologists in his realm."*

A special word about garlic: Even if garlic isn't one of your favorites, I urge you to try it. Here's why: *Garlic is a highly effective antifungal agent.* It also has other health promoting effects.

Some people eat garlic (or take garlic products) everyday. Linda Kay wrote, "Garlic controls my candida. I eat it every day. I've even used garlic enemas and douches. When I don't eat garlic, I take odor-free garlic products I get from my health food store."

Umberto Fontana, a businessman, loves to cook for his family and friends. Recently, after I'd eaten an especially tasty garlic-flavored dish, I said, "Umberto, tell me how you prepare and use garlic." Here are his comments: "Garlic tastes best when it is bruised. Instead of peeling, cutting, slicing or dicing it, just hit it with the back of a knife or the back of a pan. Then take off the skin after you've mashed it. You can then add it to soups, casseroles, salads or other dishes."

A word of caution: Anything you eat or drink can cause an allergic reaction—especially if you consume it every day. If you're like most folks with a yeast-connected health problem, you're apt to be troubled by food sensitivities, and as good as garlic is for most people, it can cause allergic reactions.

Meats

You may also eat fish and lean meats in moderate amounts. However, you don't require these food to be well nourished. Moreover, as is the case with vegetables, try to find meats and fish which are less apt to be contaminated with toxic chemicals, antibiotics and/or hormones. (See pages 71–80.)

In the December/January 1987 edition of her newsletter *Mastering Food Allergies,* Marge Jones, in discussing the early weeks on the diet, said, *"In the early weeks of the diet, the best recipes are no recipes at all.* Fresh vegetables are eaten raw, steamed, boiled or stir fried; meat, fish or fowl is broiled, baked or poached and served plain." In the section which follows, Marge gives directions for simple preparations of these basic foods.

**The Way,* an illustrated edition of the *Living Bible,* Tyndale House Publishers, Wheaton, IL, page 718.

Grain alternatives

During the past several years, I have learned about two new foods, amaranth and quinoa. When I say "new," I mean they were new to me. I hadn't heard about them before. But, according to Jane Brody, you'll be hearing a great deal about these grain substitutes in the future. After 500 years of obscurity, during which time a handful of primitive farmers kept them alive, western agriculturists have recently discovered these near-miraculous plant foods.

In discussing amaranth and quinoa in her newsletter, Marge Jones commented,

"Amaranth was a sacred food of the Aztec Indians in Mexico, from about 1200 to 1521, when they were conquered by Cortes. Quinoa was the sustaining food of the Inca Indians who lived high in the mountains of South America; it means 'mother grain,' literally the source of life. In both cases, the Indians sensed that their strength and well-being was dependent on an adequate supply of their special food.

"Centuries later, we were able to confirm their remarkable nutritional value . . . amaranth and quinoa are great foods for anyone!

"A few years ago when I learned that amaranth was not a true grain, I set out adapting its unique characteristics to grain-free recipes for people with food allergies."

The third "grain alternative," buckwheat,* is one I can remember eating in early childhood.

Quoting Jane Brody again,

"The edible part of the plant . . . is the fruit—a triangular seed that resembles a stout grain. It also cooks like a grain in about the time it takes to prepare rice or bulgur. But it is more nourishing than grains and deserves a wide audience in this country."

A word of caution about these nourishing foods. A small percentage of people will react to them. Buy them in small quantities until

---

*You'll find more information about buckwheat in *Jane Brody's Good Food Amaranth Book, Living the High Carbohydrate Way,* or you can write to the National Buckwheat Institute at P.O. Box 595, Naples, New York 14512.

you see if they agree with you. Then buy a larger quantity and store them in your refrigerator or freezer.

Water

Tap water usually contains chemicals of many types which may disagree with you and play a part in causing your symptoms. So I recommend filtered, distilled or bottled water. There are many brands including Mountain Valley, Polan, Evian, Vittel and Perrier. Bottled water comes in all sizes, varying from the six-ounce Perrier to a five-gallon jug. If you get bottled water, be sure it is stored in glass containers because chemicals leach into the water in plastic bottles.

Yeast-containing foods

Yeasts and molds live on the surface of most foods, including grains, fruits and vegetables, nuts and seeds. And they increase in number when foods are stored, especially at room temperature. However, there are a number of foods which contain large amounts of yeast. Breads, bagels, pastries, pretzels, crackers, pizza and rolls are usually made with yeast as leavening. All fermented and aged products including cheese and alcoholic beverages contain yeast. Yeasts are also found in most sauces or condiments made from vinegar or products of fermentation. Examples: salad dressings, barbecue sauces, tomato sauces, soy sauce, miso, tamari sauce, mincemeat, horseradish, sauerkraut, pickles and olives. Dried fruits are also loaded with yeasts, and as pointed out by Sidney M. Baker, "Mushrooms are nothing but a big mold." (For a further discussion of yeasts—see *The Yeast Connection and the Woman.*)

Fruits

Fruits are an excellent source of complex carbohydrates, and most people like them. However, they are quickly converted into simple sugars and may promote yeast growth. I suggest that you avoid them during the first three weeks of your diet. After you improve, you may tolerate fruits in moderate amounts. When you reintroduce fruits, take it easy. Start with 2 inches of a banana, a quarter of a pear and so on. (You'll find specific instructions for eliminating foods and adding them back in the chapter "Getting Started.")

Nuts and seeds

These foods, even though high in fat content, are loaded with vitamins, minerals and other essential nutrients. Since nuts also are apt to contain yeasts and molds, avoid them until you pass the yeast challenge. Then if yeasts and molds don't bother you, add nuts to your diet. Get nuts in the shell, or purchase shelled nuts from a health food store that refrigerates their nuts and has a large turnover. Nuts stored at room temperature are apt to be more highly contaminated with mold. After purchase, they should be kept in your refrigerator or freezer.

Coffee, tea and herb teas

During the early weeks of your diet avoid them. Then after you improve, you can cautiously experiment and see if you tolerate them.

Alcoholic beverages

Since these beverages are made with yeast and sugar, stay away from them. Even if you aren't allergic to yeast, avoid them because of the quick-acting carbohydrates.

Diet drinks

Such beverages contain no nutrients. Moreover, they often contain caffeine, artificial food coloring and flavoring, aspartame, phosphates and other ingredients which disagree with many individuals. Although these sugar-free beverages do not encourage the multiplication of yeasts in your digestive tract, I do not recommend them.

Dry cereals

Nearly all packaged cereals contain added sugar and many (like Grape Nuts) contain yeasts and malt. Others contain B vitamins which are derived from yeast.

What can you use instead? In her Breakfast chapter, Marge suggests lots of ideas for unusual (but tasty) ways to start your day avoiding dry cereals.

Grains

Whole grains are loaded with complex carbohydrates, vitamins, minerals and fiber, plus some protein and small amounts of fat. However, grains, especially wheat and corn, rank high on the list of food allergy troublemakers. So avoid wheat and corn completely until you've completed your elimination diet. Then try them on a rotated basis. Millet, brown rice and oats are less apt to cause allergies and can be used on your initial elimination diet, but alternate them with amaranth or quinoa.

Milk

Many people do not tolerate milk, including people who crave it. I've found milk to be a major troublemaker in my patients with allergies and candida-related health disorders. Avoid milk and milk-containing foods until you carry out your elimination diet and challenge. Then if it doesn't bother you, you can try yogurt and/or other milk-containing foods on a limited basis, but avoid eating them repetitiously.

Eggs

In spite of the "verbal brickbats" they have received, eggs provide nutrients that aren't found in other foods. Certainly eggs are a lot better than Egg Beaters®, in spite of their cholesterol content.

About ten years ago, I read an article which had been published in one of the medical journals. The report described the following experiment: Eggs were fed to one group of rats, and Egg Beaters® were fed to a second group. A few weeks later, the rats were examined and photographs were made of the rats in each group.

The egg-eating rats looked healthy, strong and bright-eyed; their fur was sleek and smooth. By contrast, the rats who had been eating the Egg Beaters® looked as though they'd been shipwrecked and starved for weeks. These rats appeared malnourished, scrawny and shriveled, and their furry coat was rough and irregular.

If you aren't allergic to eggs, eat them once or twice a week—especially if your cholesterol count isn't high. But make sure you cook them properly (see page 346).

More About Vegetables, Milk, Yogurt, Bread, Chicken, Fish and Fruits

Vegetables

Everyone knows that vegetables are good for you. They contain fiber, vitamins and minerals. When eaten raw or steamed, they contain no refined sugar or processed fats. Like most Americans, you're probably eating more vegatables than you used to. What's more, McDonald's and other fast-food restaurants are featuring salads and putting in salad bars.

But as good as vegetables and other fresh foods are for you, you should know that the health-promoting quality of the vegetables will depend on where and how the vegetables are grown.

1. Do they come from your back yard garden which has been enriched by compost and manure?
2. Are they grown near a heavily traveled road and contaminated with lead and other toxins found in automobile exhausts?
3. Are they grown in this country, where their production may be supervised, or are they grown in Mexico or another foreign country where such supervision is minimal or non-existent?
4. Are they loaded with insecticides, weed killers, preservatives and other chemicals?

During the past 25 years, I've seen hundreds of patients who became ill when exposed to chemicals in the air, food or water. Common troublemakers included insecticide sprays and residues in fruits and vegetables. Diesel car exhausts, gas cooking stoves, tobacco smoke, formaldehyde, perfumes, colognes and floor waxes also caused moderate to severe symptoms in some of my patients.

Yet, in spite of my interest in chemical sensitivity, until recently most people (including physicians) "looked the other way" when such sensitivity to our polluted environment was discussed. But today the public has become increasingly interested in environmental pollutants, including those which are contaminating our foods. Here are examples:

In an article, "Clean Greens," published in *Health*, Darcy Meeker commented,

> "Few of us can resist the appeal of fresh produce— succulent, tree-ripened, peaches, rich red tomatoes, or sweet corn on the cob. Fresh tastes best and it's more nutritious than canned or frozen fruits or vegetables.
>
> "But we're getting picky about the fresh produce we choose. More and more Americans are buying what they consider to be tastier, more nutritious and cleaner produce—organically grown . . . without the help of chemical pesticides, herbicides, fungicides and fertilizers.
>
> "Moreover, you don't have to go to the health food store to find organically-grown foods. Many major supermarket chains now carry organically-grown produce. Even big food companies like H.J. Heinz and Campbell's Soup company, are insisting on using produce that's free of pesticide residues."

Here are comments of a similar nature which were published in the highly respected *Nutrition Action Healthletter* in an article entitled "America's Pesticide Permeated Food," Anne Montgomery commented,

> "Conventional industry and government propaganda holds that America has the 'safest food supply in the world.' . . . But a lot of what's sold isn't safe at all. Pesticide-contaminated food has become a topic of growing concern as overuse, misuse and abuse of these toxic chemicals has escalated. . . . *Unfortunately, the very foods that health-conscious consumers are trying to eat more of— fresh fruits and vegetables—are those that are most likely to be contaminated.*"

In her interesting, comprehensive and, yes . . . frightening . . . article, Montgomery told about 1,350 people who developed symptoms ranging from nausea and diarrhea to seizures, blurred vision and irregular heartbeat. The cause: They had eaten California watermelons contaminated with the toxic insecticide, Aldicarb.

Montgomery also discussed a highly publicized incident involving apples contaminated by unacceptably high levels of Daminozide. What's more, the contamination was so certain that several major supermarket chains refused to accept further shipments of the daminozide-treated apples.

Here are other examples cited by Montgomery: A 1986 study of Kansas farmers showed that a form of cancer increased significantly with the number of days the farmers were exposed to herbicides each year. In a California study, the children born to agricultural workers were found to have deformed limbs at a rate thirteen times the rate among the general population.

In her continuing discussion, Montgomery said,

"There are no quick solutions to the pesticide dilemma. . . . It's becoming clearer to more and more farmers that pesticides are not panaceas. Despite the huge increase in insecticide use since World War II, crop losses from insect pests have increased from 7% to 13%.

"It's time to turn back the clock and take a close look at safer, non-chemical methods of growing, storing, and preserving crops . . . before the environment and food supply become even more contaminated with persistent toxic residues."

Pesticide Spraying

Vegetables are good for you if they haven't been poisoned by insecticides, chemicals and weed killers.

Here are suggestions for lessening the amount of pesticides you'll get in the vegetables you consume:*

1. Eat more root vegetables like potatoes, carrots and turnips. They're less contaminated.
2. Grow your own vegetables, or buy them from organic farmers or from a store whose manager is interested in safe foods.
3. Put 2 teaspoons of baking soda or 2 tablespoons of vinegar in a large bowl or in your sink and soak your vegetables for

---

*Further suggestions for coping with pesticides and other chemicals in your foods are found in The Chemical Problem chapter.

several minutes. Then rinse them vigorously in a stream of running water.

Milk

For many generations, Americans have been "in love" with cow milk. It's said to be pure, wholesome and loaded with nutrients of all sorts, including calcium, proteins and vitamins. Yet, *a lot of people do not tolerate milk, especially people who crave it! It's a prime offender for those with allergies and candida-related health disorders.*

Academic leaders who've expressed concern about cow milk include the late Frank A. Oski, M.D., professor and chairman, Department of Pediatrics, Johns Hopkins School of Medicine, and the late William C. Deamer, professor and chairman, Department of Pediatrics, University of California, San Francisco.

In discussing cow milk in his book *Don't Drink Your Milk*,* Dr. Oski commented,

> "Being against cow milk is equated with being un-American. It's easy to understand this view, which is inspired mainly by the advertising practices and political pressure of the American dairy industry. . . . But at last a growing number of physicians, private citizens, and even the Federal Trade Commission are planning to re-examine these long-standing and deeply ingrained beliefs in the virtue of cow milk. . . .
>
> "The fact is: The drinking of cow milk has been linked to iron deficiency anemia in infants and children. It has been named as a cause of cramps and diarrhea in much of the world's population, and the cause of multiple forms of allergy as well; the possibility has been raised that it may play a central role in the origins of atherosclerosis and heart attacks."

Dr. Oski also discussed the *allergic tension-fatigue syndrome* and other systemic and nervous symptoms which were often related to cow's-milk sensitivity.**

---

*Oski, F. *Don't Drink Your Milk*, ninth edition, Teach Services, Brushton, N.Y., 1993 (available in many Health Food Stores).
**"Most people, including physicians, believe that allergies to foods . . . produce only such classical symptoms as skin rashes, respiratory symptoms or gastrointestinal disorders. There is a growing body of evidence, however, to suggest that certain allergies may manifest themselves primarily as changes in personality, emotions, or in one's general sense of well being."

"The child or adult with motor fatigue always seems to feel weak and tired. . . . Excessive drowsiness (dullness and apathy) is typical. . . . Tension is the other manifestation of food allergy. . . . Although the *tension-fatigue syndrome* is the most common manifestation of food allergy, it is by no means the only one. Vague recurrent abdominal pains, repeated headaches, aching muscles and joints and even bedwetting have been observed as symptoms of food allergy.

"Although I've emphasized the role played by food allergies in producing symptoms in children, adults appear equally prone to the problems produced by foods. . . . The food most responsible for symptoms in both adults and children is whole cow milk."

But, in spite of my negative comments, some people may consume milk and aother dairy products and not experience problems. I tell my patients, "I'd rather have you drink milk than the sugar-containing soft drinks. But select the low-fat milks, cheeses, yogurt and other dairy products, which you'll find in every grocery store."

Now for a personal story. During the '20s and '30s, I was troubled by heavy discharge of nasal mucus, sinus infections and recurrent abdominal pain. I underwent a number of diagnostic studies, including three gastrointestinal x-rays. I also received treatments of different sorts for my nasal congestion, including repeated antibiotics and surgery. Moreover, radium rods were inserted in my nose to "dry up the mucus." Yet, my symptoms continued until 1956, when Theron Randolph of Chicago suggested that I stop drinking milk. I did, and my sinus and digestive problems went away and haven't come back.

During the thirty years of my practice since that time, I've seen thousands of patients with chronic health problems who improved significantly—even dramatically—when they stopped drinking milk, eating ice cream, and consuming other dairy products. *So if you drink milk and are bothered by a chronic health problem, milk and dairy products may be contributing to your symptoms.*

Yogurt

As is the case with carbohydrates, yogurt preparations include "good guys" and "bad guys." Commercial yogurt (the kind found in supermarkets) contains all sorts of extra ingredients, including sugar, fruit, gelatin and stabilizers of one kind or another. So it's only a distant cousin of the healthy, nutritious, homemade yogurt.

By contrast, plain yogurt found in health food stores or homemade "real" yogurt contains friendly bacteria, including *Lactobacillus acidophilus*. This bacterium and other related "good guys" which live in your intestine contribute to good health. According to Elie Metchnikoff, a Russian Nobel Prize winner who first began writing on the subject in the early 1900s, these friendly bacteria may help you live a longer and healthier life.

In a brief report in the November 1986 issue of *Natural Food and Farming*, Patricia Tirrell Ratz commented,

> "Yogurt not only aids the digestive process, it also destroys the many, harmful varieties of bacteria such as coliform. The use of antibiotics . . . kills the lacto-bacteria causing a need for replenishing it in the body. A regular diet of yogurt eaten daily enriches intestinal flora, provides vitamin B12. . . .
>
> "To make yogurt, take one quart of milk and 2 to 3 tablespoons of starter (active yogurt from a previously made batch or a starter purchased at a health food store). Heat the milk slowly in a saucepan until it almost boils. Cool until lukewarm (118 degrees Fahrenheit), stirring occasionally. Stir in the starter gently.
>
> "Cover the pan,* wrap tightly with a towel and place in a dark warm spot for 7 to 8 hours. Gas oven with a burning pilot light works perfectly. Another choice is to use an insulated cooler. Do not disturb while it is in the warm area.
>
> "Check it in a few hours, then refrigerate when it is finished or let it sit uncovered at room temperature for up to 3 days. Save some of it to start the next batch. Enjoy!"

In the conferences on candida-related disorders in Dallas, Birmingham and San Francisco (and also in a January 1987 sympo-

---

*If you leave yogurt in the pan it should be non-aluminum. Yogurt is a food which readily draws aluminum out of cookware.

sium on chronic health disorders in San Diego), Sidney M. Baker of New Haven, Connecticut, strongly recommended the use of yogurt or one of the preparations containing friendly lactobacilli. If you don't tolerate milk, you can get milk-free capsules or powders containing lactobacilli (derived from soy, carrots or other sources) from your health food store. (For further discussion, see *The Yeast Connection and the Woman.*)

Bread

If you're like most other people in the world, you eat wheat bread (and/or other wheat-containing foods) every day. So I think you'll be interested in learning more about it. I'll begin by passing along information I obtained from a fascinating book by Canadian biochemist and nutritionist Ross Hume Hall, Ph.D., McMaster University, Hamilton, Ontario, Canada.

In the first chapter of his comprehensive, illustrated, carefully researched book, Dr. Hall discusses *Lifeless Bread.* He reviews the history of bread making, beginning in the Bible (Genesis 3:19 and Leviticus 5:11) on through the ancient Egyptian, Greek and Roman civilizations.

"As early as the 6th century B.C., bread made from barley was considered less nourishing than wheat bread. . . . Wheat contains gluten, a protein mixture . . . which imparts the rubber-like quality of dough (essential for making leavened bread). Barley flour cannot be used for making leavened bread.

"We do not know precisely when yeast (obtained from wine-making) was first used to ferment bread doughs. . . . Leavened bread was the happy result of combining three technologies: Growing naked wheat, the invention of the saddle stone (by the Egyptians) and the introduction of yeast. By 500 B.C., combined flour mills and bread bakeries were operating in Athens.

"Wheat contains five distinct proteins classified by biochemists as *glutenin, gliadin, globulin, albumin* and *proteose.* The first two proteins constitute 75-80% of the total protein which forms the gluten. Gluten gives strength to the flour.

". . . During the period of Roman civilization, flour milling technology rapidly developed and soon the Romans were making four or five commercial grades of flour. The finest from which all the bran was removed was eaten only by the very rich. . . .

As the general wealth of the Roman civilization increased, the poorer classes apparently followed the lead of the rich and consumed more refined foods. . . . White was associated with goodness, purity, nobility . . . ; white flour was associated with refinement, higher standards of living, snob appeal, etc. These emotional feelings, in time, became inseparable from the texture, taste, smoothness and appearance of white bread."

In his continuing discussion, Hall also discusses chemical technology and bread making. The chemicals used by flour makers include chlorine gas, which bleaches and matures the flour. However, chlorine also reacts with other molecules in the flour, changing certain amino acids and destroying certain vitamins, including vitamin E.

Grain of Wheat

Among the deleterious effects of modern milling processes, according to Hall, are the loss of bran and fiber, the loss of nutrients found in wheat germ, plus the loss of minerals and vitamins found in the aleurone layer of the wheat kernel.

Can you include bread in your diet? My answer is no, during the first week of your diet. Here's why:

1. Nearly all breads contain yeast, and many people with candida-related health problems are allergic to food yeasts.
2. The best breads contain wheat, and allergies (and other intolerances) occur frequently in people with candida-related health problems.

What should you do? Carry out the trial diet which is described in the "Getting Started" chapter of this book. If you show reactions to yeast or wheat, avoid regular bread and bakery products. Then in a month or two, if you're improving, you may be able to rotate breads back into your diet.

Chicken

If you're like most people, you're eating more chicken and less beef. And chicken (with the fat removed) would seem to be an excellent source of meat protein. But chickens today, like the proverbial old gray mare, "ain't what they used to be." In discussing what he called "The Real Story of Chicken," Gary Null said,

"People may believe they're eating peasant food, but if they have an image of the chicken being raised in a beautiful pastoral scene at a farm—of its being fed grains by a woman wearing an apron as it clucks merrily through the day. . . that image is sure illusion.

The chicken was born and died in the factory—an animal factory.

"Today's chicken lives without ever seeing the light of day. . . . It is packed so tightly together with two to four other birds in a tiny 12-inch cage . . . it can barely move at all . . . getting no exercise or fresh air and living under such crowded conditions, such a bird is extremely susceptible to disease. By comparison, the birds that were once allowed to roam and peck and grow healthy, today's chicken is tasteless."

In his continuing discussion, Null points out that dyes are added to chicken feed, and many are injected with enzymes and given antibiotics and other drugs. After the chicken is slaughtered, more antibiotics are added and the chicken carcasses are dipped in antibiotic solutions.

Here's more. In an article in the September 17, 1987, issue of the *Wall Street Journal* entitled "Stubborn Bug: Bid to Rid Chicken of Salmonella Proves Daunting," staff reporter A. M. Freedman, in a report from Athens, Georgia, commented,

"Scientists at the U.S. Agriculture Department's Richard B. Russell Research Center here are leading the quest for salmonella-free chicken. But despite two decades of effort, the salmonella swat team has made scant progress."

In the WSJ report, Freedman stated that salmonella bacteria remain a serious problem in the U.S. food supply, accounting for about 2 million cases of food poisoning in humans annually and, sometimes, even death. Although only 1% to 4% of chickens arrive at a slaughterhouse infected with salmonella, about 35% of all the birds depart contaminated.

Leaders of the chicken industry are working to solve the problem, but answers are frustrating and hard to find. Freedman stated the frustration is so great that one government official "is seriously considering diapering the birds."

What can you do to lessen your chances of eating salmonella-contaminated chicken? Here are recommendations from Americans for Safe Food:

"At home, consumers should follow such precautions as thoroughly washing hands, cutting boards, plates and other utensils with soap and water after cutting or preparing raw meat, fish or poultry. A cutting board used for meat should not be used for vegetables until it's been washed. Because heat kills bacteria, it's important to cook meat thoroughly and refrigerate all leftovers promptly. At room temperature, salmonella bacteria can double their population every 25 minutes, so keep cold foods cold and hot foods hot."

Fish

In their booklet *Guess What's Coming to Dinner—Contaminants in Our Food,* Ben McKelway and the staff of Americans for Safe Food (ASF) discussed the pesticides, antibiotics, hormones and other animal drugs, microbial contaminants, aflatoxins and other hazardous substances which are found in just about any food you eat. And in discussing seafood, they commented,

"Americans are eating more fish and shellfish than ever before . . . Unfortunately, seafood caught in polluted waters is often contaminated with industrial or agricultural chemicals. Mercury, lead, DDT, dioxin and polychlorinated biphenyls (PCBs) are just a few of the dangerous chemicals that have been found at alarming levels in some fish. . . .

"PCB concentrations are highest in the fattier species of fish such as the carp, catfish . . ."

In their discussion of fish, they point out that fish caught almost anywhere and everywhere can be contaminated, including perch found in the polluted waters of the Great Lakes and fish caught in the Santa Monica Bay off the coast of the Northeast.

Here are their concluding comments in a section called "Play It Safe":

"When possible, buy smaller fish. Salmon is one species that still seems relatively low in contaminants. Learn what species are likely to have high residues and try to eat them no more than once a month."

Here's more. In an article in *Natural Food and Farming,* "Perils of the Catch, A Safe Eating Guide for Fish Lovers," Frances Sheraton Goulart quoted the 18th-century English writer Samuel Johnson who said,

"The fishing rod is a stick with a hook in one end and a fool at the other."

Goulart continued,

"What Johnson didn't say was that you're twice a fool if you eat a catch that's unfit for human consumption."

In her interesting article, she discussed seafood toxins of different sorts which can be found in shellfish or any saltwater or freshwater fish. She also discussed the contamination of fish by brown worms, tapeworms and salmonella bacteria. She recommended several measures to lessen your chances of eating contaminated fish. Included were safety checking the source, eating more lean fish and carefully inspecting the fish. Make sure the flesh is firm and moist, doesn't smell bad and that the eyes are clean, bright and shiny as marble.

Here's more. In an article in the *Nutrition Action Health Letter*, Lisa Y. Lefferts provided further information about the chemical contamination of domestic fish. Here are a few excerpts from her article, "Good Fish, Bad Fish":

"Among the worst offenders are polychlorinated biphenyls, or PCBs. Although the manufacturing of PCBs was banned in the United States in 1979, the pollutant continues to show up in high concentrations in wildlife and fish.

"In 1984, researchers at Wayne State and other universities examined the infants of women who reported regularly eating an average of two or three meals per week of PCB-contaminated fish from Lake Michigan. At birth, the babies showed weak reflexes and sluggish movements, as well as other signs of "worrisome" behavioral development.

"In 1983, the Food and Drug Administration found DDT in 334 of the 386 samples of domestic fish it tested, even though the use of this 'probable human carcinogen' was halted in 1972.

"Low levels of lead, cadmium, chromium and arsenic frequently turn up in shellfish."

In discussing her recommendations for safe seafood, Lefferts said,

"The best fish to choose are offshore species, particularly those low in fat."

Cod, haddock, pollock, yellow fin, tuna and flounder caught offshore tend to be relatively safe, but catfish and carp are bottom feeders and particularly vulnerable to contamination from tainted sediments. Migratory fish, such as striped bass and bluefish, are frequently tainted with PCBs, even if they're caught offshore. Swordfish frequently exceed allowable levels of methyl mercury.

The bottom line: Don't stop eating seafood, but to be safe, eat a variety. Ask where the fish was caught, and trim away the fat and dark meat. When you cook your fish, use methods which allow the fat to be removed. Don't make sauces out of the liquid drippings or cooking water.

Also, avoid stews that call for whole fish with internal organs intact, since toxins accumulate there. Avoid raw shellfish entirely if you have cancer, diabetes or any disease that impairs immunity.

Based on these and other reports I've read in the past year or two, I am eating more and more vegetables and less animal foods and fish.

Fruits

These plant foods are not only delicious, they are good for you. In discussing fruits in his book, *The Healing Power of Foods*, Dr. Michael T. Murray said,

> Fruits are excellent sources of many vital antioxidant nutrients, especially Vitamin C, carotenes, flavonoids and polyphenols like ellagic acid. Regular fruit consumption, like regular vegetable consumption, has been shown to offer significant protection against many chronic degenerative diseases, including cancer, heart disease, cataracts and strokes.

Here are further comments about fruits which I included in *The Yeast Connection Handbook*.

> How often or how much fruit you can take is an individual matter. After a month or so, some people seem to be able to eat one or two fruits every day without experiencing problems. Yet, in the occasional person, fruits must be avoided completely for many months. To determine your own tolerance—*experiment*.
>
> One more word of caution about fruits, expecially if you are yeast sensitive. Avoid the juices—except for freshly squeezed juice—because they are loaded with yeast.

The Chemical Problem

If your problems are candida related, you're apt to be more sensitive to environmental chemicals. These include chemicals you breathe, touch, eat or drink.

You may react to chemicals in or on your foods, or to those present in food containers (including cans, plastic wrappings and boxes). Chemical contaminants can come from many sources, including herbicides (weed killers), fungicides, insecticides and food colors, additives and flavors. These toxic (or potentially toxic) substances are added to (or sprayed on) foods to prevent deterioration or to improve their *appearance* or taste.

APPLES Golden Delish!
49¢/lb.
(colorants added)

Lead and other chemicals from *automobile exhaust* can contaminate vegetables, fruits or grains from fields adjacent to heavily traveled roads. And aflatoxin (a powerful carcinogen), produced naturally by a mold, may grow on field corn, peanuts and other crops.

Here are examples of contaminants found in foods and beverages: Bananas picked green are usually exposed to a petroleum-derived gas, ethylene. So are apples, pears, oranges and tomatoes.

Chickens may contain *antibiotics*, hormones and other chemicals.

Tetracycline (for animal use)

Sugar is usually treated with chemicals of various sorts during processing.

Peelings on fresh fruits and vegetables often contain insecticide and herbicide residues. They also may be coated with mineral oils and waxes to give them an attractive shine.

French-fried potatoes may be treated with chemicals to prevent discoloration.

Beef and pork are loaded with insecticides. They also contain chemicals and hormones of various sorts. Some are administered to the animal before slaughtering; some are added to the meat as preservatives.

Tap water often contains chemicals from a variety of sources.

These include insecticides and weed killers which remain in the water in spite of purification and filtration; fluorine and chlorine and other chemicals which are added to the water; chemicals picked up from plastic pipes or copper pipes.

Here are suggestions that may help you lighten your chemical load.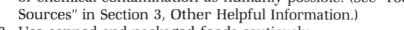

1. Use well, spring or distilled water—glass bottles only.
2. Obtain foods from organic sources. Some farmers, growers, and packers specialize in raising and producing foods which are as free of chemical contamination as humanly possible. (See "Food Sources" in Section 3, Other Helpful Information.)
3. Use canned and packaged foods cautiously.
4. If you use commercial foods, purchase those in glass containers.
5. Use glass jars or containers (rather than plastic) to store foods in your own refrigerator.
6. Purchase meats, fruits, vegetables and grains from growers in your area who use organic farming methods.* Or subscribe to *Natural Food and Farming*. Listed in this magazine are many sources of chemically uncontaminated food.

Foods Which Are Less Apt to Be Chemically Contaminated

Fish and Meat—Seafood and meat from which the fat has been stripped prior to cooking.

Vegetables—Potato (undyed and home-peeled), turnips, eggplant, tomato (if field ripened), carrots (but not bagged in plastic), squash, okra, green peas and green beans.

Fruit—Canteloupe or watermelon from a local farmer's market.

---

*You can obtain more information about organic foods, publications and growers from Community Alliance with Family Farmers (CAFF), P.O. Box 363, Davis, CA 95617, phone (1-800-852-3832.

Miscellaneous—Nuts (in shell only), Brazil nuts, coconut, walnut, hickory nut, pecan, filbert, hazel nut.

Fats and Oils—Olive, cottonseed, soy, safflower, sunflower.

Chemical contamination of our food seems to be increasing. It's a subject you should know more about. The best current source of information: Americans for Safe Food* (ASF).

Here are excerpts from a 50-page booklet, *Guess What's Coming to Dinner*, published by ASF.

> "Our food is contaminated. From pesticide residues on fruits, vegetables and grains to antibiotic-resistant strains of Salmonella bacteria in our meat, to traces of powerful animal drugs in poultry, invisible chemicals and germs permeate our food supply. . . . You

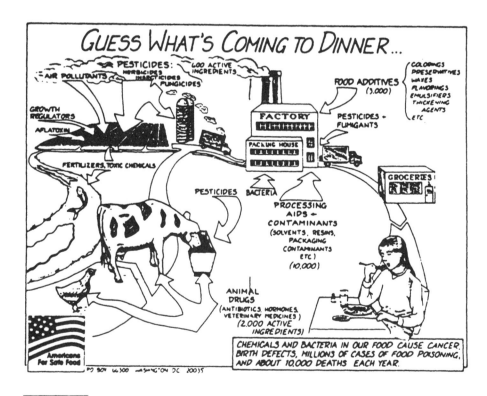

---

*Available from this organization are books, booklets, newsletters, posters and other material about foods that are good for you and foods that may be harmful. To obtain information, write to CSPI, 1875 Connecticut Ave. N.W., Washington, DC 20009-5728.

won't see these dangerous residues on any ingredient list . . . the law doesn't require it. . . .

"Consumers feel betrayed. Having learned about the dietary causes of heart disease, cancer, stroke and diabetes, millions of Americans have been eating more fish and poultry, whole grains, fresh produce and low-fat dairy products. All too often, however, these otherwise wholesome foods are tainted, and government regulation amounts to little more than a false promise of protection. . . .

Chemicals also poison our environment. They contaminate ground waters, rivers and lakes; kill wildlife; and trigger the spread of bugs and weeds that are resistant to pesticides. . . . Once consumers learn about the dangers associated with so many of our foods, the next step is to press for safe alternatives.

A growing demand for safe food will eventually cause grocers and farmers to make changes . . . changes that will be to everyone's advantage in the long run, with the possible exception of the chemical and drug manufacturers. *That is the goal of Americans for Safe Food,* and the shelves of some supermarkets bear evidence that the process has already begun. . . .

The campaign is a positive one . . . (its) goal is realistic . . . crops and animals can be grown with far fewer chemicals than they are today. Furthermore, *Americans for Safe Food* is not calling for an immediate end to the production of chemically-treated food. It is simply demanding what many consumers are demanding: A safe *alternative.*"

Here are a few of the suggestions in the booklet under the heading "What You Can Do":

1. Organize an Americans for Safe Food coalition in your community (write to ASF to find out how).
2. Get informed, then organize a local "Safe Food Day" community forum, or public debate on contaminants in food.
3. Prepare a list of local sources of contaminant-free food.
4. Write, and tell your friends to write, letters to the editor of your local newspaper. The shorter your letters are, the more likely they are to be published.

Editor
Daily News
Anytown, USA
12345

Now here's still another suggestion: Raise some of your own food. Or, find a farmer's market which features produce which has been grown "organically." Such food has been fertilized with natural compost (a fertilizing mixture composed of manure, peat, leaf mold, lime, food scraps, etc., mingled and decomposed).

More About the Chemical Pollution of Our Foods, Homes, Schools and Workplaces

If you're bothered by chemicals, get a copy of Lynn Lawson's magnificent book, *Staying Well in a Toxic World.* It is carefully researched and clearly written by a woman who's been there. To obtain this book, send your check for $18.95 to Lynn Lawson, P.O. Box 1732, Evanston, IL 60201.

If you're concerned about the chemical pollutants that are affecting your children, you may be already aware of the crusading work of Dr. Doris Rapp. To learn more, get a copy of Dr. Rapp's book, *Is This Your Child's World?—How to Fix the Schools and Homes That Are Making Your Children Sick.* You'll find this book in bookstores and health food stores throughout North America.

Here's another important book by a Yale University professor, *Our Children's Toxic Legacy—How Science and Law Fail to Protect Us From Pesticides,* by John Wargo, Yale University Press, 1996.

Here's more. A picture of Robert Redford appeared on the cover of a recent issue issue of *American Health.* Also featured on the cover were a series of articles in a section entitled "Clean Up Time: Fighting For Our Environment." These articles told about Robert Redford's fight for a cleaner environment, pesticides and strawberries, a mother's fight for cleaner water and how and why to plant a garden.

Here are excerpts from the article "Taming the Killer Strawberries."

"Once, strawberries blossomed briefly in mid-summer, then skipped town. Now, you can find picture perfect berries all year long.

"Pesticides help make this marvel possible. But, it's hard to keep these chemicals down on the farm. Chances are better than even that the strawberries you buy in the supermarket will have residues of pesticides on them. In fact, fruits and vegetables in general—key elements of a healthy diet—are, ironically, a major source of pesticide residues in our food supply."

One of the *American Health* authors suggests writing to Americans for Safe Food (ASF). He also recommends the book *Pesticide Alert*, which is available from bookstores. It can also be ordered from the National Resources Defense Council. Send $6.95 plus $1.55 shipping to NRDC, Publications Department, 40 West 20th Street, New York, NY 10011.

Here's more. In his new book, *Choose to Live* (Grove Press, 920 Broadway, New York, NY 10010, published July 1988), Joseph D. Weissman, clinical assistant professor of medicine at UCLA, in discussing the "X factor" in disease said:

> "During the last 200 years . . . the world has undergone a unique period of rapid industrialization. The Industrial Revolution brought with it new man-made chemicals: chlorine and its compounds, coal-tar derivatives, pharmaceuticals, petrochemicals, etc. . . . All industry, past and present, creates by-products and waste that require disposal. The only means of eliminating them are burning (with the subsequent development of toxic smoke), disposal in nearby waterways, or burial. . . .
>
> "Underground waste disposal ultimately intrudes upon water aquifers, and burning waste pollutes the air; thus, toxic materials are deposited in farming areas and finally make their way into water and food supplies.
>
> "All foods are affected: fruits, vegetables, grains, fish, poultry, meat, eggs, dairy products. Some foods store more toxins than others, for some are bioconcentrators and biomagnifiers. . . . *Generally, all animals are bioconcentrators—from fish, mollusks, and birds to cattle, sheep and humans.*
>
> "The absorption or retention of poisons in animals is far greater than in plants. The greatest concentrations of toxins occur in animal fat and cholesterol, for many chemical toxins are fat soluble; muscle tissue, egg and milk are not exempt, however."*

In his continuing discussion, Dr. Weissman commented,

> "The various toxic substances in the environment constitute the X factor. This term is derived from the Greek, *xenobiotics*, a word research scientists used to describe substances, foreign and harmful to living creatures, including man. . . . These include man-made poisons, pollutants, reactive chemicals, free radicals, radioactive substances, heavy metals and most pharmaceutical and chemical food additives.

---

*This quotation and the illustration which follows are used with permission.

"It is the intrusion of the X factor that has been the major cause of both the decline of infections and the appearance of the new man-made diseases."

In his book, Dr. Weissman included a chart showing pesticides in the U.S. diet based on studies carried out in the 1960s. Researchers found that pesticide residues in meat, fish and poultry were over 10 times higher than in leafy vegetables, fruits and legumes. And they were 30 or 40 times higher than in grains, cereals and root vegetables.

While animal products contain high levels of pesticides, studies in the 1980s and 1990s show that pesticides on fruits and vegetables and other imported foods may be even more important. In his 1996 book, *Our Children's Toxic Legacy, How Science and Law Fail to Protest Us from Pesticides* (Yale University Press, 1996), John Wargo said,

"Some U.S. companies manufacture pesticides that the Environmental Protection Agency (EPA) has prohibited from domestic use . . . These banned pesticides, however, may reappear as residues in imported foods, a phenomenon termed the 'circle of poison' by U.S. environmental and consumer interest groups . . .

"Children are especially vulnerable to health damage from pesticides. . . . They may be more susceptible to loss of brain function if exposed to neurotoxins during critical periods of development . . . Young children often eat more of fewer foods than adults . . . Higher intakes of some types of foods such as fruits, fruit juices and some vegetables could in turn lead to a greater consumption of pesticide residues on these foods."

As a pediatrician, I'm deeply concerned about the "epidemic" of children with behavior and learning problems, including ADHD and autism. And I feel that pesticides in the foods children are consuming may be playing an important role in causing these problems.

A conference co-sponsored by the International Health Foundation (IHF) and the International Center for Interdisciplinary Studies of Immunology (ICISI) at Georgetown University Medical Center, was held in Washington, D.C. in November 1999. Its title is *ADHD: Causes and Possible Solutions*. Among the causes that were discussed were the toxins in the air, food, soil and water.

For information about this conference write to IHF, Box 3494, Jackson, TN 38303, or to ICISI, Georgetown University Medical Center, 3800 Reservoir Rd., Washington, DC 20007.

Obtaining the Foods You'll Need

If your health problems are yeast connected, go to your kitchen and pantry and *get rid of the sugar, corn syrup, white bread, and other white-flour products, soda pop, most ready-to-eat cereals and all of the sweet-fat snack foods.* Foods or beverages containing these nutritionally deficient simple carbohydrates promote poor health. To overcome a candida-related disorder, you'll need to avoid them.

Replace them with more vegetables, including some you don't usually eat. Here are some suggestions with some you've heard of and some that may be strangers to you: asparagus, artichoke, boniata (white sweet potato), brussels sprouts, chayote, daikon, fennel, jicama and rutabaga. Also, buy the grain alternatives, including amaranth, buckwheat and quinoa. (Marge provides you with instructions and recipes for preparing and serving all of these foods in the recipe section of the book.)

Also get rid of the processed and prepared junk foods which contain coconut oil, palm oil, palm kernel oil and/or hydrogenated or partially hydrogenated fats, as well as those containing food coloring and additives. Replace them with modest amounts of linseed, canola, olive, walnut, sunflower, safflower, sesame and other unprocessed, unrefined oils.

Select and buy the purest foods you can find. If you're like most people with a yeast-connected health problem, you're bothered by chemicals of different kinds. These include insecticides, traffic fumes, formaldehyde, perfume, tobacco smoke and chemical contaminants in your food. Yet, finding foods that aren't chemically contaminated isn't easy.*

Visit the manager of your supermarket or specialty food store. Ask him if his store offers contaminant-free foods. He won't think you're crazy, because he's been reading and hearing about contaminated watermelons and apples and sick chickens. Moreover, he may have heard that the Grand Union Supermarket chain is successfully marketing "natural chicken" and "beef raised without additives and growth stimulants."

Even if your supermarket manager can't answer your questions about safe foods, ask him to look into the situation. Then shop mainly around the outer edges of your supermarket. Look for fresh and frozen vegetables, fresh meat, poultry, fish, seafood, eggs, olive oil, pure butter, and sardines packed in sardine oil.

Talk with other people in your community about establishing a co-op. Also, go to a farmer's market and see if you can find growers who raise their own vegetables (and other foods) "organically." And if you have space for a garden, begin raising some of your own food.

To get more information on how to get started, subscribe to *Natural Food and Farming,* the official journal of Natural Food Associates. This journal contains many interesting articles about organic gardening, plus advertisements from producers of chemically free vegetables, fruits, grains and meats. The cost of the journal and membership in Natural Food Associates is $15 a year. Send your check to Circulation Manager, P.O. Box 2110, Atlanta, Texas 75551.

Go to your health food store and purchase the following good foods:

Whole grains: Whole wheat, stone ground corn meal, short and long grain brown rice, barley, rye, oats and millet. Also the grain alternatives, quinoa, amaranth and buckwheat. You'll find those last three "new" foods useful for preparing breads and other baked goods if you do not tolerate grains. (See page 58.)

Unprocessed, unrefined vegetable oils: You need these oils to conquer your candida-related health problems. As I've already discussed in this book (pages 36–38) and in *The Yeast Connection*

---

*See my discussion of *The Chemical Problem* (pages 74–80).

and the Woman (pages 315–324) and in *The Yeast Connection Hand-book* (pages 99–100), you need the good essential fatty acids to conquer your yeast-connected health problems and regain your health. And food-grade flaxseed oil is the richest source of the essential Omega 3 fatty acids.

Other unprocessed vegetable oils include safflower, sunflower, soy, sesame, walnut, corn, olive and canola. According to Dr. Leo Galland of New York, an authority in treating candida-related health problems,

> "Olive oil is a rich source of antioxidants. . . . Symptomatic improvement for some candidiasis patients with olive oil supplementation is probably attributable to this antioxidant effect."

Oils tend to become rancid when they remain on a shelf at room temperature. So purchase your oils from a store with rapid turnover and keep them refrigerated.*

---

*Dated flaxseed oil is now available in many health food stores. Antioxidants are important in restoring immune function and combatting free radical pathology. For a comprehensive discussion of free radicals and other antioxidants, see *The Yeast Connection and the Woman*.

Food Allergies and the Rotated Diet

Candida-related health problems and food allergies go "hand-in-hand." In a questionnaire and telephone survey of 25 knowledgeable and experienced physicians, each respondent said, "All of my patients with candida-related health problems are troubled by food sensitivities."

Why do individuals with CRC develop food hypersensitivities? Here's a probable explanation. Research studies by W. Allan Walker, professor of pediatrics, Harvard Medical School, show that the lining of the intestinal tract (the mucosal barrier) can be adversely affected through many different mechanisms. And he stated,

> "There is increasing experimental and clinical evidence to suggest that large antigenically-active molecules can penetrate the intestinal epithelial surface—in quantities that may be of immunological importance. This observation could mean that the intestinal tract represents a potential site for the absorption of ingested food antigens that normally exist in the intestinal lumen."

Walker does not mention the possible role of candida in compromising the mucosal barrier. Yet the observations of both practicing physicians and researchers suggest that candida overgrowth in the gut may harm the mucosal barrier. This may lead to the absorption of incompletely digested food molecules, which may then cause food sensitivities.

The most frequent food offenders in my patients—and in the experience of other physicians—are yeast, wheat, milk, corn, eggs and legumes. However, *any food may cause an adverse reaction.* Such reactions are divided into two general types:

A. Obvious food allergies with prompt reactions
B. Hidden food allergies with delayed or masked reactions

Obvious food allergies are usually caused by uncommonly eaten foods including shrimp, cashew nuts, strawberries and lobster. However, obvious allergies may also be caused by eggs, peanuts, chocolate, tomato, citrus and other foods you eat frequently.

Hidden food allergies are usually caused by foods you eat every day—foods you crave, especially milk, corn, wheat, sugar, yeast and citrus. What's more, you may be "addicted" to a food causing your symptoms.* And as is the case with other addictive substances, you're apt to feel better when you eat the food you crave, even though you're allergic to it.

Here's an example. You're tired and feel you need a pickup. After drinking a glass of milk, you feel better. So you may say to yourself, "Milk really agrees with me." Then in an hour or so, you develop a headache and feel tired again. So you drink another glass of milk and again feel better, only to develop symptoms again in an hour or so. The same sort of "up-and-down" reaction can occur with coffee, orange juice, bread and other foods.

How do you know if you're sensitive to a food? With an obvious allergy, identifying the offender presents no problem. By contrast, tracking down a hidden food allergy requires a well-organized and properly executed bit of detective work.

Here's what you do:

1. Avoid a food or foods you suspect *completely* for five to seven days. Keep a diet diary for three days *before* you omit the suspected food or foods. Continue the diary during the period of elimination.

2. When you notice a *convincing improvement* in your symptoms lasting 48 hours, return the eliminated foods to your diet, one food each day and see if your symptoms return. In this way you "challenge" the offending food. You may notice a flare-up in your symptoms within a few minutes, or they may not occur for several hours or even until the next day. (You'll find detailed instructions for carrying out an elimination diet in the chapter "Getting Started.")

---

*I've included more information about allergies and especially hidden food allergies in my 2001 book *Tired—So Tired! and the "yeast connection."* You'll find this book in most general bookstores and health food stores, or you can order it from Wellness Health & Pharmaceuticals in Birmingham, AL, 800-227-2627.

Rotated Diets

A rotated diet means a varied diet. If you are bothered by food allergies (and most individuals with a candida-related disorder have them), you'll control them a lot better if you do not repeat a food more often than every fourth day.

Examples: Carrots on Monday, white potato on Tuesday, sweet potato on Wednesday, peas and beans on Thursday and carrots again on Friday.

Beef on Monday, shrimp on Tuesday, chicken on Wednesday, salmon on Thursday, etc.

Apples on Monday, pineapple on Tuesday, bananas on Wednesday, citrus on Thursday and apples again on Friday.

Rotating grains requires a different approach. Here's why: Wheat, rye, corn, oats, millet and rice all belong to the same food family—the grasses or grains. Cross-sensitivity reactions seem to occur more frequently than with fruits, vegetables and meats. For example, people who do not tolerate wheat usually experience problems with barley and rye, often are allergic to corn or oats, and sometimes, are bothered by rice, especially if they eat these grains every day.

To lessen your chances of developing "grain problems," eat more starchy vegetables and fewer grains. And try the grain alternatives, buckwheat, amaranth and quinoa (see also page 58). You can also learn more about grain alternatives in Marge Jones' monthly newsletter, *Mastering Food Allergies*. This newsletter contains a number of articles especially designed for the person with candida-related disorders and associated food allergies. To obtain more information, write to Marge at 2615 North 4th Street, Suite 677, Coeur d'Alene, ID 83814.

By following a rotated diet, you achieve the following advantages:

1. You're *treating* your food-allergy problems.
2. You're *diagnosing* the problem every time you eat a food and detect a reaction.
3. You're *preventing* further food allergies by reducing repetitious eating.

While on a rotation diet, keep the number of foods on your diet to a minimum until you find out which foods you tolerate and which foods cause symptoms. Here's an example of the sort of detective work you may need to do. Suppose you develop symptoms after a meal consisting of baked chicken breast, baked potato, steamed green beans and whole wheat bread.

Suspect 1. Which of these foods do you eat most often? Focus on this food first.

Suspect 2. Which food do you really love? This is sometimes an important clue.

If, like most people, you eat bread every day, eliminate it. Continue to eat the chicken, potato and beans on the appropriate day of your rotation.

Then if eliminating bread makes your symptoms disappear, you'll then need to identify the troublemaking ingredient of your bread. To do this, the next time your chicken, potato, beans, wheat meal is scheduled, eat a large portion of pure wheat-containing cereal. The best way to do this is to get whole-grain wheat from a health food store and cook it. A second choice would be shredded wheat.

If eating pure wheat doesn't bother you, chances are it's the yeast in the bread causing your problems. To make sure, try eating some pure baker's yeast. (For further instructions in testing for yeast sensitivity, see *The Yeast Connection and the Woman*.)

If you eliminate bread and still develop symptoms after a meal consisting of chicken, potatoes and beans, eliminate another food suspect. If potatoes have been one of your favorite foods, eliminate them and see what happens. If potatoes don't bother you, eliminate the beans and then the chicken.

By continuing to experiment, you can usually find out which foods cause symptoms and which ones do not.

Here are more comments on rotated diets and food allergies. Although you may not have been aware of it, you've probably been eating wheat, corn, eggs, milk, sugar, yeast and soy every day. Here's why: They're present in just about every commercially prepared food. To avoid these hidden foods, you need to cook "from scratch."

When you eat any food every day, your body may lose its tolerance to the food. Here's an example: Corn is used in many commercially prepared foods, and it's apt to be hidden in the form of dextrose, fructose, corn syrup or corn starch. Because most Americans consume corn-containing foods several times a day, hidden allergies to corn occur frequently. According to food allergy pioneer Theron Randolph, corn is the most common food allergen.

Regaining tolerance: When you follow the other parts of your candida treatment program and your health improves, your food allergies usually lessen.

Here's an example. You've identified milk as an allergy troublemaker. However, if you avoid milk and dairy products for six to eight weeks or longer, your milk sensitivity will usually lessen—like a *fire that dies down.* How do you find out? You experiment.

Drink two or three ounces of milk and see if you develop symptoms. If the milk doesn't cause a reaction, you may be able to use milk, yogurt or another dairy product every fourth day.* This will make your diet more enjoyable. However, if you resume eating milk-containing foods every day, your milk allergy will return.

You'll find more information about rotated diets in the following publications:

---

*Each person is different. To determine how often you'll tolerate a food that has bothered you in the past will require experimentation. You may tolerate it once a week, once every two weeks, or once a month. And some food sensitivities persist even though you avoid the food for many months.

If Today Is Tuesday, It Must Be Chicken by Natalie Golos. Human Ecology Research Foundation of the Southwest, 12110 Webbs Chapel Road, Dute 305E, Dallas, TX 75234.

The Allergy Self-Help Cookbook by Marge Jones (pages 31-46) Rodale Press, Emmaus, PA 18049.

Allergy and Candida Cooking Made Easy, by Sondra K. Lewis. Canary Connect Publications, P.O. Box 5317, Coralville, Iowa 52241-0317, 1996.

Allergy Cooking with Ease," by Nicolette M. Dumke. Starburst Publishers, P.O. Box 4123, Lancaster, PA 17604, 1992.

The Rotation Diet Game, by Dr. Sally Rockwell, Box 31065, Seattle, WA 98103. Send for free newsletter.

Coping with Candida Cookbook, by Dr. Sally Rockwell, Box 31065, Seattle, WA 98103. For more information, call (206) 547-1814.

5 Years Without Food: The Food Allergy Survival Guide, by Nicolette M. Dumke, Allergy Adapt, Inc., 1877 Polk Avenue, Louisville, CO 80027, (303) 666-8253, 1997.

Getting Started

I've talked about avoiding sugar and junk food and eating more complex carbohydrates and less protein and fat. I've also discussed the chemical contamination of many of our foods. I've also talked about food allergies and other sensitivities. Yet, your head may be spinning and you may be asking, "How do I get started?" "What do I do first?"

Almost without exception, every person with a candida-related health problem is bothered by allergies and other sensitivities. Although tests by your physicians can reliably indicate sensitivities to house dust mites, pollens, molds and animal danders, tests are only of a limited value in detecting food allergies and other adverse food reactions.

Such sensitivities are usually "hidden" and are caused by foods you crave and are eating every day. To identify the foods that bother you, you must carry out a carefully planned elimination diet. I recommend such a diet as your first step. To make things easier for you to understand, I've put my recommendations in question-and-answer form.

Q: How do I find out if my symptoms are caused by sensitivities to foods I'm eating every day?

A: You eliminate the foods which are most apt to be causing your symptoms.

Q: What will I look for? How will I know I'm allergic to a food?

A: If you're allergic to one or more of the foods you avoid, your symptoms will diminish after a few days. And they will return when you eat the food again.

Q: What foods should I eliminate?

A: You'll need to avoid many of your favorite foods. Here's why:

The more of a food you eat, the greater your chance of developing a sensitivity to the food. So while you're following the elimination diet you'll avoid many of the foods you've been eating every day, including milk and all dairy products, wheat, corn, corn syrup and corn sweeteners, yeast, eggs, peas, beans and other legumes, cane and beet sugar, chocolate, tea and coffee, food colors and flavors, food additives, processed foods and all fruits.

Q: I can see that this diet won't be easy. Can I get enough to eat?

A: Yes. Although you'll probably suffer food cravings during the first several days of your diet, you can get plenty of calories by filling up on the permitted foods.

Q: What food can I eat?

A: Vegetables of all kinds, except for corn and the legumes. Here are some of them: white potatoes, tomatoes, sweet potatoes, cabbage, lettuce, carrots, squash, asparagus, cauliflower, broccoli, onions, celery, green peppers, cucumbers, plus some vegetables you may not be familiar with, such as rutabaga, jicama, fennel, leek and many others. (Marge gives you detailed instructions for selecting and preparing these vegetables in her recipe section.) You can also eat lean meats of any kind, including turkey, chicken, beef, lamb and pork. Also fish and other seafood.

Q: How about breads or crackers?

A: Because wheat, corn and rye are common causes of chronic allergy, avoid these grains while you're on this diet. However, you can eat rice and oats and the grain alternatives, amaranth, quinoa and buckwheat, to make homemade breads, pancakes and crackers. (See the recipe section.)

Q: How about fruits? Do they cause allergies? Why do I need to avoid them?

A: Allergies or sensitivities to fruits do occur. However, they aren't nearly as common as allergies to yeast, milk, wheat and corn. Yet many people with yeast-connected health problems find their symptoms flare when they eat fruits—especially during the early weeks of their diet. Here's why: In spite of their fiber content, fruits are readily converted to fructose and other simple sugars in the intestinal tract. So avoid them until things "settle down," and this generally takes about three weeks.

Q: What can I drink?

A: Water. I recommend mineral water, distilled water, well water, spring water or herb tea.

Q: Is there anything else I can eat on this diet?

A: Yes. Nuts that are freshly shelled and untreated, including English walnuts, pecans, almonds, Brazil nuts, hazel nuts, pine nuts and macadamia nuts. Avoid peanuts. Also avoid pistachios because they're often contaminated with mold. Avoid processed nuts because they often contain sugar or other additives.

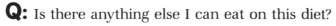

ALMONDS   PECANS

Q: Anything else?

A: Yes. You can use the unprocessed oils found in health food stores, including safflower, sunflower, sesame, canola, walnut, linseed and olive.

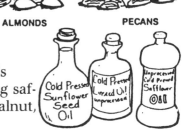

Q: How do I start this diet? What do I do first?

A: Discuss the diet with your spouse and other family members. Study the list of foods that are permitted and feature those that you and other members of your family enjoy. If they'll eat the same diet you eat, things will be easier, but if they feel deprived, they can eat other things that you're avoiding. Next, purchase foods and prepare menus you'll need. (You'll find menu suggestions for your elimination diet on pages 100–101.)

Q: What will I need to do to carry out this diet?

A: The diet is divided into two parts:

Part 1: During the initial elimination phase of the diet, you'll avoid many of the foods you usually eat to see if your symptoms improve or disappear.

Part 2: During the second phase of the diet, eat the foods you've eliminated one at a time and note which foods cause your symptoms to return. This is called a food challenge.

Q: How will I know the diet is making a difference?

A: Buy an 8″×10″ notebook and keep a detailed record of the foods you eat and record your symptoms.

    a. Start three days (or more) before you begin your diet.

    b. Continue your record while you're following the diet, five to seven days (sometimes longer).

    c. Be especially attentive while you're eating the eliminated foods again—one at a time.

Q: How will I feel on the diet?

A: During the first two to four days on your diet, you're apt to feel irritable and hungry. And you won't feel satisfied even though

you fill up on the permitted foods. You may feel restless and fidgety or tired and droopy.

You're apt to develop a headache or leg cramps and feel "mad at the world" because you aren't getting foods you crave—especially sweets. You may feel like a two-pack-a-day smoker who has just given up the "weed." (People with hidden food allergies are usually addicted to the foods they're allergic to.)

Here's some good news. If foods you've avoided are causing your symptoms, you'll usually feel better by the fourth, fifth or sixth day of your diet. Almost always, you'll improve by the tenth day. Occasionally, it will take two to three weeks before your symptoms go away.

Q: If I improve on the diet, what do I do then? When and how do I return foods to my diet?

A: After you're certain that all or most of your symptoms are better and your improvement has lasted for at least 2 days, start eating the foods again—one food each day. If you're allergic to a food you've eliminated, you should develop symptoms when you eat the food again.

Q: What symptoms should I look for and how soon will I notice them?

A: Usually, but not always, your main symptoms will reappear. You'd probably develop a headache or your nose would stuff up and you'd feel tired and depressed. However, sometimes you'll notice other symptoms, including some that haven't bothered you before, including itching, coughing or urinary frequency.

Your symptoms will usually reappear within a few minutes to a few hours. However, some people may not notice a significant symptom until the next day. Nearly always, if you avoid an allergy-causing food for a short period—five to twelve days—you'll develop symptoms promptly when you eat the food again. By contrast, if you avoid a food one to two months, your sensitivity will usually lessen and you won't show any symptoms unless you eat the food two or three days in a row.

Q: When I eat a food again, does it make any difference what form the food is in?

A: Yes! Yes! Yes! Add the food in pure form. For example, when you eat wheat, use pure whole wheat (obtainable from a health food store) rather than bread, since bread contains milk and other ingredients. If you're adding milk, use whole milk rather than ice cream, since ice cream contains sugar, corn syrup and other ingredients.

Here are suggestions for returning foods to your diet:

Milk—Drink an ounce or so for breakfast. If it causes no symptoms, drink a couple of ounces in the middle of the morning. Then, if you still show no symptoms, drink as much as you want later in the day.

Wheat—On the second day add wheat. Get pure whole wheat from your health food store, add water and cook it for 25 minutes. Add sea salt if you wish.

Eggs—Eat eggs on the third day. Make sure they're well cooked (see page 346).

Yeast—Use brewer's yeast tablets, baker's yeast and/or mushrooms. Here's a suggestion for challenging with yeast: break off a crumb of brewer's yeast and eat it, if you show no reaction in ten minutes, eat a bigger crumb. Continue to eat additional pieces of yeast tablets during the next hour. If you show no reaction to the first tablet, eat a second tablet several hours later. Then eat a mushroom and, if drinking milk didn't bother you, eat some moldy cheese.

Corn—Use fresh corn on the cob, pure corn syrup, grits or hominy, or eat some plain popcorn. Eat a small amount in the morning, then gradually increase the amounts just as you did with yeast.

Legumes—Eat some peanuts, peas, string beans, lima beans, soy beans, or black-eyed peas.

Q: How about sugar, chocolate, food coloring, tea, coffee and some of the other foods I've avoided? Do I challenge with them?

A: Yes. Challenge with any food or beverage you've been eating or drinking frequently. And add it back just as you did with the milk, wheat, yeast, legumes, eggs and corn. Start with a small amount in the morning and gradually increase it during the day.

Q: I think I understand what you want me to do. However, a few points aren't clear and I'd appreciate it if you would review them for me and give me any additional suggestions you feel are important.

A: Okay. Here they are. Plan ahead. Go shopping. Purchase the foods you'll need. Then ask—even beg—other family members to help you and to cooperate.

Keep a diary of your symptoms for at least 3 days before you begin your diet. Continue your diary until you've eliminated the foods and added them back again.

If you're sensitive to a food you've been avoiding, you'll usually show a significant improvement in four to seven days. Then to tell which of the foods bother you, eat the eliminated foods again one food per day and see if your symptoms return.

Keep the rest of your diet the same while you're carrying out the challenges. If you show an obvious reaction after eating a food, eliminate it again, then wait until the reaction subsides (usually 24 to 48 hours) before you test another food.

If a food challenge causes severe symptoms, you can shorten the reaction by taking a teaspoon of "soda mixture" (two parts baking soda and one part potassium bicarbonate)—your pharmacist can prepare this mixture for you. Or dissolve two tablets of Alka Seltzer Gold in a glass of water and drink it. You can also take a laxative such as Milk of Magnesia, Magnesium Citrate or Epsom Salts to eliminate the offending food from your digestive tract rapidly.

Q: Suppose I'm allergic to milk, yeast, wheat, corn legumes or other foods? Does this mean that I'll always be allergic to these foods?

A: No. If you avoid a food you're allergic to for one to two months, your sensitivities to the food will usually decrease so that you can eat the food occasionally. Taking antifungal medication and following a comprehensive treatment program will also help you overcome your food sensitivities.

My good friend, the late William C. Deamer, professor of pediatrics at the University of California, compared food allergy to a fire that gradually dies down. Yet, Dr. Deamer pointed out that blowing on the embers (like eating a lot of the food) will cause the allergy to return.

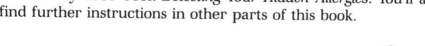

You'll find further discussion of food allergies and elimination diets in my 1988 book *Detecting Your Hidden Allergies*. You'll also find further instructions in other parts of this book.

Foods You Can Eat on Your Trial Diet

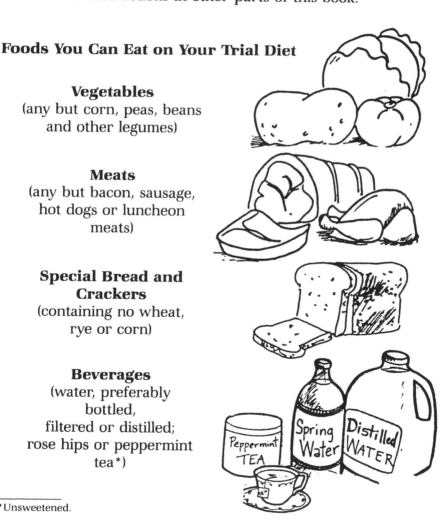

Vegetables
(any but corn, peas, beans and other legumes)

Meats
(any but bacon, sausage, hot dogs or luncheon meats)

Special Bread and Crackers
(containing no wheat, rye or corn)

Beverages
(water, preferably bottled, filtered or distilled; rose hips or peppermint tea*)

*Unsweetened.

Miscellaneous
(fresh shelled unprocessed
nuts, seeds and oils—no
peanuts or pistachios)

Foods You Must Avoid

Milk, cheese, yogurt and other dairy products

Eggs or egg-containing foods

Foods containing wheat or rye

Foods containing corn

**Fruits and foods
containing sugar**

Chocolate and colas

Yeast-containing foods

Coffee and alcohol

**Soy, peanuts, beans and
other legumes**

Coloring and additives

Menu Suggestions

Here are menu suggestions that may help you carry out your elimination diet. As you'll see, only a few foods are included in each meal. Here's why: the fewer the ingredients, the better your chances for successfully completing your trial diet.

If you're a person who likes to get the day started with a hearty meal, the breakfast menus (no orange juice, coffee, sugar, eggs, bacon, wheat, cereal or toast) will look especially skimpy. Yet, if you'll look at Marge's recipes in her breakfast and bread section, you'll find specific instructions for preparing grain-free pancakes, amaranth soda bread and waffles, cooked quinoa and quinoa crackers.

You'll also find a recipe for wheat and corn-free tortillas. However, if you aren't up to cooking and preparing all of these foods, you can fill up on some or all of the following foods: Oats, rice, quinoa, buckwheat, nuts, meats, fish, potatoes and other vegetables. (Yes, you can eat meat and vegetables for breakfast!)

Your lunches and evening meals should be easier. Eat mainly vegetables of all sorts, plus some meats and nuts. Bake or broil your meats and steam your vegetables. Remember, you can eat any vegetable but corn and the legumes. Vary your diet as much as possible.

For between-meal snacks, go to your health food store and load up on nuts and seeds of all kinds (except peanuts and pistachios). You can also snack on raw vegetables and rice cakes or crackers.

For beverages, use spring, filtered or bottled water and a simple herb tea, such as peppermint tea or rose hips tea.

If you don't like the vegetables suggested on the menus, look in Marge's section for other ideas. Also, check at your farmer's market or supermarket for some of the "new" vegetables, including rutabaga, jicama, fennel, leek, turnips, eggplant, okra, radishes and many others.

You can also get nut butters other than peanut butter and the unprocessed oils, including sunflower, safflower, olive, linseed, walnut and canola. You can mix these oils with lemon juice for seasoning your vegetables or making salad dressings. And of course you can use your imagination and ingenuity in putting together vegetable or vegetable and nut salads of all sorts.

SEVEN-DAY MEAL PLAN

DAY	BREAKFAST	LUNCH	SUPPER	SNACKS
1	Cooked oatmeal, pork chop, cashew nuts	Pork chop, broccoli, Sesame-Oat Crackers, sliced tomatoes	Shrimp, broccoli, lettuce and tomato salad, squash	Broccoli or squash, cashew nuts, Sesame-Oat Crackers
2	Cooked brown rice, filberts, sardines packed in sardine oil, rice cakes	Kasha and cabbage soup, cauliflower, carrots, rice cakes	Baked chicken, rice, carrots, filberts, rice cakes	Raw carrots, filberts, sunflower seeds, rice cakes
3	Cooked Quinoa, lamb patty, pecans	Turkey breast, baked sweet potato, beets	Lamb chops, spinach, vegetable salad (use your imagination)	Celery and carrot sticks, crackers, celery
4	Sesame Walnut Pancakes, chopped walnuts, peppermint tea	Beef patty, asparagus, squash	Small steak, baked potato, brussels sprouts, tossed salad	Walnuts
5	Oatmeal, pork chop, cashew Nuts	Salmon, broccoli, sliced tomatoes, Sesame-Oat Crackers	Baked snapper, broccoli, squash	Squash, celery, broccoli
6	Brown rice, sardines in sardine oil, rice crackers, filberts	Kasha and cabbage soup, carrots, rice cakes, cauliflower	Baked chicken, rice, filberts, carrots	Filberts, sunflower seeds, rice cakes
7	Cooked Quinoa, sweet potato, pecans	Turkey breast, sweet potato, beets	Lamb chops, sweet potato, spinach	Pumpkin seeds, pecans

Bake or broil the meats and steam the vegetables. Suggestions for breads, pancakes, waffles, soups, salads and dressings can be found in the recipe section.

The Cave Man Diet

If you're following a comprehensive treatment program for your yeast-related health problems and . . .

- You have identified several foods that bother you and are avoiding them
- You're continuing to experience symptoms
- You suspect that you are sensitive to other foods

. . . you may wish to try the Cave Man Diet. This term is used to describe a diet which avoids every food you eat more than once a week. This diet requires careful planning, preparation, shopping and execution.

Here's what you can eat and drink on the Cave Man Diet:

Oils
Safflower, sunflower, walnut, olive or canola

Grain Alternatives
Amaranth, buckwheat, quinoa

Meats, Fish and Seafood
Lamb, shrimp, cod, salmon (or other fish), lobster, scallops, wild game

Vegetables
any but corn, white potato, tomato and legumes

Beverages
Mineral water, spring water

Nuts
Filbert, Brazil nut, English walnut, almond, pecan

ALMONDS   PECANS

Here are the foods you must avoid:

processed and packaged foods

chocolate

white potato

apple

egg

beef

pork

citrus

legumes
beans, peas, peanuts

food coloring,
additives, emulsifiers,
preservatives

yeast

milk, cheese, yogurt

sugar

coffee, tea and alcohol

All grains

Although you may think you'll starve on the Cave Man Diet, you can take in plenty of calories by eating six or more times a day. Bake or broil your meats and fish and steam your vegetables. You'll find vegetable suggestions and detailed instructions for preparing them in Marge's Recipe Section of this book.

You can also obtain many of the calories you need from unprocessed nuts and the grain alternatives, and Marge provides you with detailed instructions for making bread, waffles and pancakes in the Breakfast and Bread Section of this book.

Continue the Cave Man Diet for 5 to 10 days. As soon as you show a significant lessening of your symptoms lasting 2 days, start challenging with the foods you've eliminated

Return the foods that you have eliminated* *one at a time* at breakfast, lunch, supper and bedtime (four times a day). Eat the food in large quantities—as for example, six eggs for breakfast, two or three baked potatoes for lunch and a half to whole chicken for supper and four bananas at bedtime.

If a food causes a reaction, a laxative is taken to expedite or remove the foods from the digestive tract. Additional food challenges are delayed until your symptoms have subsided.

---

*Here's a different method George and Leslie Peickert-Kroker have found effective in managing their patients. They call it gradual rotation. Here's how they do it. One new food is returned to the diet each week at a specific time. For example on Friday evening, a permitted or tolerated food is eaten at 5 P.M. Then a test food is eaten (in moderate to large amounts) at 7 P.M. as the last meal of the day. Symptoms are noted and recorded before the meal is eaten and during the minutes and hours before and after bedtime. They're also noted the next morning.

Here's why. Food reactions often delayed may cause hangovers similar to those which follow alcohol ingestion. In discussing this plan, the Krokers said, "This method enables our patients to gradually increase the number and variety of tolerated foods over a period of weeks and months."

Moving Ahead

Bringing yeast-connected health problems under control is sometimes easy. For example, Emily wrote me recently from Utah and said:

"Thank you, Dr. Crook, for helping me get well. I was bothered by fatigue, headache, depression, PMS and many other symptoms. I had visited many different doctors looking in vain for help. Then after reading your book, I eliminated sugar and yeast from my diet. I immediately began to improve. When I also avoided wheat and milk, and took antifungal medicine and nutritional supplements, within a couple of months I felt like a new person.

It's been a little over two years since I started on the program and now I'm a well person—full of energy. I rarely develop symptoms unless I *really* cheat on my diet, or I'm exposed to tobacco smoke or strong perfumes."

Yet, I've also heard from people who aren't doing so well. For example, Rita called me from New York recently, and said:

"I'm bothered by persistent vaginal yeast infections, headache, fatigue, chemical sensitivities, intolerance to many foods, itching and burning of my skin all over. Although I've followed a yeast-free, sugar-free diet and have been helped by nystatin and Nizoral, I continue to have symptoms. What do you advise?"

Responding to Rita, I told her I could understand why she might feel frustrated and discouraged. Then I told her that I thought the chances were excellent that she could overcome her problems and that she should persist in efforts.

I pointed out that in the years 1993–1996, a number of my physician consultants told me of the effectiveness of Diflucan and Sporanox in treating some of their difficult patients, and during 1997, Dr. Sidney Baker and Dr. Charles Resseger, told me of the successful use of the new antifungal medication, Lamisil, in helping their patients who had failed to respond to other antifungal drugs and now I tell my own patients like Rita, who are continuing to experience problems.

Your yeast-connected health problems are related to what

might be called "lowered resistance" or a *weakened immune system*. And you may be able to strengthen your immune system and regain your health in a few weeks or months.

More often, however, it will take time, patience, persistence and careful management of the multiple factors contributing to your illness. The example of the overburdened camel illustrates this important point. So to regain your health—to look good, feel good and enjoy life, you'll need to unload many "bundles of straw."

Now then. *In moving ahead, what you eat will depend on your answers to many different questions,* including:

1. What foods are you allergic to?
2. What foods are available to you?
3. Do you live alone?
4. If you have a roommate or a spouse and/ or children, are they interested and supportive?
5. Does your work require you to travel and eat many meals on the road?
6. Can you prepare your lunch at home and take it to work with you ("brown bagging")?
7. Have you found a physician (or other professional) interested in the Candida-Related Complex (CRC), who can help you?

Other pertinent questions include: Do you like to cook? How big is your freezer? Do you raise any of your own fruits, vegetables, meats or nuts? Are there organic farmers in your community? Can you obtain fish from uncontaminated sources?

No matter what your answers are to these questions, here are simple instructions that should help you:

1. Avoid any food you're allergic to for a month or two. Then, because food allergy is "like a fire that dies down," cautiously try eating a food troublemaker again. If it doesn't trigger your symptoms, eat it occasionally, but no more often than every 4 to 7 days.
2. Include more vegetables in your diet—vegetables of all kinds, even some you don't usually eat.

3. Bake, broil or steam your vegetables. You can use herbs, fresh or dried, to season them (if you aren't unusually sensitive to molds).

4. Lean meats and fish are okay. Yet, you don't need to eat them every day and certainly not every meal.

5. Eggs are okay if you aren't allergic to them. However, eating them once or twice a week is enough.

6. Grain products, including oatmeal, oat bran, whole wheat, shredded wheat, brown rice, rice cakes, barley and millet, are nutritious foods. They contain fiber and lots of trace minerals. Include them in your diet if you aren't allergic to them.

7. Become familiar with and use the grain alternatives, amaranth, quinoa and buckwheat. You can find these products in almost any health food store, and Marge's recipes will tell you how to use them.

8. Avoid sugar and foods that contain simple carbohydrates, including corn syrup, white flour, white rice and honey.

9. How about dairy products? Many people, including those with CRC, are bothered by intolerances and allergies to milk—especially whole milk. (It also contains lots of undesirable saturated fat.) So use dairy products with caution.

   However, sugar-free, fruit-free yogurt is generally well tolerated, even by some people who are sensitive to other milk products. Home-prepared yogurt (using yogurt starter) is especially good because it contains more friendly yeast-fighting lactobacilli.

10. How about fruits?* Along with many other specialists, I've found that fruits often trigger symptoms in patients with CRC. So I usually tell my patients to avoid fruits for the first three weeks, until they improve. Then begin eating them on a trial basis—cautiously.

---

*Dr. Harold Hedges and Penny Fox of Little Rock, Arkansas, include fruits during the early weeks of the diet. Recently Penny commented, "Our patients usually arrive so sick and so stressed out that even doing your complete elimination diet is more than they can handle. In such patients, we begin with these very simple instructions. Absolutely no sugar, alcohol or moldy cheese. Yet we permit them to have a couple of pieces of bread and two servings of fruit a day.

"We've found that most patients have to get better before they can follow more difficult and complex instructions. Then as we see patients for return visits, especially those who aren't doing better, we provide them with additional information. And we've arranged cooking classes for some of our highly motivated patients."

11. How about yeast-containing foods? Many people with CRC develop symptoms when they eat raised breads, moldy cheeses, drink beer or canned fruit juices (such juices are loaded with yeast). Moreover, some highly sensitive people may react to small amounts of yeast in salad dressings or leftovers. Still others develop symptoms when they drink coffee or tea.

   In discussing fermented and aged products, juices and other beverages, yeast authority Sidney M. Baker commented,* "Everyone is different. Individual tolerances for coffee, tea, cheeses, juices, and alcohol have to be determined on a trial and error basis by each person."

   He also stated that freshly squeezed juices stored for a day or two in the refrigerator don't usually cause problems and that some people can "consume high 100 proof alcoholic beverages with fewer problems than if they consumed beers or wines."

   If you passed the "yeast challenge test" you may be able to consume some yeasty foods, but don't go overboard.

12. What can you drink? I especially recommend bottled or filtered water. Here's why: It contains fewer chemical contaminants. For a hot beverage, add a squeeze of lemon or orange juice. Herb teas are also usually well tolerated—if you aren't highly sensitive to yeast and molds.

   How about coffee and regular tea? Some people with CRC tolerate them, while others do not. If you're sensitive to yeast, you'll have to experiment. And even if yeasty foods and beverages don't bother you, eating or drinking the same substances every day often causes problems.

13. How about the artificial sweeteners? Many people with CRC tolerate them in limited amounts. You can try them and see if they agree. I prefer the liquid saccharin preparations including *Fasweet* and *Sweeta*. (For a further discussion of artificial and other sweeteners see pages 355–366 of *The Yeast Connection and the Woman,*and pages 180–183 of *The Yeast Connection Handbook*.)

14. Expand and diversify your diet to avoid repetitive eating.

---

*You'll find further information about Dr. Baker's theories on yeast on pages 336–337 of *The Yeast Connection and the Woman*.

Nearly all people with CRC develop food allergies. Here's the apparent reason:

Increased candida in the gut irritates the membrane lining of the intestinal tract, including its mucus covering. Experimental studies by several scientists show that this results in a "leaky gut," which allows microscopic amounts of food particles to enter the body, leading to allergic reactions.

The more frequently you eat a food, the more apt you are to develop an allergy to that food. Accordingly, rotating your diet, i.e., eating foods no more often than every fourth day helps keep food allergies from developing.

15. Menu suggestions: Use the 7-day meal plan as a starting point, and use any foods you aren't allergic to. Become familiar with and use Marge's recipes. They're tasty and loaded with all sorts of nutrients which promote good health, and they've all been carefully and lovingly kitchen tested by a real expert.

    Look especially at her magnificent section on the many different varieties of vegetables. (Marge provides you with detailed instructions for selecting, purchasing, preparing and cooking these vegetables.)

16. Take charge of your life and health, and do the other things you need to do to strengthen your immune system and maintain your health. (You'll find a 10-step program in chapter 9 of *The Yeast Connection Handbook,* "Steps You'll Need to Take to Regain Your Health.")

    Diets aren't forever: At the Memphis Candida Update Conference, George and Leslie Peickert-Kroker comprehensively reviewed and analyzed the various diets used by different professionals in treating CRC. They stress many things including the importance of providing diets—

which include all the important nutrients

which recognize the importance of food sensitivities and help people deal with them

They also said,

"Diets shouldn't be too difficult to follow and should not become boring and cause frustration and depression."

They pointed out that such feelings often lead to poor compliance and failure to improve. And they said in effect,

"Diets aren't forever and diet restrictions should be periodically re-evaluated by the person with CRC and the professionals who care for them."

SECTION 2

Recipes

Introduction

A few years ago I experienced a variety of health problems that my family doctor dismissed as "that time" for a woman. He suggested that I busy myself as a volunteer in a hospital. Without benefit of testing, he gave me his diagnosis: 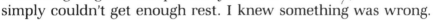 Empty Nest Syndrome!

I didn't believe it for a minute! I felt fatigued . . . spacey . . . with all-over muscle weakness. My attention wandered so much that I had trouble concentrating. I found myself crying easily—for no reason. And sometimes after meals I felt an overwhelming urge to sleep. Always tired, I simply couldn't get enough rest. I knew something was wrong.

After a comprehensive treatment program that included an anti-candida diet, anti-fungal medication and nutritional supplements, I'm a new person. Cured? I didn't say that. But my head is clear and I have a ton of energy. Yet, I know problems still exist.

What's different now? These things occur to me:

1. *I did (and do) my "homework"*—I attend health lectures and study many resources to better understand my health problems.
2. *I changed my attitude.* As I gained information, I became more hopeful and positive. Instead of "Poor me, I'm a victim," I became a participant in my recovery. I charted my course of action and worked hard to stay on track.
3. *I made a commitment to getting well.* I decided to do everything possible to help my body heal—and to avoid doing anything that would harm it.
4. *I learned to select and prepare the food that I need*—including meals to eat on the run or while traveling. Now I plan my food for a trip as routinely as I pack my suitcase!
5. *I started to exercise* as soon as I regained a little energy. I learned that I feel better when I stick to a routine of regular exercise. Mostly I walk briskly. But sometimes I pedal and

pump a dual-action exercise bike. Or I swim. I've learned to work at my own pace to avoid feeling overtired.

Clearly the recipes in this section focus on food selection and preparation. Yet, I want to emphasize that my own recovery required *more* than a special diet. In overcoming my problem, I learned to cook without sugar, honey, maple syrup and vinegar.

I even discovered foods I'd never heard of. I also learned better ways to select and store foods. In the pages that follow, I share those discoveries with you. I hope they'll help you as much as they've helped me!

What You'll Find In My Recipes

If you're like many folks I've talked to who have looked at the list of foods to avoid, you're apt to wail, "What's left for me to eat?" So I've designed my recipes so that they focus on foods that most people can eat and enjoy.

I have emphasized tasty vegetables of all sorts which will make your diet more enjoyable and less apt to cause allergies. I also use a variety of grains, rather than just wheat

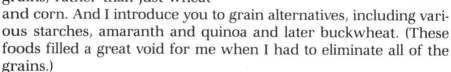

and corn. And I introduce you to grain alternatives, including various starches, amaranth and quinoa and later buckwheat. (These foods filled a great void for me when I had to eliminate all of the grains.)

Because milk intolerance or sensitivity causes problems for so many people, I include only a few recipes that contain a dairy product (yogurt), and I suggest alternatives like Nut Milk or Nutty "Mayo." Fewer than 10% of my recipes contain egg, and only one bread recipe calls for yeast.

With my specially designed recipes you shouldn't need to do much adapting. I've done most of it for you. But I often include suggestions for other ingredients, in case you wish to substitute.

Getting It Together

If, like most folks, you rely on packaged mixes, fast food restaurants or carry-outs from the "deli," you may find it difficult to start cooking "from scratch." I can't deny that cooking takes time. I can only suggest that *if you really want to enjoy better health, planning and preparing nutritious meals is the place to start.*

As I've counseled people about their diets, I've found that folks who take the time to prepare delicious, attractively served meals, don't feel deprived. Attitude and planning make all the difference in the world!

You can expect your candida-control diet to be different from meals you usually eat—and different from the "typical" American diet. But that's not all bad. Here's why: Diets loaded with refined carbohydrates, fat, protein and salt contribute to many different degenerative diseases. So while you're overcoming your candida-related problems, you'll be lessening chances of developing heart disease, osteoporosis, diabetes and cancer.

I wrote the recipe directions in great detail so you'll know what to do, how to do it and what to watch for. You can prevent many culinary catastrophes by reading through the directions (as well as the ingredients) before you start, so you're sure you understand each step of the process. Assemble both your equipment and ingredients before you start.

In introducing my recipes, I often suggest shortcuts and time-saving tips. With practice, you'll probably devise your own tricks to reduce the time you spend in the kitchen. For instance, you might decide to cook double the quantity you need and freeze the rest. Or you might decide to cook your breakfast (and maybe lunch) before you go to bed.

Recipes which contain common allergy troublemakers are coded to help you:

[C]	= Corn	[E]	= Egg	[L]	= Legumes
[M]	= Milk	[W]	= Wheat	[Y]	= Yeast

Nuts and herbs may also trigger symptoms in some yeast-sensitive people, especially if stored at room temperature. Recipes containing these items are *not* coded, however; use cautiously, initially.

I realize that cooking and preparing special recipes takes time—lots of time. Yet, you might look at your special requirements as an adventure or a game, rather than a hassle. Begin with one or more of my simple recipes. And when you succeed with them, I hope you'll return to these pages again and again and try more of them.

Okay! Get ready (study this book) . . . get set (send for or buy the ingredients you'll need) . . . and go for it!

Meal Planning

In planning your candida-control diet, you first identify the foods that bother you, using Dr. Crook's elimination diet and challenge.

If you found that you're extra sensitive to yeast, you'll need to avoid yeast-containing foods for many, many weeks before you try them again. Similarly, if you're allergic to milk, egg, corn, wheat—or other foods, you must avoid them until things "settle down" and you're improving.

Whether you're allergic to these foods or whether you aren't, your first step toward easing the hassle is to relax and take the task in stride. Forget about the typical American breakfast of bacon and eggs or cereal with milk. Forget about rigid "shoulds" and "oughts" that you've accumulated in your head over the years.

I was surprised to find a new sense of freedom in planning my menus when I threw out the "rules." I make "dinner" (that is the main meal of the day) anytime it's convenient for me—even first thing in the morning. I eat food that's appropriate for my diet at any hour of the day, without apology (fish and vegetables for breakfast and cereal for supper, for example).

Vegetables

A high-vegetable diet is a healthy diet—high in fiber, complex carbohydrates, vitamins and minerals. And it's low in fat. Veggies should constitute 70–80% of your diet. Keep this in mind when you see fish, chicken (and/or other lean meats) and vegetables listed in my recipes. So load up on veggies and eat smaller amounts of meats. Also, eat some of the grains and fruits if they don't trigger your symptoms.

Food Allergies

I omitted yeast, wheat, corn, milk and eggs from many of my recipes. Even if you've found that you aren't allergic to these foods,

I wouldn't eat them more often than every fourth day because they're so apt to cause sensitivity reactions. I also eliminated chocolate, food coloring and food additives and sugars of all kinds.

If you've found that you're sensitive to many foods, including potatoes, tomatoes, oats, and rice, you may have to do even more detective work. *Any food can cause problems, especially those you eat everyday.* By varying your diet and keeping a written record of what you eat and what symptoms you're experiencing, you may be able to identify foods that agree with you and the foods that do not.

No single method works best for the person with multiple food allergies. However, if you find you're reacting to many foods, here are my suggestions:

1. Rotate your diet and do not repeat any food more often than every fourth day. You'll find menus and other instructions which will help you in Section III of this book. You can also achieve variety in your meals by utilizing many different vegetables and other foods.

2. Find a physician who is interested and knowledgeable in dealing with food allergies to guide you. You'll also find helpful information about food allergies in my newsletter, *Mastering Food Allergies,** and in Dr. Crook's book *Detecting Your Hidden Allergies.*

DETECTING YOUR HIDDEN ALLERGIES

Foods you eat everyday can cause asthma, "sinus", headaches, fatigue, nervousness, digestive problems, arthritis ... and many other disorders.

By William G. Crook, M.D.

Nuts and Seeds

Nuts and seeds contain a lot of nutrients, and I include them in many of my recipes. Purchase them from a busy store with a rapid turnover. When you get to know the clerks in the store, ask them when they expect a fresh shipment. Then go in and buy a couple of months supply and store them in your freezer. Discard shriveled or "runt" nuts, and avoid pistachios, because they are loaded with mold.

---

*Mastering Food Allergies, 2615 N. 4th St., Suite 677, Coeur d' Alene, Idaho 83814.

Leftovers

Mold growth occurs on food stored in your refrigerator. So put your leftovers in glass jars, date them and put them in your freezer.

Fruits

Because they are rapidly converted into simple sugars in the intestinal tract, fruits may trigger your symptoms. Wait until you're feeling better before trying them. Begin with ¼ of a banana, apple or pear. If it agrees with you, gradually increase your fruit intake over the course of the next several weeks.

Later, you can eat fruits as a snack, add them to cereals or salads, or use them in preparing all-fruit sorbet or other desserts.

How about juices? Wait many months before trying them. Here's why: they contain little or no fiber to slow their absorption, and unless freshly prepared, juices contain a lot of molds.

Breakfasts

"What can I eat for breakfast?" Time and time again I hear this. And it's a valid concern for people who are on a diet to control candida.

If you strip breakfast of yeast, you eliminate toast, French toast, bagels, sweet rolls—even sourdough bread (See Breads). If you also omit wheat, milk, corn, sugar, soy and egg, as many of us do, you end up with a gaping void in your menus where breakfast used to be.

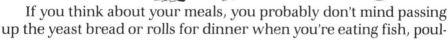

If you think about your meals, you probably don't mind passing up the yeast bread or rolls for dinner when you're eating fish, poultry or meat, served with plenty of vegetables. But toastless breakfast seems hardest hit, followed closely by bread-oriented lunches (We'll discuss lunch in the next chapter). It takes imagination and a little creative problem solving to cope with these limitations, but that's what this book is all about.

Some of the ingredients may be unfamiliar to you. Look in the chapter on helpful hints for descriptions and uses of them.

Pancakes? or Flatbread?

You can do a lot more with pancakes than drown them in a puddle of syrup! You can make them a few days ahead, package and refrigerate or freeze them. To use, crisp them in a toaster oven or on a rack in a (conventional) low-temperature oven.

Eat these versatile little treasures with your fingers, like dainty pieces of toast. Or top them with your favorite filling or bean dip for open-faced mini-sandwiches. They go brown-bagging easily and travel well on trips, too.

You can make simple, flat pancakes by adding enough water *to any flour* to make a medium batter. Everything added beyond that point only embellishes. A little oil often makes the cakes more tender and helps you turn them more easily. Eggs lighten and bind foods. A little salt, cinnamon, vanilla or anise enhances or adds flavor. Arrowroot and tapioca starches hold moisture and tend to "soften" the taste of the stronger flours such as amaranth, dark buckwheat or rye. But remember, *except for flour and water, they're all optional.*

Leavening

Leavening is a hallmark of civilization. It produces light textured breads. Historically, however, man simply combined flour and water with a pinch of salt to pat into hearty flatbread.

Today cooks use baking powder in their breadmaking. Yet, I'm concerned about most of the commercial, double-acting baking powders. Here's why: They contain aluminum. And, as you may have heard, some authorities feel that aluminum may play a role in causing Alzheimer's disease.

Even baking powder in your health food store can cause problems for people who are allergic to corn or potato. Sometimes I make single-acting baking powder at home (see page 324). However, since it's less effective, I've come up with still another alternative.

I mix baking soda and an acidic food—lemon juice, cream of tartar or unbuffered vitamin C crystals. Then, when the liquid and dry mixtures are combined, the soda and acid react, releasing CO_2 (carbon dioxide). If the CO_2 is trapped in the batter, the baked item is lightened or "raised."

Bake the food promptly after mixing, to catch whatever CO_2 action you've generated. The gluten in wheat is tops at this function. But the flours that I usually work with lack gluten and don't respond much to the bubbling action. So I often omit leavening altogether (unless I add a gum to help—read on).

Pancakes tend to go flat because the batter has to stand, while the first batch of cakes is cooking. Leavened muffins, nutbread and coffeecake are different. To prepare them, I preheat the oven, prepare the pans, assemble all dry ingredients in one bowl and all of the liquids in another bowl or blender jar. I combine the two mixtures with a few swift strokes and pop the item into the oven.

Interestingly, as I learned about leavening, I found that guar and other natural gums form a "net" in baked goods that traps the CO_2. You'll obtain a lighter, slightly higher end product when you add ½ teaspoon of guar or other gum (per cup of flour) to the recipe. So experiment with these gums from your health food store. They hail from the legume family.

Breakfast Strategies

- Discover Breakfast Pudding and experiment with the many variations.
- Learn how to make Nutri-Ola in its many forms—a favorite at home and a must for travel.
- Learn about the non-grain alternatives to grains—amaranth, buckwheat, quinoa (pronounced keen-wa) and teff.
- Use grains with discretion, if you tolerate them at all. Wheat and corn are prime allergy offenders. Even if you are lucky enough to tolerate them, don't eat them every day. By varying your diet, you're less apt to develop sensitivities. Barley, oat and rye are closely related to wheat and cause problems in wheat-sensitive people. Here are suggestions for a common-sense approach to grains:
  1. Alternate the grains with non-grain alternatives—amaranth, buckwheat quinoa and teff.
  2. Use more of the less-commonly used grains—millet, milo (sorghum) and wild rice.
  3. Eat more vegetables and less bread.
- Try fish or meat with vegetables for your morning meal. It's internationally chic to do so! The English enjoy fish for breakfast, and the Japanese often start their day with tofu—or fish-vegetable soup. I devised a way to eat sweet potato for breakfast that I really enjoy.
- Plan ahead. Allow time to shop for the foods you need, and give yourself more time for food preparation. At least at first, try preparing your breakfast in the evening—possible candi-

dates include Breakfast or Creamy Pudding, Nutri-Ola, and any of the pancakes in this chapter.

- Try to avoid feeling frantic and rushed. If you oversleep and worry about missing the bus, you'll experience "dietary desperation." And you'll pop absolutely anything into your mouth.

Breakfast Pudding

Serves 1

This is it. You may decide this recipe is worth the price of the whole book! It's so versatile you can enjoy it warm or cold. If you choose "cold," plan ahead by cooking enough for three or four meals. Package in individual portions, label and freeze until needed. Or cook the sweet potato, quinoa or whatever the night before and chill overnight.

Note the wide range of variations. Some are grains, others are the non-grain alternatives and a few are vegetables. Breakfast Pudding solves the problem of family members who require or prefer different foods for breakfast. You aren't apt to miss cereal with milk after trying it.

1   cup cooked diced sweet potato, warm or cold

2-4 ripe apricots, or 1 or 2 cubes of pine-
    apple Fruit Sweetener, page 322

¼   cup chopped almonds or other nuts,
    optional

Put the cubes of sweet potato in a cereal bowl. Purée the apricots in a blender and pour over the sweet potato. (If you're only having 2 apricots you may wish to add 2 or more tablespoons of water for more juiciness.) Sprinkle the almonds on top. Enjoy.

❖ VARIATIONS ❖

Use a different starch with different fruits and different nuts. The sky's the limit!

The Starch—Use a cup or more of cooked quinoa, millet, buckwheat, rice, rye, barley, oat or diced, baked butternut squash. Use the whole groats form of the grains.

The Fruit—Try puréed fresh peach, banana, kiwi, pear, apple, pineapple, plums, or berries. Vary the *amount* of fruit to suit your tolerance for sweets—for instance ⅓ of a banana, a few tablespoons of fresh pineapple or half of a pear may be best for you.

When you tolerate more fruit, purée part of it and dice the rest to stir into the pudding. The flavor and sweetness depend solely on the fruit—ripe, sweet fruit will produce the best results. Berries, some plums, and certain varieties of apples can be quite tart, so select your fruit with this in mind.

Or see Fruit Sweetener, page 322, for how to purée and cook a fresh pineapple, and store it safely without losing it to mold. Later, when you can eat dried fruit, experiment with dates.

The Nuts—Optional, nevertheless they add flavor, interest and nutrients to the total meal. For a creamier version, add half of your nuts and a little water to the blender when puréeing the fruit. (It's like a fruity nut milk.) Scatter the rest, chopped, on top.

Experiment with these combinations:
Cooked rice or millet, nectarines or peaches, and almonds
Cooked quinoa, seedless grapes, and Brazil nuts
Cooked buckwheat, pineapple, and walnuts or pecans
Baked, diced butternut squash, kiwi and hazelnuts
Cooked, diced sweet potato, banana and pecans

Creamy Nut Pudding

Serves 1

I designed this pudding for those first few weeks when you can't eat fruit and may not tolerate grains. The non-grain alternatives contain more protein and are lower in carbohydrates than true grains. Expect "creamy," not "sweet."

1   cup cooked quinoa, amaranth or buckwheat
    OR
    diced, cooked sweet potato or butternut squash
⅓   cup Brazil or other nuts
⅓   cup water
½   teaspoon vanilla, optional

Put the hot or cold quinoa, amaranth or buckwheat in a cereal bowl. In a blender, grind the nuts to a fine meal. Add the water, vanilla and 2–4 tablespoons of the quinoa, amaranth or buckwheat and blend until smooth and slightly thickened. Taste. Add salt if necessary. Pour into the cereal bowl, stir and enjoy.

> ❖ **NOTE:** Minimize the inevitable mold that nuts contain by or- ❖ dering them fresh from a supplier. Refrigerate (or freeze) them promptly. I buy them in a health food store where their nuts are refrigerated and are frequently replenished.

Millet-Peach Pudding

Serves 2

This recipe differs from Breakfast Pudding by including oil, spices and nuts. The combination makes a fragrant, satisfying end product. If you forget the overnight soak you can still make the recipe (see Note).

- ¹/₂   cup whole millet, rinsed
- 2   cups water
- ¹/₄   teaspoon salt
- 1   ripe peach or 1–2 ripe nectarines, puréed
- ¹/₄–¹/₂ teaspoon ground cinnamon
- ¹/₈   teaspoon ground cloves
- 1–2 tablespoons almond oil
- ¹/₄   teaspoon pure almond extract
- 3   tablespoons chopped, toasted almonds, optional
- ¹/₂   ripe peach or 1 nectarine, diced

Soak the millet in 2 cups of water overnight. Without draining, bring the millet, water, and salt to a boil. Reduce the heat and let the pudding simmer about 25 minutes until tender.

Remove the pot from heat and add the fruit, spices, oil and extract. Beat hard for a few strokes. Gently stir in the diced fruit. Divide into two bowls and top them with chopped almonds.

> ❖ **NOTE:** If you want to make this pudding but forgot to soak the ❖ millet overnight, simmer it 35 minutes over very low heat. Remove from the stove, fluff with a fork and cover for 10 more minutes. Millet or any grain, however, is more digestible when soaked or slow-cooked for hours. (See Porridge for slow-cooking directions, page 141.)

Cooked Quinoa or Teff

Serves 4

1   cup quinoa or ½ cup teff
2   cups water
¼   teaspoon salt, optional

Quinoa only: measure into a saucepan half-full of cold water. Swish quinoa briskly with your hand, then pour it into a fine strainer to drain. Repeat two or more times, until your water runs clear and doesn't foam when agitated. Drain again.

Bring quinoa or teff, water and salt to a boil. Reduce heat and simmer, covered, for 15 to 20 minutes, until the water is absorbed. Remove from heat, and cover for 5 minutes more.

> ❖ **NOTE:** Add quinoa or teff to soups in either of two ways—1) ❖ Add them, uncooked to the pot a half hour before serving time, or 2) Add them cooked (left-over) to the pot 10 minutes before serving. (If frozen, allow 20 minutes.)

Sally Rockwell's Nutri-Ola*

Most granolas contain oats, but in this recipe you may use either the non-grain alternatives (buckwheat, amaranth and quinoa) or the less common grains or oats. By selecting ingredients that agree with you, you'll create your own custom-made food product. Enjoy it as a breakfast cereal, snack bar or as an improvised cookie.

I made several different versions of this for my breakfasts on a two-week trip. Impressed with my success, I asked Sally's permission to share the recipe with you. I adapted it slightly to use fresh fruit, rather than dried—but the credit is hers. Thanks, Sally!

---

*Adapted from *The Rotation Game* and *Coping with Candida Cookbook,* by Sally J. Rockwell, P.O. Box 31065, Seattle, WA 98103.

Nutri-Ola Non-Grain Variations

AMARANTH	BUCKWHEAT	QUINOA
2 cups amaranth flour	2 cups white buckwheat groats, ground	2 cups quinoa flour
2 cups puffed amaranth	1 cup sunflower seeds, ground	1 cup cooked quinoa
1 cup pecans or walnuts, or mixture	1 cup cashews or part whole buckwheat groats	1 cup Brazil nuts, sliced
1½ cups pear Fruit Sweetener, page 322	1½ cups pineapple Fruit Sweetener	1½ cups mashed banana
½ cup walnut oil	½ cup sunflower oil	½ cup canola oil
2 teaspoons cinnamon		2 teaspoons vanilla
	salt to taste	

Nutri-Ola Grain Variations

MILLET	MILO (sorghum)	OAT
2 cups millet flour	2 cups milo flour	2 cups rolled oats (not ground)
1 cup ground hazelnuts	1 cup sunflower seeds, ground	1 cup oat bran
1 cup hazelnuts, halved or whole	1 cup whole sunflower seeds or any nuts	1–2 cups almonds, halved or sliced
1 cup grape Fruit Sweetener	1 cup pineapple Fruit Sweetener, page 322	1 cup mashed banana OR puréed peach-nectarine mixture
½ cup hazelnut or canola oil	½ cup sunflower oil	½ cup almond oil
2 teaspoons cinnamon	2 teaspoons vanilla	1 teaspoon pure almond
	salt to taste	

Directions For All Variations

Preheat oven to 325°. MIX DRY INGREDIENTS in a large bowl. MIX OIL AND FRUIT in a small container. If Fruit Sweetener is frozen, melt over low heat. Remove from heat and stir in oil. Use a blender to liquefy banana. Add vanilla, if using.

COMBINE MIXTURES. Pour liquids over dry ingredients and mix well to moisten. The Nutri-Ola mixture is dry, almost crumbly. Yet you need to moisten the dry ingredients. If needed, add from 1 to 4 tablespoons of water, to mix well. (The trick here is to add only enough liquid to moisten *without getting it too wet, like a batter.*)

BAKE on an oiled jelly roll pan, in a single layer, for 50–60 minutes. Stir twice to break clumps. Nutri-Ola crisps as it cools. If not crisp enough, return to the turned-off oven for another 20–30 minutes to dry out.

Notes on Adapting Recipes

Knowledge of the Biological Classification of Foods is useful— for example, almond, peach and nectarine all belong to the Plum family, so putting them together on the same day makes sense.

Similarly, if a nut or seed oil is commercially available, use the whole nuts or seeds *with* their matching oil. If you can't find an ingredient, don't throw out the recipe! Use cashews with canola oil or olive oil. If you can't find milo flour, order it in your health food store.

I developed these ideas to help you get started—they're not written in stone. Experiment!

Oat Granola

About 6 cups

Commercial granolas will sabotage your special diet. Here's why: They're usually sweetened with sugar, honey or maple syrup and are loaded with fat. Besides that, wheat germ or bran fortify some brands and many contain raisins, dates or other dried fruit.

This granola contains only 2 tablespoons of fruit and 2 teaspoons of oil in a whole cup of granola. When you make your own granola, use different nuts, seeds, oil or fruits to customize the recipe.

3   cups rolled oats
½   cup sunflower seeds
½   cup almonds, halved or coarsely chopped
1-2 teaspoons cinnamon
¼   teaspoon salt, optional
¼   cup almond or sunflower oil
¼   cup pineapple juice
½   cup mashed banana

Preheat oven to 350°. Combine oats, seeds, almonds, cinnamon and salt in a large mixing bowl. In a blender jar combine the oil, pineapple juice and mashed banana, and blend briefly. Pour the thick liquid over the oat mixture and blend well.

Spread on a large jelly roll pan (cookie sheet with edges) and bake for about 45 minutes, stirring the granola 2 or 3 times. When light brown, remove from oven—it crisps as it cools. Store the cooled granola in tightly capped glass jars, in a cool place. Serve with Almond Milk, page 320, or Pineapple-Banana Milk, page 321.

Three-Seed Pancakes (Grain-free)

Serves 2

These pancakes are a regular part of my diet, at home or on the road. Yet, when I asked a home economist to test them, she called and said, "There must be some mistake—there is no flour, egg or milk listed—and those three ingredients DEFINE pancakes."

Maybe she's right, and we need a new word to describe these thin, crisp cakes—perhaps they're un-sweet cookies? In any case, try them. The proof is in the eating.

1   cup raw pumpkin seeds
1-2 tablespoons whole anise seeds
2   tablespoons whole flax seeds
¼   cup any starch*
1   cup warm water
1   tablespoon oil
¼   teaspoon salt, optional
¼   cup water

---

*Arrowroot, kudzu and tapioca starches, and carob and chestnut flours all tested well. And if you find another kind of non-grain starch or flour, try it, too!

Combine the pumpkin, anise and flax seeds with the starch in a bowl. Whisk it, to mix. Grind ½ cup of the mixture at a time in a blender. Process on "high" for 30 seconds. Stop to scrape the bottom and sides of jar. Process again for 30 seconds, or until mixture is fine meal. Pour the meal into a mixing bowl and repeat.

When you grind the last of the seeds, add the water, oil and ground meal; blend again. Taste the batter and add salt if you want it.

Pour the batter into a bowl. Rinse the blender jar with the remaining 2 tablespoons of water and stir into the batter. Let batter stand 10 minutes to absorb the liquids. Batter may rest overnight, refrigerated. Spoon a tablespoon at a time onto a hot griddle.

You won't need oil if you use non-stick cookware. However, you may wish to add another ½ teaspoon of oil to the batter and/or to your griddle to help you turn the cakes more easily. They'll be flat, thin and crisp. Serves 2. If you have some left, freeze them.

❖ SERVING SUGGESTIONS ❖

Eat them like cookies. They're delicious. Or crown them with mashed banana or any fruit topping. (See the "ETC." chapter.)

Sesame-Walnut Pancakes (Grain-free)

Serves 2

One day when I didn't have my usual three seeds for pancakes, I started experimenting with what I could find. I couldn't believe the results! Though I haven't made these as many times as the Three-Seed Pancakes, they're so good I wanted to share them with you.

½   cup sesame flour (or ground sesame seeds)
½   cup ground walnuts
½   cup tapioca starch flour
2   tablespoons whole sesame seeds, optional
¼   teaspoon salt
⅔   cup warm water or Stevia Tea
⅜   teaspoon unbuffered, corn-free vitamin C crystals
1   tablespoon walnut or light sesame oil
¼   cup boiling water
1   teaspoon baking soda

In a bowl, combine sesame flour, walnuts, starch, seeds and salt. Whisk to mix.

Dissolve the vitamin C crystals in the warm water or Stevia Tea. Add this liquid and the oil to the nut-seed mixture. Whisk to blend.

Preheat your griddle. Wait until a drop of water "dances" across the hot griddle before you finish mixing the batter.

Add the baking soda to boiling water. Stir to dissolve. Whisk this mixture into the batter (it will foam). Immediately spoon batter onto the griddle, using 1–2 tablespoons for each pancake. (Small cakes are easier to turn.)

Cook over medium to medium-high heat. When the cakes bubble and the edges start to brown, turn to cook the other side. Top with any fruit or fruit sauce. (See "ETC." chapter.)

Before starting the pancakes, simmer ¼ to ½ teaspoon of stevia powder in ¾ cup of water for a few minutes. Set it aside to cool to lukewarm. Measure again—you should have ⅔ cup.

If the murky appearance bothers you, strain it when adding to the batter. (I don't.) While stevia lends a faint sweetness to baked goods, it isn't "sugar" or a concentrated sweet.

Banana-Plantain Pancakes (Non-grain)   E

16 Four-inch Pancakes

Occasionally a treasure of a recipe, like this one, comes to my attention in letters from *Mastering Food Allergies* readers. I've made it several times—it's a big hit with my husband! And as long as we're eating egg, I make hard-boiled eggs to accompany the pancakes.

These non-grain pancakes will surprise you with their delicious, slightly sweet flavor. You don't even need a fruit topping. Just munch them out of hand—flat, folded or they're soft enough to roll.

In the absence of grain, the egg provides both structure and texture. So if you can't eat egg, don't try to improvise without it.

2   egg whites
1   egg yolk
¼   cup water
1   medium banana
1   plantain
1   tablespoon oil
2   tablespoons arrowroot or tapioca starch
¼   teaspoon salt
³/₈ teaspoon vitamin C crystals

Preheat your electric griddle to 325°, or put your non-electric griddle over medium heat.

Combine all ingredients in a blender. Process for a minute or more, until the batter is thick and very smooth. Pour the batter into a small bowl. Spoon rounded tablespoons of batter onto the hot griddle.

Let them cook a little longer than grain pancakes. When the bottom is quite brown—but not burned—turn them over to bake the other side.

❖ VARIATION ❖

Banana-Sweet Potato Pancakes—Omit the starch. Substitute a medium-sized sweet potato for the plantain. In mixing, blend the eggs, water, banana, oil, salt and vitamin C crystals before you add a few cubes of peeled sweet potato. Continue to add pieces of sweet potato until they're all in the batter. Optional: Stir in ½ cup coarsely chopped pecans after you pour the batter into a bowl.

Adapted from Margot Engleman,
Green Valley, Arizona

Amaranth Pancakes/Flatbread

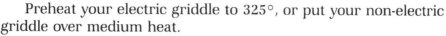

Serves 2–3

Allow enough time to bake Amaranth Cakes sufficiently, over moderate heat. If you use too much heat, they appear to be done before they are cooked in the middle.

I made that mistake once with a double batch I was hurrying to cook for a trip. When I realized how gummy the middles were I spread them on wire racks on cookie sheets and put them in a slow

(300°) oven for 20 minutes or so. They dried out all right and crunched when I ate them! I learned that they're more stable and less likely to promote mold growth when oven-dried.

1	cup amaranth flour
1	tablespoon arrowroot starch
¹/₄	teaspoon salt
1	cup water
1	tablespoon oil

Whisk together the ingredients and allow to stand a few minutes, or even refrigerate overnight. Preheat a griddle until a drop of water "dances" on it. If necessary, add a bit more water to the batter to keep it a medium-thin consistency so the pancakes stay relatively thin.

Drop 1 or 2 tablespoons batter on a hot griddle, making 4- to 6-inch cakes. Cook until they appear dry around the edges, turn and bake the other side. These require a bit more time to cook than wheat pancakes do. Serve with any fruit topping, such as Pineapple Jam or banana Fresh Fruit Jam, or eat out of hand, like toast.

> ❖ **TIP:** These freeze well. Make a bunch when you have some ❖ time and freeze them in single-serving portions.

Quinoa Pancakes/Flatbread

Serves 2–3

Pale yellow, delicious and versatile, these cakes are sturdy enough to spread with nut butter and send to school. Because they're so nourishing, they seem to stick to your ribs longer, too.

1	cup quinoa flour
1	cup water
¹/₄	teaspoon salt, optional
1	teaspoon oil

Whisk ingredients together and let stand a few minutes while griddle preheats. Spoon batter onto hot griddle, spreading cakes with a spoon, if necessary, to keep them from being too thick. Or add another tablespoon or two of water. Turn and bake the other side.

No oil is required on most non-stick griddles, but use oil if you need it for your cooking surface. Serve with Applesauce, Blueberry Sauce or your choice of topping.

Buckwheat Pancakes/Flatbread

Serves 2–3

Enjoy Buckwheat Cakes morning, night or noon. Top them with fruit for breakfast or make your favorite sandwiches to take brown-bagging. Simple to make and sturdy to handle, they freeze well for future quick meals.

1 cup white buckwheat flour
¼ teaspoon salt, optional
1 cup water, or a little more
½ to 1 tablespoon oil

Combine ingredients using enough water to make a medium-thin batter. Let it stand a few minutes while the griddle preheats. Spoon tablespoonsful onto hot griddle. As batter thickens, add a little more water, so cakes will stay thin.

❖ VARIATION ❖

Replace up to ⅓ of the flour with ground nuts or seeds. Add ¼ teaspoon of cinnamon to the batter. Use up to 1 tablespoon of oil in the batter if your griddle tends to stick and oil the griddle, if you need to.

Rice Pancakes/Flatbread

Serves 4–5

Most rice pancakes turn out dry, but by including some cooked rice, I found I could overcome this tendency. I admit the results pleasantly surprised me.

1 cup brown rice flour
1/4 teaspoon salt
2/3 cup *cooked* brown rice
1 cup tepid water
1 1/2 tablespoons oil

In a small bowl combine the dry ingredients and stir them, mixing well. Add the cooked rice and toss lightly. Add the water and oil and whisk the batter together. Preheat your griddle. Spoon the batter onto the hot griddle. A non-stick griddle won't need oil, but if you need some for your equipment, use it. Yields 30 4-inch cakes. Freeze some for another day.

About Waffles

When I started designing recipes for waffles free of wheat, milk
and eggs, I hoped to produce an adequate substitute for the real thing. I was
stunned when I tasted the Oat, Carob-
Buckwheat, Quinoa and Amaranth Waffles. They're so much better than "adequate," they're hard to describe. You can't possibly eat
them and feel deprived!

WAFFLES AS BREAD: Never underestimate the usefulness of
waffles. It's hard to bake breads and crackers often enough to supply a family. And in hot weather, who wants to heat the oven? So in
summer, I make a zillion kinds of pancakes, 3–4 kinds of waffles
and a variety of flatbreads.

While I'm mixing the batter, I preheat the waffle iron on my
screened porch or at the dining table. Then I sit and read a book, or
visit, while I "bake bread." (My new waffle iron has reversible grids,
so I can bake the pancakes and flatbreads on the griddle side.)

Just find a spot near an electric outlet where you can make
yourself comfortable—waffles take 10–14 minutes each. So if
you're making four waffles you must commit 45–55 minutes to the
job, plus mixing time. Why not get comfortable and enjoy that
time?

If you're enjoying a leisurely breakfast rather than "baking
bread," producing a waffle every so often paces the meal. And you
can quarter each waffle to keep 2–4 people happily munching.

Equipment

I did all testing with a standard, 9x9 non-stick waffle iron
(Sears, about $45). It makes excellent thin, crisp waffles. I find rec-
ipes made with alternative flours, water, herbal teas
or Nut Milk, page 320, and no eggs, make better thin
waffles than the Belgian (thick) kind.

All waffle irons today are coated with teflon. If
you need the old-fashioned, uncoated steel grids, try
shopping at garage sales or raid someone's attic.

I wash the grids after each use and brush across them lightly with oil before using again. The directions usually say to wash the grids and oil them *once,* then just brush the crumbs away and store. It's now considered "seasoned" and ready to use. But if you don't want to have traces of oat in your quinoa waffles, I suggest swishing them in suds—or holding them under a faucet between uses.

Tips

- *Never* put batter in a waffle iron until it's properly preheated.
- To make lighter, textured waffles, dissolve unbuffered, corn-free vitamin C crystals in most of the liquid for the batter. Separately, dissolve the baking soda in a small amount of boiling water. When the acid and alkaline liquids mix, they foam up, releasing carbon dioxide gas. This action raises the waffles instead of baking powder. Whisk in baking soda water at the last minute, when you're ready to start cooking.
- Work quickly when your waffle iron is open, and close it as soon as you can to keep from losing too much heat.
- When you pour waffle batter onto the grid it should be thicker than pancake batter—yet it must "flow" through the grids to fill out the shape of the waffle.
- Don't use too much batter. The overflow tends to cement the waffle in place, causing it to stick. Start with ¾ to ⅞ of a cup of batter. Use a glass measuring cup to pour the batter into the grids.
- If your batter thickens too much to flow into the corners, whisk in 1–2 tablespoons more water.
- Don't peek until the steam almost stops rising from the waffle iron.
- Lift the lid slowly so you can see if the waffle is intact. If it starts to separate, drop the lid for another minute or two—it may rebond.
- With proper cleaning, oiling and preheating of your waffle iron, plus following these "TIPS" and my recipe directions, sticking waffles are almost a thing of the past.
- Use a fork to ease the waffle gently off of the grid. Don't use a sharp knife.
- Have handy: wire racks for cooling baked waffles, foil and a marking pen for packaging.

- Always cool waffles completely before packaging them to freeze.
- To reheat and crisp waffles again (they become limp temporarily) put them in a warm oven, on a wire rack, for 3–5 minutes, or put in a toaster turned to the lightest setting—they're already baked.

Amaranth Waffles

4, 9x9 waffles

Great, crisp waffles. Top with sliced or puréed fruit; eat out of hand. Please read "About Waffles" before you start.

3/4 teaspoon unbuffered, corn-free vitamin C crystals
1²/₃ cups cool water, Nut Milk, page 320, or Stevia Tea
2 1/4 cups amaranth flour
1/₃ cup arrowroot or tapioca starch
1/₂ teaspoon salt
1/4 cup oil
1/₃ cup boiling water
2 teaspoons baking soda

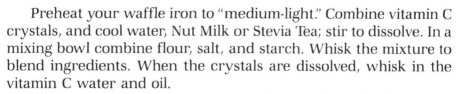

Preheat your waffle iron to "medium-light." Combine vitamin C crystals, and cool water, Nut Milk or Stevia Tea; stir to dissolve. In a mixing bowl combine flour, salt, and starch. Whisk the mixture to blend ingredients. When the crystals are dissolved, whisk in the vitamin C water and oil.

When the waffle iron is ready, combine soda and boiling water in a small bowl—it will foam. Stir to dissolve; whisk into the batter.

Using a measuring cup, pour a scant cup of batter onto the hot waffle iron. *Do not peek for the first 10 minutes.* When it's done, use a spatula or fork to loosen the waffle around the edges and slide it to a plate or wire rack. Repeat until your batter is gone.

Quinoa Waffles

4, 9x9 waffles

Light, crisp and delicious—a real winner. Please read "About Waffles" at the beginning of this chapter before you start.

You can do anything with Quinoa Waffles—make an open-faced sandwich, pulverize for crumbs, serve a stew or something "creamed" over them—or just munch out of hand like cookies.

- 2 cups cool water, Nut Milk or Stevia Tea
- ³/₄ teaspoon unbuffered, corn-free vitamin C crystals
- 2 cups quinoa flour
- ¹/₂ teaspoon salt
- ¹/₄ cup oil
- 2 tablespoons boiling water
- 2 teaspoons baking soda

Combine the cool water, Nut Milk or Stevia Tea with the vitamin C crystals and stir to dissolve. Combine the flour and salt. Add the cool liquid mixture and oil. Beat or whisk hard for 2 minutes. Set aside to rest for 10 minutes.

Preheat your waffle iron to "medium-light." In a small cup dissolve the baking soda in boiling water—it will foam up. Whisk the soda water into the batter.

Use a glass measuring cup to pour a scant cup of batter onto the hot iron. Wait for the waffle iron's light to signal that your waffles are done—about 10–14 minutes. *Do not peek in the first 10 minutes.* Remove to a plate with a fork.

Carob-Buckwheat Waffles (Grain-free)

4, 9x9 waffles

These brownie-like waffles are delicious. They accept a fruit topping—but taste good enough to nibble alone. The nuts are optional, but if you remember loving walnuts or pecans in your brownies, include them when you can.

If you're adding the chopped nuts, use the same kind to grind for the Nut Milk. If you're not adding them, try using Brazil nuts, almonds, macadamias, or pine nuts for your Nut Milk.

1 cup white, unroasted buckwheat groats
2 ½ tablespoons starch (arrowroot, tapioca, kudzu, potato)
½ cup carob flour
½ teaspoon salt
½ cup chopped walnuts or pecans, optional
1 ½ teaspoons baking soda

Nut Milk:

½ cup any nuts, raw or lightly roasted
2 cups boiling water or Stevia Tea, divided
½ teaspoon unbuffered, corn-free vitamin C crystals
⅓ cup walnut (or other) oil
1 tablespoon vanilla

Preheat waffle iron to "medium." If it's well seasoned, you won't need oil, but follow manufacturer's directions.

Grind ⅓ cup groats at a time in a blender. Pour the flour into a large mixing bowl. Add the starch, carob flour, salt and *chopped* nuts.

In the same blender (without washing), grind the remaining nuts to a fine meal. Scrape the bottom and sides of the jar; add 1¾ cups of boiling water or Stevia Tea, vitamin C crystals, oil and vanilla; blend for one minute.

Pour the liquids over the dry ingredients. Whisk lightly until the mixture is blended.

Combine the remaining ¼ cup of boiling water with the baking soda (it will foam up). Stir to dissolve. Whisk it into the batter.

Use a measuring cup to pour 1 cup of batter into the heated waffle iron. Depending on your equipment, these waffles take 10–14 minutes to bake. (Don't peek for at least 10 minutes.)

Oat Waffles

3–4, 9x9″ waffles

If you love crispy, crunchy food, you'll love these waffles. Use them for bread and crackers as well as a breakfast main course. If you want to "bake bread" for future use, double the recipe. Please read "About Waffles" at the beginning of this chapter.

2   cups rolled oats
¼   cup oat bran
2¼   cups water
½   teaspoon sea salt
2   tablespoons oil
½   cup pecans or walnuts, chopped, optional

Grind the oats in a blender. Add the remaining ingredients. Blend the batter until light and foamy. Let it rest for 10 minutes, or more (see Note), to thicken. Preheat waffle iron. Just before baking the waffles, stir in nuts.

Pour one cup of the batter onto a 9x9-inch waffle iron and *quickly* spread it almost to the edges. Bake 10–15 minutes—a little longer than traditional egg-milk batters bake. Don't peek for the first 10 minutes.

Waffles are best served promptly.

> ❖ **NOTE:** When possible, put the batter *in your refrigerator* 30 ❖ minutes to overnight. Beat vigorously before baking the waffles. The chilled batter seems to promote natural rising action by creating more steam. (Thanks to Elizabeth Pettus, Hurst, TX, for this helpful tip. She shared it in the *Mastering Food Allergies* newsletter—and she's right!)

❖ VARIATION ❖

If you didn't make the batter the night before cooking, yet you want to make lighter waffles, try this: Dissolve ¾ teaspoon unbuffered, corn-free vitamin C crystals in 2 cups of water. Use for the liquid in Oat Waffles. Just before baking, dissolve 1½ teaspoons of baking soda in ¼ cup boiling water. Whisk into the batter and bake at once.

Adapted from Natalie Golos'
If This Is Tuesday It Must Be Chicken

Light Egg Waffles   E

Here's an egg-containing variation for all four kinds of waffles in this chapter—oat, buckwheat, amaranth and quinoa. You'll probably make about two more light, airy waffles from each recipe.

1   recipe of waffle batter
2   eggs, separated

Put the egg whites in a small bowl. Either discard the yolks or whisk them lightly and add them to your waffle batter.

Beat the egg whites to soft peaks—but don't beat them until they're stiff and dry. Use a rubber spatula to fold them into your waffle batter gently but thoroughly. Bake one cup of batter at a time.

Steamy Breakfast Porridge

You may have limited your hot cereal consumption to oats or wheat, or in the South, corn. Let's look further, to see the delicious dishes we can make from the less common grains and non-grain alternatives. I can't think of a more nutritious, comforting way to start a day than with a steamy bowl of porridge.

Overnight Cooking

Cooking cereals slowly, preferably overnight, is advantageous for several reasons—

1. Phytates bind minerals. They are found in all grains and to a lesser extent in the non-grain alternatives. The binding causes a high percentage of the minerals to be unavailable to the body. When we say a cereal provides us with so-much iron and calcium, that's rather hypothetical. The food may *contain* that much, but the amount our bodies can actually utilize is generally much, much less.

Long, slow cooking breaks down the phytates without destroying the other nutrients. And we have a much better chance of absorbing and utilizing those nutrients—especially if our digestive system is compromised.

2. Digestion. Nearly everyone with food allergies has compromised digestion. It seems to be part of the package. Slow cooking is a way to provide ourselves with more usable nutrients from our food without eating more of it.

3. Minerals. Not everyone tolerates supplements. If you rely on your food to provide 100% of your nutrients, you need to obtain every bit that food has to offer.

4. Fiber. Surprisingly, although the phytates are broken down, the fiber is left intact. The long, slow cooking does not destroy it. Remember, all grains are an excellent source of fiber.

5. Convenience. Imagine spending about 2 minutes each evening assembling a few things and rising in the morning to find a hot, nutritious breakfast ready and waiting. That's more "instant" than most fast foods are!

6. Flavor. Slow cooking makes the flavor more mellow, with a little more natural sweetness coming through. And since you're avoiding sweeteners, that improved flavor can be very important.

7. Convalescence. Anyone who is recuperating from illness with minimal appetite needs to maximize nutrients in their most digestible form for optimal nourishment.

Overnight Cooking Instructions

Add ¼ teaspoon of salt to any recipe on page 143. Combine ingredients in slow cooker the night before. Cook all night. In the morning beat until creamy; divide into 2 hearty servings. Enjoy "as is" or top with fresh fruit or Nut Milk, page 320. I always start with cool, room-temperature water to keep the cereal from lumping in boiling water.

> ❖ **NOTE:** The one-quart–size slow cooker is ideal for cooking ❖ porridge for one to three people. Or double the recipe and use the low setting for larger slow-cookers.

Porridge Proportions—adapted for slow cooking

CEREAL		WATER	COMMENTS
Amaranth*	¾ cup, whole	3½ cups	Whole seeds for best porridge.
	OR		OR
	¾ cup flour	3 cups	Whisk flour into the water and cook to a smooth gruel for small children, invalids.
Buckwheat*	½ cup	3 cups	Grind unroasted groats to *coarse* meal in a blender OR use Cream of Buckwheat cereal.
Millet	½ cup	2 cups	Use whole grains of millet.
Oats, rolled	⅓ cup	2 cups	Combine rolled oats and the oat bran, stir in water. Oat bran lowers
+			cholesterol + produces creamier
Oat bran	⅓ cup		porridge.
Quinoa*	½ cup, whole	2 cups	Rinse whole quinoa 3 or 4 times, for best flavor. Flour version is extra creamy.
	OR		
	⅓ cup, whole		
	+ 2 tablespoons		
	flour	2 cups	
Rice	⅓ cup	2 cups	Tested with Rice & Shine from health food store. Be sure to read labels. *Supermarket* Cream of Rice is white and refined.
Rye	½ cup	1¾ cups	Tested with Cream of Rye from health store (rolled flakes). Flavor is pleasant and mild.

*Amaranth, Buckwheat and Quinoa are *not* true cereal grains.

Banana Shortcake

Serves 1

This Banana Shortcake makes a satisfying, whole breakfast—it's not a dessert shortcake. Because the Banana Bread is made in advance—and probably frozen—the shortcake is quick and easy to put together. I sometimes serve it for "normal eating" house guests who devour every last crumb!

½ to 1 ripe banana

1-2 teaspoons lemon juice
    OR a pinch of unbuffered, corn-free vitamin C crystals, to
    taste, optional

2   slices Buckwheat Banana Bread, page 160

Mash banana with a fork; whip until light and frothy. If you enjoy a little tang, add the lemon juice or the pinch of vitamin C crystals. Toast the bread lightly either in a toaster oven or in a dry frypan—homemade quickbreads don't do well in a traditional pop-up toaster.

To assemble: Lay toasted bread on a plate; top with a dollop of mashed banana.

> ❖ **NOTE:** If your Banana Bread is frozen be sure to take it out the ❖
> evening before you want it for breakfast. Use a serrated bread
> knife for slicing.

Fried Mush

This is one of the few recipes for fried food you'll find in this book. Fried Mush is an age-old way to use leftover cooked cereal. And if you take certain precautions about the frying process, an occasional treat shouldn't hurt you.

Rules: Never reuse old oils or rendered fats. Never use the oil if you preheat it so long that it starts to smoke—throw it out, wipe the pan with a paper towel and start over. Avoid using excessive fat, as in deep frying. Do not overcook the food to the point of being burned.

1   cup or more of cooked cereal—any kind

1-2 tablespoons vegetable oil

Pour cereal into small oiled mold or bread pan. Smooth the top surface and press out large air pockets. Chill several hours or overnight. When set, cut in ½-inch slices, "bread" them by coating both sides with the same kind of flour as the cereal you're using.

Heat oil until it sizzles when a crumb of cereal is dropped into it, *but it must not be smoking.* Fry a few slices at a time, turning to brown the second side. Drain on paper towels; patting tops with more paper towels to remove surface fat. Keep warm until all are cooked. Serve with applesauce or other fruit.

> ❖ **NOTE:** If preparing slow-cooking Porridge to use for Mush, ❖ reduce the water by ½ cup. This gives the Mush a little firmer consistency that holds together when it's turned over.

Fried Plantain

Serves 1–2

Fried plantain you'll find makes a satisfying non-grain accompaniment to eggs, meat, poultry or fish. I think of it as a substitute for hash-brown potatoes. Because I haven't eaten it frequently in the past, I am much more likely to tolerate it now. Plantain, a fruit, is an oversized cousin of the banana, with one important difference—it must be cooked.

1   large plantain, half ripe or ripe*
2   tablespoons of oil, your choice

Wash the plantain to remove surface mold; pat it dry. Cut into thirds. Cut lengthwise just through the skin, so you can more easily remove the peel. Try to remove the peel with your fingers. (It will pull away only if plantain is ripe.) If it's too tight, stand the piece of plantain on one end and cut the peel away. Slice the peeled pieces ³⁄₈ of an inch thick.

Heat oil over moderate heat. When oil is heated,** arrange the slices in a single layer to cook. Turn when golden brown and cook the other side. Watch the plantain carefully—it burns easily.

Drain on paper towels. Using another paper towel, pat the top surface. Keep warm until all slices are cooked.

---

*NOTE on ripening plantain: Let the green plantain ripen at room temperature in a paper bag. It's half ripe when it turns yellow and fully ripe when a few black spots appear. Either stage is delicious. When it's ready, use at once or hold it in your refrigerator a few days.
**Properly heated oil sizzles when a test piece of food is dropped in it, but it *does not smoke.* See recipe for Fried Mush, page 145, for safe frying methods.

Breakfast Turkey Sausage

6 patties

I save turkey sausages for special occasions—a company brunch, a birthday or holiday. I prefer to mix and shape them the night before the brunch. I put the patties on a cookie sheet, cover and refrigerate them overnight. I think the sage has more of a chance to permeate the turkey that way, too.

I used to buy chicken breasts when I wanted to make sausage— the food processor grinds them in no time. But now many markets carry ground turkey, making this recipe even easier to prepare. When you grind your own chicken or turkey, however, you avoid more fat and unknown additives.

1   pound ground turkey
³/₄   teaspoon sea salt
¹/₄ – ¹/₂ teaspoon black pepper
¹/₂ – 1 teaspoon dried sage
      OR
10 – 12 fresh sage leaves, minced

Mix turkey with salt, pepper and sage. Use a fork or a food processor for less than one minute. Shape into 6 thin patties or several links. Fry or bake until browned.

You can freeze the sausages, either raw or cooked, for future fast breakfasts.

Adapted from *Beat The Yeast Cookbook,* by permission of the author, Charlene Grimmett (P.O. Box 1769, Aurora, Illinois 60507)

Lunches

Lunch in the United States seems to be synonymous with fast food—sandwiches—something between two slices of yeast bread. If that isn't problem enough, that "something" is apt to be topped with yeasty, mold-laden cheese.

Understanding the booby traps that await you, helps you avoid them. You can forget about most fast food eateries. Safe lunches away from home boil down to two choices: You can eat in a cooked-to-order, sit-down restaurant and take your chances on being able to find safe food; or you must carry your own food from home. Until you improve, you'll find "brown-bagging" works best.

Whether you realize it or not, if a candida infection triggers your health problems, food allergies and other hypersensitivities play a role in causing your symptoms. Accordingly, your health will improve if you interrupt your cycle of repetitiously eating a few favorite foods over and over again.

Here are suggestions to help you.

1. Try millet, wild rice, or milo in place of wheat.
2. Include buckwheat, amaranth quinoa and teff in your diet to help minimize the grains.
3. Eat cherries, pineapple, mangoes and other less common fruit in place of apples, oranges and bananas.
4. Try rutabaga, jicama, turnips and other less common vegetables instead of your old standbys, probably green beans and corn.
5. Eat more lamb and pork instead of so much beef. Watch for "beefalo" or buffalo in your markets, and sample them when they appear. If you don't tolerate these choices see Food and Product Sources in Section 3 for sources of exotic game meats.

6. Buy Cornish game hens and turkey to alternate with chicken. Order duck in a restaurant
   for a change.

7. Select grouper, orange roughy, oreo dory and other less
   common fish in place of tuna and your other usual choices.
   (See the fish chapter for each preparation.)

By reducing or eliminating your pattern of repetitious eating,
you'll feel better—more energetic—perhaps even brighter.

Lunch Strategies

- *Plan ahead* so you don't find yourself ravenous and rapidly
  becoming frantic for anything.
- Use fresh, whole foods and avoid aged ones, such as cheeses,
  vinegar, soy sauce, tamari, miso, etc.
- What about leftovers? They're OK if you
  1) Refrigerate them promptly and eat
     them the next day, see Next-Day
     Lunch Salad, page 195.
  2) Freeze them for future meals.
- If you conscientiously rotate foods, you can still eat leftovers
  (from the night before). Count one "day" from 3 PM of one
  day until 3 PM the next day.
- Eat a variety of unusual foods
  for breakfast (rather than
  eggs); carry hard-boiled eggs
  for lunch, to eat with raw vegetables. When you eat in a restaurant, order eggs as a vegetable omelet, perhaps with
  baked potato or plain rice. Skip the yeast rolls.
- By eating less common fish at home, you can
  save tuna for a lunch out. Both Bumble Bee and
  Star Kist offer individual-sized (3 oz.) cans of
  water-packed white albacore tuna. A pull-ring top makes
  them easy to open away from home. Eat it plain, right out of
  the can. See Salad Dressings for ideas. Add raw veggies and
  you have a fine lunch. (Of course many restaurant menus offer tuna salad but you'll never know what's in it, so you'd be
  taking a chance.)
- By consuming less common poultry at home you can occasionally carry (or order) plain chicken for lunch. Try this:
  About once a month arrange 4 fryer chickens on a cookie

sheet and roast them. Discard the skin. Carve all legs and wings and package promptly for the freezer (perhaps 1 leg + 1 wing together, or whatever your appetite dictates). Serve the breast and thigh meat for dinner, and dice the remainder for future salads, then package, label and freeze promptly. Carry a package of frozen chicken for lunch with lots of veggies. It thaws by noon.

- Homemade soups are tops for lunch at home, and they carry well in a thermos, too. Or carry a jar of frozen soup to microwave at work. Thick and hearty soups make satisfying meals. Prepare in large batches and freeze in individual or family-sized portions. (See "Soups.")
- You can find what you're looking for more readily in your freezer by color-coding your food bins. For example: red for chicken, green for all varieties of fish, blue for turkey, yellow for lamb and white for soups of all kinds. Even with color-coded bins, always label your packages clearly. Remember, use your lunch bins only for cooked, ready-to-go foods.

Sweet Potato-Banana-Pecan "Quickie" Meal

Serves 1

This combination makes a simple, speedy and satisfying lunch, breakfast or light supper. Remember to add a little protein to balance the meal. If you like it as much as I do, you'll make a habit of fixing an extra sweet potato, in readiness for this dish.

¹/₄ cup broken pecans
¹/₂ ripe banana, peeled, cut in half lengthwise
1   sweet potato, baked or steamed,* peeled
1   teaspoon walnut oil

*If you want to prepare this dish but forgot to precook a sweet potato, refer to *15-Minute Sweet Potatoes*, page 266.

Dry-roast the pecans in a 10-inch skillet over medium heat. Shake or stir them to prevent burning. When they smell toasty (only a few minutes), remove the pecans. Add the oil to the skillet; immediately add the banana halves, flat side down, and ¾-inch slices of sweet potato.

Cover and cook 5–10 minutes, until the bananas are golden brown and the lightly browned sweet potatoes are heated through. NO NEED TO TURN THEM. Remove to a plate, turning both the bananas and sweet potatoes so their brown sides are up. Scatter the pecans on top and enjoy!

Sandwiches Supreme

Serves 1

This simple "recipe" demonstrates that you can make an interesting sandwich even if you can't have lettuce, tomato and mayonnaise.

Pancakes/Flatbreads, any kind
Turkey, chicken, duck or Cornish game hen, thinly sliced
Avocado slices
Carrot, shredded
Alfalfa sprouts
OPTIONAL: Avocado "Mayo," see page 209

Prepare open-faced sandwiches, layering ingredients in the order listed. Serve at once.

Sunny Apple Sandwiches   Y

Serves 1

Here's a Mom's answer to peanut butter 'n jelly. Kids of all ages love these mini-sandwiches. To send them brown-bagging, pack the fruit slices and seeds separately. Then put two pancakes spread with nut butter face-to-face, lightly.

Pancakes/Flatbread, any kind
Roasted sunflower butter
Sprinkle of sunflower seeds
Thinly sliced raw apple

Spread the flatbread thinly with sunflower butter, sprinkle a few sunflower seeds on it for "crunch" and top with the apple slices.

❖ VARIATIONS ❖

Use roasted almond or cashew butter in place of the sunflower butter and either omit the seeds or use sesame seeds. Try sliced pear, apricots, peaches, nectarines or banana instead of the apple slices.

> ❖ **TIP:** To prevent fruit from turning brown, rub with lemon or ❖
> lime juice or dip in a solution of ¼ teaspoon unbuffered, corn-
> free vitamin C crystals and water. Drain well, then package for
> the lunch bag.

Hidden Sandwich Salad

Serves 1

Don't ask why the tortilla "sandwich" tastes so much better buried in salad—just accept that it does. It's a knife and fork affair to savor!

1   large or 2 small E-Z Tortillas, page 159
Nutty Mayo, page 208, to taste
Shredded turkey, chicken, duck or Cornish hen
Sliced tomato
Green pepper rings
Shredded lettuce or sprouts
Salsa, guacamole or more mayonnaise

Arrange the tortilla(s) on a luncheon plate. Spread them thinly with mayonnaise and assemble the remaining ingredients in the order listed.

Bean-Topped Tortillas

Serves 2

Do you miss ethnic food? I do. That's why I developed this Mexican recipe. No cheese, no corn or wheat, no yeast-laden chili powder. Yet you can still make them as highly seasoned as you like—and fun!

Here's the gameplan: Bake your tortillas in advance. Allow about 45 minutes to prepare the rest of the dish. Add your beans to the sharply seasoned sauté. While they simmer together, mash the avocado. When you're ready to eat, assemble it all quickly and easily. Serve to raves.

4   E-Z Tortillas, baked, any kind, page 159
1   tablespoon olive oil
3/4 cup chopped onions, optional
1   clove garlic, minced, optional
1/2 small jalapeño pepper, more or less to taste, minced (See "Peppers, Hot" for cautions)
2   cups of pinto beans with their liquid
1   avocado
1-2 tablespoons lime juice
     OR
1/8 - 1/4 teaspoon vitamin C crystals, unbuffered, corn-free dissolved in 2 tablespoons of water
1/2 cup onion, chopped
1   large red, yellow or green bell pepper

Put two tortillas on each plate and set aside. In a large skillet, sauté the ¾ cup onions in olive oil over medium heat until half-done (about 5 minutes). Add the garlic and jalapeño pepper; cook few minutes longer. Before the veggies brown, add the beans and their liquid.

Using a potato masher or a fork, mash about half the beans. Stir occasionally while they simmer. In 15–20 minutes the beans become thick enough to spread. Canned beans contain plenty of salt—don't add any. If you're using dried beans that you cooked, add a little salt to taste.

Meanwhile, mash the avocado and season it to taste with the lime juice or vitamin C crystals in water. Have ready the ½ cup chopped onions, and slice the bell pepper into 8 thin rings.

To assemble: Spread the bean mixture on the tortillas. Top each with a dollop of mashed avocado, 2 tablespoons chopped onion and 2 colorful pepper rings.

Shrimp-Stuffed Tomatoes

Serves 4

This salad makes a lovely do-ahead lunch that's especially good in late summer when fresh tomatoes are at their best.

4   large, ripe tomatoes
1   cup peas, fresh or frozen
12 medium shrimp, cleaned and cooked
Pinch of sea salt to taste
Generous pinch of dill weed

Core tomatoes; scoop out and reserve pulp. Be sure to leave a sturdy bottom in the tomato. Steam fresh peas for 5–10 minutes until tender, or thaw frozen peas. Chop the shrimp. Combine the peas, chopped shrimp, tomato pulp, salt and dill. Spoon the mixture into the tomato shells and chill. Serve cold.

Fruit 'N Nuts

Serves 1

While this combination may sound like a snack, it isn't. We sometimes need a portable, no-fuss meal—this one slips easily into your purse or briefcase. It enables you to meet your social, economic or family obligations away from home.

If you have a stray piece of duck or flounder to add lean protein, so much the better. Clearly, this suggestion applies to your maintenance diet, after you've found that you tolerate fruit.

SELECT A COMBINATION, or make up new ones. Notice how related fruits and nuts can comprise a one-family meal. Some of the fruits require a glass jar and a spoon.

#1　1 ripe mango
　　　Cashews, raw or home-roasted

#2　Nectarines, peaches, plums, cherries or apricots
　　　Almonds, raw or home-roasted

#3　Grapefruit sections
　　　Pecans or Walnuts, raw

#4　Pineapple, diced or puréed
　　　Macadamia nuts

#5　Apples or pears
　　　Hazelnuts

#6　Honeydew, or other melon,* diced or in balls
　　　Pumpkin Seeds

---

*Wash the skin well before you cut a melon. This helps reduce the contamination that occurs when the knife blade cuts through, dragging surface mold and yeast into the fruit.

Breads, Muffins and Crackers

Few—if any—commercial bread products will meet your individual dietary requirements. Yeast-containing commercial bread products trigger symptoms in many (perhaps most) people with a candida-related illness. Wheat and the other gluten grains such as rye and barley provoke symptoms in others. Some people with persistent yeast-connected illness may not tolerate any true cereal grain—rice, millet, milo and wild rice. Unless you're very astute and "tuned in" to interpreting the signals of your body, chances are you'll need diagnostic help to determine into which category you fall.

In any case, the good news is that you can definitely enjoy simple bread products that fill the bill for you. Most recipes in this chapter do not contain yeast or wheat. Because corn is such a common allergen, I limit it, too. Many allergists believe that barley is so close to wheat that it's not a good choice either.

The recipes in this book may require that you shop in a health food store for the less common grains and unroasted buckwheat groats. You can also send away for exotic new grain-like foods such as amaranth and quinoa. Remember, the shape and texture of the bread will differ from the light, airy slices you may be used to. Still, it you accept new ideas—and are hungry enough to try them—you'll find a gold mine in this chapter.

"New" Ideas From History

Every ancient culture had its version of a simple flour and water flatbread similar to the ones in this section. The most common example today is the Mexican tortilla, made with either corn or wheat flour. But going back further, the shepherds of biblical times probably carried flour and salt with their supplies. They'd combine the flour and a pinch of salt with water, pat the dough thin for quick cooking and bake the resulting tortillas or chapatis on a hot rock at the edge of a fire.

Moving on through time, the Aztec and
Inca Indians of sixteenth-century South
and Central America thrived on their
own locally grown "superfoods"—
amaranth and quinoa. While not exactly
common supermarket items, you can buy
both of these grain alternatives by mail. (See
page 354 in the third section.)

The people of Eastern Europe ate a lot of buckwheat, a plentiful, grain-like plant. For centuries they thrived on it, using it in
many ways. They ground and used it as we do wheat, corn, rice
and oats.

What's so special about amaranth, quinoa and buckwheat? Besides fantastic nutritional attributes, these foods are *not true cereal
grains*. This means that even if you must avoid *all* of the grains,
you'll probably tolerate one or more of these alternatives.

Sourdough Is Yeast Bread

During the California gold rush, some of the miners devised a
special bread—almost by accident. They noticed that when they
mixed their bread for the evening meal in the morning, by night-
time it rose a little and fermented, developing an interesting, tart,
unique flavor. Of course, I'm describing the prototype for the bread
we know as San Francisco sourdough.

Even though no yeast starter was deliberately added, we now
know that the full day of "proofing" allowed the bread to pick up
the free-floating wild yeast drifting in off the Pacific Ocean. The
balmy temperature helped the wild yeasts grow and multiply. And
as they flourished and fermented throughout the day, they flavored and slowly raised the bread. Today most San Francisco sourdough bread is made with a wild-yeast starter rather than trusting
the ocean breezes. But whether the starter is added or a long
proofing develops the wild yeast in the air, *sourdough bread is not
yeast-free*. Don't believe it if someone tries to sell you "yeast-free
sourdough bread." There's no such thing.

Differences Inevitable

When you bake a gluten-free bread, you must
expect a different end-product. A certain magic is missing. Here's
why: Gluten makes dough elastic; it traps the carbon dioxide that

makes the bread rise and develop a "light" texture. Without gluten, you can't expect to make extremely light bread.

Breads, muffins or crackers made with alternative flours turn out dense and solid. They resemble pumpernickel bread or bran muffins in texture. They rise only minimally, but have wonderful, hearty flavors and are very, very satisfying.

Leavening In Quickbreads

Nutbreads and muffins are usually leavened with baking powder. But all commercial baking powders contain booby traps. Popular supermarket brands almost always contain corn and aluminum. The corn is a problem for many—and the aluminum isn't good for anybody. The aluminum-free, corn-free baking powder in health food stores contains potato starch—another potential problem.

Consequently, I improvise for the leavening by adding an acid and an alkaline to the batter, separately. I dissolve unbuffered, corn-free vitamin C crystals (the acid) in most of the liquid of my recipes. I also dissolve baking soda (the alkaline) in a few tablespoonsful of boiling water.

To be effective, the vitamin C (ascorbic acid) crystals must *not* be buffered. Yet in many health food stores the staff seems determined to push *buffered* C products, implying that "buffered is better." And that may be true, if you're going to drink it. However, if you plan to use the vitamin C for leavening, insist on ascorbic acid crystals.

If you can't find unbuffered vitamin C crystals, see pages 354-359 for several suppliers, many with a toll-free number. Most suppliers ship promptly, often the same day. Corn-free, unbuffered vitamin C crystals are usually derived from sago palm—and are generally well tolerated.

Vitamin C crystals are pure ascorbic acid. But I find one product easier to work with—"Dull C" from Freeda. It dissolves almost instantly—and my baking goes faster. Other brands take from 10 to 15 minutes to dissolve in room-temperature water. Sometimes I specify barely warm water to help the crystals dissolve a little more quickly.

I develop recipes using the vitamin C crystals because they are so well tolerated. However, here are two more acid alternatives that you might use in place of the crystals:

1. Use 3 times as much lemon or lime juice as the measure of baking soda. However, lemon and

lime carry a strong flavor that may or may not go well in a particular dish. And this won't work if citrus disagrees with you.

2. Another alternative acid is cream of tartar. It's derived from grapes. Use twice as much as the measure of baking soda.

Leavening of non-wheat breads can be enhanced by following a few basic guidelines:

1. Have everything ready for baking before you combine the dry and liquid ingredients.
2. Preheat your oven.
3. Dissolve the vitamin C crystals in water or juice (about 5 minutes in warm water, about 12–15 minutes in cool water).
4. Either dissolve baking soda in a little boiling water and stir in last, just before baking, or combine it with the flour and other dry ingredients.
5. Oil and flour the pans or put muffin papers in place.
6. Mix *all* dry ingredients (except the vitamin C or other acid, and maybe the baking soda) in one bowl and blend *all* liquids together in your blender or another bowl. To combine, pour the liquids over the dry ingredients. Use a rubber spatula to combine them, mixing only until everything appears moist. If baking soda is not in the dry ingredients, dissolve it and add now.
7. Don't beat quickbreads unless recipe indicates and don't worry about a few lumps. *Quickly* scrape the batter into the prepared pan and pop it into the oven. Don't allow the batter to linger at room temperature. Here's why: The acid and alkaline start "fizzing" right away. So if you delay, you'll reduce their leavening action in the oven, where it counts.

Flatbreads Are Flat

You'll find traditional tortillas and chapatis easy to make. Roll them thin, in 6-inch circles and bake quickly. In this chapter I selected only unleavened flatbreads, not pita or "pocket" breads that require yeast.

Traditional flour-and-water flatbreads are simple and quick. They didn't survive for many, many centuries by accident. They became classic because of that ease of preparation, because they're so versatile to use, and so satisfying to eat. See "E-Z Tortillas" for a universal, any-flour flatbread.

More Breads

Several waffles and pancakes in the Breakfast chapter lead double lives— they make wonderful "toast" or supporting surfaces for open-faced sandwiches. Make them when you have time and freeze for future "quickie" meals. You'll be glad you did!

E-Z Tortillas

Quick and easy to prepare, satisfying to eat. They make salads into meals, or go brown-bagging (with topping packed separately). And they freeze well, too.

> 1¼ cup any flour (not starch): amaranth, buckwheat,
>   corn, millet, milo, oat, quinoa, rye or wheat
> ¼ teaspoon salt
> ½ cup water, room temperature
> ½–1 teaspoon oil, optional (use it especially with quinoa
>   and millet)

Whisk 1 cup of flour and the salt together in a bowl. Make a "well" in the center and pour in the oil and water. Stir several strokes with a fork until the dough clumps together in a ball.

Preheat a large griddle or 2 skillets. Scatter the remaining ¼ cup of flour on a bread board or piece of wax paper.

Break off balls of dough the size of a golf ball. Roll them in flour. Flatten with your hand, turning often to keep them floured. As the dough absorbs flour, the texture becomes more workable—like "Playdough."

Roll each tortilla thinner with a rolling pin or a smooth, clean bottle. When thin, and 6–7 inches across, check both sides to see they're well floured. Bake them on the hot griddle, one or more at a time (depending on your equipment). Use no oil.

Bake about 3 minutes on each side. Once you get the feel of making and baking tortillas, you'll do it quickly and easily.

Put the baked tortillas on wire racks or lay them on cotton towels. See the Lunch and Salad chapters for creative ways to use tortillas.

> ❖ **E-Z MIX TIP:** To work on wax paper—wipe your counter with ❖
> a damp sponge, lay the wax paper flat. The dampness holds the
> paper in place and keeps it from slipping. When finished, fold
> the paper several times and discard. Out goes most of your
> mess! (Wax paper may contain traces of corn starch.)

Buckwheat Banana Bread

1 Loaf

You get the delightful mild flavor by using unroasted groats and grinding them in your blender. This adds only 5–7 minutes to your preparation time, and it's worth it!

2	tablespoons flax seeds, ground
1/3	cup water
1 1/3	cups "white" (unroasted) buckwheat groats, divided
1/2	cup pumpkin (or other) seeds
2	tablespoons tapioca (or other) starch flour
1/2	teaspoon salt
1/2	teaspoon guar gum,* optional
1/2	teaspoon nutmeg or cinnamon, optional
2/3	cup chopped walnuts or other nuts, optional
1/4	cup walnut or other oil
2	cups mashed bananas, about 4 medium (see Variations)
1/2	teaspoon unbuffered, corn-free vitamin C crystals
2	teaspoons baking soda
2	tablespoons boiling water

Preheat oven to 400°. Combine flax seeds with water in a small saucepan. Bring to a rolling boil and immediately remove from heat. Set aside to soak until needed.

In a blender, grind 1/3 cup of the groats into fine flour. Place strainer over a mixing bowl and pour in flour. Rub the flour

---

*You'll find guar gum in a health food store. It helps trap carbon dioxide, producing bread with a slightly lighter texture. It doesn't affect the flavor.

through with a spoon, returning unground pieces to blender. Repeat three times or until all groats have been ground.

Oil and flour an 8- x 4-inch loaf pan. Tap the pan gently to coat the bottom and sides with flour. Tap any extra flour back into the mixing bowl.

Combine pumpkin seeds, tapioca starch, salt, guar gum and spices. Blend on high 1 minute, stopping twice to scrape the bottom. Add seed mixture and nuts directly into the flour, and whisk together well.

❖ **E-Z MIX TIP:** Measure 2¼-cups of water; pour into the ❖
blender jar. *Mark that level* and discard the water.

Combine in blender oil and add 2 ripe bananas, broken into 1″ chunks. Blend. Continue to add banana chunks until the 2¼-cup level is reached. Add the corn-free vitamin C crystals and flax mixture. Blend one minute.

Pour the liquid mixture over dry ingredients and mix thoroughly. Dissolve baking soda in boiling water. Add to the batter and stir with a few swift strokes until water disappears (don't beat it). Quickly scrape batter into pan and place in hot oven.

Immediately reduce temperature to 325°. Bake for 70 minutes, or until a toothpick thrust in the middle comes out dry. Remove from the oven and cool in the pan for 10 minutes. Turn it out on a wire rack and cool completely before slicing.

❖ VARIATIONS ❖

The following fruits may be used in place of banana in the above recipe.

Pineapple Bread—Simmer fresh pineapple purée 10 minutes. Substitute 2 cups of purée in place of bananas and proceed as above. (Save the remaining pineapple purée to use as "jam" on the bread.)

Applesauce Bread—Substitute 2 cups of Real Applesauce, page 214. Proceed as above.

Pear Bread—Use 2 cups of chopped, ripe pears. For a pear spread, see Pear Honey.

Mystery Bread—Blend fresh, sweet, green seedless grapes, to make 2 cups of purée.

Amaranth Soda Bread

1 Round Loaf

I'm delighted to share this recipe with you! It's a godsend when you're avoiding grains. Even if you've never made bread before, this is so simple you're sure to succeed.

This round loaf is delicious "real" bread. You'll enjoy it most while it's still warm or in the first 24 hours. Egg-free soda bread just doesn't keep well, and freezing doesn't capture that fresh-from-the-oven goodness, either. I do freeze leftovers for bread crumbs or poultry stuffing, however.

Because all soda breads are crumbly, they are best for open-faced sandwiches, or with soup or stew. My favorite? I cut a wedge of bread, split it into top and bottom halves, top them like shortcake with mashed and seasoned avocado, plus tomato or onion slices, sprouts, chunks of tuna or slices of cold, roasted turkey. It's a knife-and-fork affair to savor!

³/₄ cup warm water, Nut Milk, page 320, or Stevia Tea, page 329

³/₄ teaspoon unbuffered, corn-free vitamin C crystals

2³/₄ cups amaranth flour, divided

³/₄ cup arrowroot or tapioca starch

¹/₂ teaspoon salt

1 tablespoon anise or fennel seeds, ground, optional

2–4 tablespoons oil*

2 tablespoons boiling water

2 teaspoons baking soda

Preheat oven to 400°. Combine water and vitamin C crystals; stir and let stand to dissolve. In a large mixing bowl, combine 2¹/₄ cups of the flour with starch, salt and ground seeds; whisk together lightly.

Add liquid with dissolved crystals and oil to the flour mixture. Mix batter with a spoon. Sprinkle a little of the remaining half-cup of flour in a circle centered on a baking sheet. Put the rest of the flour on a bread board or a piece of waxed paper.

---

*Although you can make this recipe with as little as 2 tablespoons of oil, it tastes better when it contains the 4 tablespoons (¼ cup). Because there's no fat from egg yolks, the additional oil helps avoid dryness. This is especially important if you plan to eat the bread unbuttered.

Dissolve baking soda in boiling water; add to the dough and stir. The dough will be very stiff. When the water disappears, beat hard for 10 strokes. Turn the dough onto the floured board or waxed paper.

Roll the dough to coat it with flour. Working quickly, knead for 2–3 minutes. The dough will absorb enough flour to handle easily, yet remain soft.

Gather dough into a smooth ball and put it on the floured baking sheet. Pat into an 8-inch round, 1-inch thick at the edges and mounded slightly in the center.

Use a sharp knife or razor blade to slash a deep "X" in the top of the dough. Pop into the oven at once, and reduce temperature to 325°.

Bake 55–65 minutes. "Done" may be a little tricky to determine (the toothpick test isn't enough). I suggest this: Using clean oven mittens or paper towels, grasp the loaf and crack it open. Look deep inside—uncooked dough appears darker in color, so is easily detected. If you see that, put the loaf back in the oven another 10 minutes.

When the inside of the bread is uniformly pale tan, it's done. Note the exact cooking time for your oven in the margin on this page. Assuming you shape future loaves approximately the same, you'll know how long to bake your next batch.

Rye Soda Bread

A delicious, yeast-free, 100% rye bread. For some reason, this recipe rises more and makes a better loaf when it's round—with a deep "X" slashed in the top. (In a loaf pan, it's disappointing.) Time your baking so the bread can cool 15–30 minutes before you cut it.

Most soda breads include eggs and a sweetener, but I've designed this one to rise well without eggs, and a sweetener is strictly optional—see "Variations."

This relatively small round loaf rises better than larger loaves that contain 4–5 cups of flour. If you need more bread, make more loaves.

I took two loaves of hot-from-the-oven Rye Soda Bread to a pot-luck luncheon when I was working on this chapter. The response? Unanimous approval—and everyone wanted the recipe!

$3/4$ cup warm water
$3/4$ teaspoon unbuffered, corn-free vitamin C crystals
3   cups rye flour plus $1/2$ cup for the baking sheet and bread board
$1^{1}/_{2}$ teaspoons ground caraway seeds, optional
$1/2$ teaspoon salt
$1/3$ cup oil
$1/4$ cup boiling water
2   teaspoons baking soda

Preheat oven to 400°.

Combine water and vitamin C crystals; stir to dissolve. Put 3 cups of rye flour, ground caraway and salt in a large mixing bowl. Whisk them together lightly.

Add liquid with dissolved vitamin C crystals and oil to the flour. Mix the batter with a spoon (it will be stiff). Sprinkle a little of the remaining half-cup flour in a circle, centered on a dry baking sheet; put the rest on the bread board.

Combine the boiling water and baking soda—stir to dissolve— add to the batter. Stir. After the water is absorbed, beat hard for 10 strokes. Turn the dough out on the floured bread board.

Roll the dough in flour—turn it over several times to flour the surface, pat flat (to about $3/4$-inch thickness). Fold in half pressing the dough with your palm. Repeat.

Gather the soft dough into a ball, flatten, fold and press it again. Repeat a few times, working quickly. (This takes about 2–3 minutes.) Don't worry when you have flour left on the board—the dough will absorb as much as it needs. Discard the rest.

Shape the dough into a smooth round ball and put it on the floured baking sheet. Pat the dough so it's about 8 inches across, an inch thick at the edges and gently mounded in the center. With a sharp knife, cut a deep "X" in the top and pop the bread in the oven.

Immediately reduce the oven temperature to 325°. Bake the bread for 55–60 minutes. To determine if the bread is done, break the loaf in half. (Because ovens differ, you must find the time it takes this bread to bake completely *in your oven*. Jot that time down in the margin. For future loaves, use that baking time and you won't need to break the loaf open to confirm doneness.)

❖ VARIATIONS ❖

"Pumpernickel" Rye Bread—Add 1–2 tablespoons carob powder to the rye flour. This amount of carob darkens the color of the bread and only seems to enhance the other flavors. You can't detect its flavor—and it certainly doesn't make "chocolate bread."

Traditional Soda Bread—Traditionally, soda breads are lightly sweetened. Add 1 teaspoon to 2 tablespoons of aguamiel, see page 354 (or any other sweetener you tolerate) to the vitamin C water. OR make Stevia Tea, page 329, with 1/8 teaspoon of stevia. Cool the tea to lukewarm, measure 3/4 cup, and add the vitamin C crystals. Proceed with the recipe, using the tea for the liquid.

Country "Corn" Bread

I adapted this simple recipe that I found in the office of Thomas Stone, M.D., in Rolling Meadows, IL. No one there remembers who originated it, so I can't even acknowledge his or her achievement. It's so versatile I couldn't resist adding the Variations. I think you'll agree this recipe is a treasure!

1	cup water or fresh fruit juice (or part water and part fruit purée)
1/2	teaspoon unbuffered, corn-free vitamin C crystals
2	cups flour—*choose one or create a mixture*: amaranth, buckwheat, quinoa or any grain—barley, kamut, millet, oat, rice, rye, spelt or teff
1	teaspoon baking soda
1/2	teaspoon salt
1/3	cup oil
1–2	tablespoons water, juice or purée, optional

Preheat oven to 400°. Oil and flour a pie plate or an 8- or 9-inch baking pan. Combine the water or juice with vitamin C crystals and stir. Set aside to dissolve.

Combine flour, baking soda and salt in a bowl. Whisk well to distribute the soda.

Add liquid with dissolved crystals and oil at the same time. Stir quickly with a few swift strokes, only until the dry ingredients become moist. The batter should be heavy but pourable. If necessary, add another 1 or 2 tablespoons of liquid. Scrape batter into the pan and bake 16–20 minutes, or until a toothpick thrust in the center comes out clean and dry.

❖ VARIATIONS ❖

1. Add chopped nuts.

2. Use Stevia Tea, page 329, or a non-caloric, herbal sweetener in place of the water.

3. Add from a teaspoon to a tablespoon of aguamiel, see Ingredients and Techniques in Section 3, when you tolerate a small amount of concentrated sweets.

4. Add 1 teaspoon of guar gum to the dry ingredients for a little lighter bread (you may also need to add an extra 2 tablespoons of water).

5. Carob Bread: Substitute ¼ cup of carob powder for ¼ cup of amaranth or other flour. Add chopped walnuts. Sweeten the bread with aguamiel (#3, above) or use fruit juice or Stevia Tea for liquid. Produces delicious mock "brownie" bread. Better for munching than sandwiches.

6. Liquefy ripe bananas, peeled pears or seedless grapes. Use 1 cup of thin fruit purée in place of the water. Be ready to add 2 to 4 tablespoons of water, if needed, for proper "heavy batter" consistency.

7. Use a slightly sweet version (above) as your base for a biscuit-like shortcake. See "Strawberry Shortcake," page 295. Choose from strawberries, *ripe* peaches, nectarines, bananas, or any sweet berries—blueberries, raspberries, blackberries. "Creamy Nut Topping," page 325, provides a convincing "whipped cream" touch.

Irene Corwin's Whole Wheat Bread

2 Loaves

Whole grain wheat bread MEANS "health food." Yet, ironically, most whole wheat bread contains enough phytic acid to cause two problems in the body: It pulls calcium out of the bones, leaving them more vulnerable to rickets and osteoporosis and it destroys some of the zinc.

The first consequence is by far the more serious. Not that zinc isn't important—but you can meet your need for it by eating vegetables, seafood, liver, nuts and seeds. So in a good diet, when you eat those foods *without* whole wheat bread, you're probably getting enough to compensate for your losses. Or you can take a supplement.

Alsoph Corwin, M.D., told me this story behind his wife's unique formula for bread: During World War II the British turned to minimally processed whole grain cereals and breads to save energy so they could spend the time, labor and fuel it took to refine flour on the war effort.

At first, all went well. But soon, increasing cases of rickets suggested that something was amiss. Scientists pondered the problem. "Perhaps," they said, "it's the phytic acid in the whole grains drawing calcium out of the bones and binding other minerals."

So they added a minute amount of calcium carbonate to neutralize the phytic acid in the whole grains—and the rickets "epidemic" promptly stopped. It took just half a teaspoon per loaf of bread to do it! Ever since, the British have included calcium carbonate in their whole grain products—by law.

Surely, if you're going to make your own whole wheat bread, you want to receive all of its potential benefits. See the footnote for help in locating calcium carbonate.

6   cups whole wheat flour, finely ground*
2   rounded tablespoons dry, granular yeast**
1½ to 2 teaspoons salt
1   teaspoon calcium carbonate***
3   cups spring water, lukewarm

In a large bowl, sift 3 cups of flour with the yeast, salt and calcium carbonate. Add water and mix with electric beaters, medium speed. Replace the beaters with a dough hook. Keeping the motor at medium speed, gradually add the remaining flour. Process until dry spots disappear and the dough leaves the sides of the bowl.

---

*To protect the freshness of whole wheat flour, store it, sealed airtight, in your freezer.
**Buy refrigerated yeast, usually packaged in glass jars, from a health food store.
***Ask for pure, powdered calcium carbonate in your health food store. Some drug stores may carry it as "precipitated chalk." If you still can't find it, order by mail from Freeda Vitamins. They're listed under Food and Products Sources in Section 3.

If the dough feels sticky, add a little more flour and mix it in thoroughly. Place the dough in a well-oiled bowl, cover with a damp towel and place it in a warm spot (82–85°). The dough should double in size in about 45 minutes.

Punch the dough down, re-cover with towel and let rise again. Generously oil two bread pans. Turn dough out on a floured board. Knead vigorously. Divide into two equal parts and shape into a loaf and place in the prepared pans. Cover with a damp towel and let rise again for 30–45 minutes, at 85°.

Preheat oven to 425°. Handling gently, remove the towel and place the loaves in the oven. Bake 15 minutes. Reduce the oven temperature to 375° and bake 25 minutes more. These times and temperatures fit aluminum pans. (The pans don't transfer aluminum to the bread.) Pyrex dishes will take a little longer.

Remove bread from pans and allow to cool on wire racks.

> ❖ **TIPS: For Baking Successful Whole Wheat Bread**   ❖
> - Don't let the dough rise too much—overinflation will cause it to collapse.
> - It's important to preheat your oven—don't bake the bread until you're sure the temperature has reached 425°.
> - Crust of this bread is hard. For a softer crust, gently spread a thin layer of butter or oil on the loaves before baking.
> - Fresh bread cuts better if you allow it to cool.
> - Expect a few more crumbs than from white bread.
> - Restore fresh-from-the-oven taste and texture by warming a slice 15–20 *seconds* in a microwave oven, or wrap and heat it a few minutes in a warm oven.
> - If you don't need the second loaf right away, wrap it in a moisture-proof wrapper and freeze. Don't refrigerate.
> - You learn to recognize the proper "feel" of the dough through experience. Don't be afraid to try! Failure to achieve a perfect loaf is usually only cosmetic. Imperfect loaves are quite satisfactory—and nourishing.

❖ VARIATIONS ❖

Triticale Bread—Substitute triticale flour for all the flour in this recipe.

Rye Bread—Use half rye and half whole wheat flours.

Quinoa Crackers

3 Dozen

Making your own crackers can seem like the straw that broke the camel's back—especially when you're preparing everything else from scratch, too.

Here's what works for me: On a day when I'm serving soup or stew from my freezer, I bake crackers. By combining a quick dish with a time-consuming one, I don't feel like I'm spending my whole day cooking.

½   cup of cool water
¼   teaspoon unbuffered, corn-free vitamin C crystals
1   cup quinoa flour
⅓   cup tapioca starch flour
2   tablespoons sesame seeds
1   teaspoon baking soda
¼   teaspoon salt
2½ tablespoons oil

Combine the cool water and vitamin C crystals. Stir to dissolve and set aside.

Preheat oven to 350°. Combine the flours, seeds, baking soda and salt in a mixing bowl. Make a well in the middle. Pour water with dissolved crystals and oil into the well.

Stir with a fork until the dough clumps together. Add another tablespoon of water, if necessary, to help the dough form a smooth ball.

Working on an ungreased cookie sheet, put a piece of wax paper over the dough and roll it to about ⅛-inch thickness. Cut into 2-inch squares. (A pizza-cutting wheel makes cutting crackers a speedy job.) Prick tops with fork.

Bake 20–22 minutes, or until the crackers are lightly browned. Remove crackers to a wire rack to cool. The crackers crisp as they cool.

If you want yours extra crispy, just remove the irregular-shaped crackers from the outer edges and separate the remaining crackers. Return them to the oven (heat turned off) for another 10–20 minutes. When cool, store in an airtight container.

Adapted from *Free and Easy Eating: An Allergy Cookbook*, by permission of the author, Nicolette Dumke (1877 Polk Avenue, Louisville, CO 80027)

Amaranth Crackers

About 3 dozen

Amaranth Crackers are so versatile that every batch can have a different flavor. I suggest rolling them on the baking sheet to reduce handling.

4	tablespoons cool water
¹/₄	teaspoon unbuffered, corn-free vitamin C crystals
¹/₂	cup pumpkin, sunflower or sesame seeds, divided
³/₄	amaranth flour
¹/₂	cup arrowroot starch
¹/₄	teaspoon salt
3	tablespoons olive or other oil
2	tablespoons boiling water
1	teaspoon baking soda

OPTIONAL ADDITIONS:

1 teaspoon of any one of the following: chili powder, dried oregano, basil, dill weed, or ground anise, fennel, cumin or caraway seeds*

Combine the cool water and vitamin C crystals. Stir and set aside for the crystals to dissolve.

Finely chop or coarsely grind ¼ cup of the pumpkin (or sunflower) seeds until they're about the size of sesame seeds. Scatter them on a non-stick or oiled baking sheet.

Grind the other ¼ cup of seeds into a fine meal. Combine with the flour, starch and salt. Whisk the dry ingredients together well.

Dribble the oil over the flour mixture and stir. When large clumps form, lay spoon aside and use a table knife in each hand to cut through the clumps. Stop when the particles are the size of small peas. (Takes two minutes or less.)

With a fork, stir in liquid with dissolved vitamin C crystals. Dough will be dry, but starting to come together in a ball. Preheat oven to 350°.

Combine the boiling water and baking soda, stirring to dissolve. Pour it onto the dough and stir it in. The dough will form a smooth, cohesive ball.

Turn the dough onto the prepared baking sheet. Put a sheet of

---

*To substitute fresh herbs (basil, parsley, oregano, thyme), add a *tablespoon* of chopped leaves to the seeds before grinding.

oiled wax paper over the dough and pat the ball down to about an inch thick. Using a rolling pin, or a tall, smooth bottle, roll the dough thinner. It will nearly cover the baking sheet. Try to make the dough as uniformly thin as possible—about ⅛ inch.

Remove the wax paper carefully. Use a knife to separate it from the dough, if necessary. Cut 1½- to 2-inch squares. Prick the tops with a fork. Bake 22 minutes.

Remove from oven, and remove the irregular crackers from around the edges. Separate the rest of the crackers. If you like extra-crisp crackers, return them to the hot oven (with the heat turned off) for another 10–20 minutes.

Sesame Oat Crackers

A cracker this good might easily take the place of cookies during the months you omit sweets.

¼   cup sesame seeds
1½ cups oat flour
¼   cup oat bran
½   teaspoon salt
¼–½ teaspoon chili powder, optional
¼   cup olive oil
¼   cup water
1   teaspoon toasted sesame oil (oriental type)

Preheat oven to 350°. Toast the sesame seeds until golden brown in a dry skillet or oven. In a mixing bowl, whisk together the seeds, flour, bran, salt and chili powder.

Stir in the oil, water and sesame oil; mix thoroughly. Roll out on a baking sheet, with a sheet of oiled wax paper over the dough. Cut into squares with a knife or pizza-cutting wheel.

Bake for 10–12 minutes until lightly brown. When cool, store in an airtight container.

Adapted from Nutrition for Optimal Health Assoc. Developed by Jacqueline Marcus, R.D., Skokie Valley Hospital, Good Health Program

Oat Bran Muffins

1 Dozen

²/₃ cups rolled oats

2 teaspoons baking soda

³/₄ teaspoon unbuffered, corn-free vitamin C crystals

¹/₂ teaspoon salt

1¹/₂ teaspoons cinnamon, optional

¹/₂ cup chopped walnuts, optional

1¹/₂ cups oat bran

1¹/₂ cups applesauce, puréed raw banana or seedless grapes, OR puréed, cooked carrots*

¹/₂ cup water OR Stevia Tea, page 329

¹/₄ cup oil

2 eggs

In a blender, grind the rolled oats, half at a time, into flour. In a small bowl combine the oat flour with baking soda, vitamin C crystals and salt. Add the cinnamon and nuts, if you want them. Whisk the dry ingredients together and set aside.

Measure oat bran into a larger bowl. Without washing the blender, combine in it the puréed fruit or carrots, water or Stevia Tea, oil, and egg yolks. Blend for 60 seconds; pour over the oat bran. Stir to blend. Set aside to soak for 10 minutes.

Preheat oven to 400°. Prepare a muffin pan with oil and a dusting of flour, or cupcake papers. In a small bowl beat the egg whites until they hold soft peaks.

Working quickly, add the dry ingredients to the bran mixture all at once. Stir to moisten. Fold in the beaten egg whites with a rubber spatula. Divide into 12 muffin cups, pop in the oven for 14–16 min. or until light brown and crusty.

Serve with Fresh Fruit Jam, page 317.

---

*A time- and work-saving way to bake with carrot purée is to buy junior baby food.

Quinoa Applesauce Bread

1 Loaf

Nickie Dumke developed this bread based on the methods she learned from *The Allergy Self-Help Cookbook*. If you notice the techniques behind the simple combining of ingredients in this book, your creative juices may start to flow, too!

I think you'll treasure Quinoa Applesauce Bread—it's a delicious (non-grain) treat that you can make sweet or savory, to suit your needs.

1½ cups applesauce, room temperature or slightly warmed
¾   teaspoon unbuffered, corn-free vitamin C crystals
2½ cups quinoa flour
¾   cup arrowroot or tapioca starch, or sesame flour
2½ teaspoons baking soda
½   teaspoon salt
1-2 teaspoons cinnamon, optional
1   cup water, apple juice or apple juice concentrate, thawed (sweetness of bread depends on this choice)
⅓   cup oil

Preheat oven to 400°. Oil and flour an 8x4-inch loaf pan.

In a small bowl, combine the applesauce and vitamin C crystals; stir to dissolve the crystals. Combine the quinoa flour with one of the starches or sesame flour. Whisk in the baking soda, salt and cinnamon, mixing them well.

Add the liquid and oil to the applesauce. Whisk them together and pour over the dry ingredients. Whisk only enough for the dry ingredients to disappear.

Quickly scrape the batter into the prepared pan. Pop it in the oven and reduce the oven temperature to 350°. Bake 55–60 minutes, or until a toothpick inserted into the center comes out dry.

Cool the loaf in the pan for 10 minutes, then turn it out on a wire rack to finish cooling.

❖ **SERVING TIP:** For a light meal morning, night or noon, toast ❖ slices of this bread in a dry skillet (take care not to burn them). Top each with a spoonful of unsweetened applesauce, shortcake style. Delicious and very nutritious.

Adapted from *Free and Easy Eating: An Allergy Cookbook,* by permission of the author, Nicolette Dumke (1877 Polk Avenue, Louisville, CO 80027)

Buckwheat Crackers

Some people who react to wheat also experience problems with buckwheat—though the two are totally unrelated. Experiment to determine your own tolerance.

I settled on this recipe because you can roll this quantity of dough on a cookie sheet. If you need more crackers, double the recipe and divide the dough into two balls. Roll on two cookie sheets.

1	cup "white" buckwheat flour*
1/4	cup arrowroot or tapioca starch
1/4	teaspoon salt
3	tablespoons sesame seeds
2	tablespoons cold-pressed sesame oil
1/2	cup water

Preheat oven to 400°. Mix the flour, starch, salt and seeds in a small bowl. Make a "well" in the center of the flour and pour in the oil and water.

Stir with a fork. As the flour absorbs the liquid, the dough will start to clump into a ball.

Oil the center of a cookie sheet (the flat kind without edges is easiest to work on). Leave the outer edge, about 1 inch, unoiled. Scrape the ball of dough onto the middle of the cookie sheet. Pat it into a flat rectangle.

Oil one side of a sheet of waxed paper or foil. Place the oiled side down on the dough. Using a rolling pin or the side of a smooth bottle, roll the dough out very thin. (It will approximately fill the oiled space on the cookie sheet.)

Cut the dough into 2-inch squares. Salt the tops lightly if you wish (use a salt shaker to control the flow—and don't overdo it!).

Place crackers in the oven; immediately reduce oven temperature to 350°. In 12 minutes remove them from the oven and lift off the crispy crackers around the outer edge. Put them on a wire rack to cool.

---

*Buy *unroasted* buckwheat groats and grind them into flour in your blender. Measure the flour after grinding.

Separate the remaining crackers with a spatula. Turn the oven off and return those crackers to the oven for 10–20 minutes until they're crisp enough for your taste.

> ❖ **NOTE:** No matter how many times I roll crackers, I still leave ❖ the center ones thicker than the ones at the outer edges. I think you'll do this, too. So I adapted my recipe to reflect this tendency. Now they'll all be crisp!

Soups

I find something comforting about a steamy bowl of soup, especially in the winter! Those of us on special diets have even more reasons to like and make soup. Soups make plain foods more delicious. They provide flavors we can't achieve when we cook those same ingredients separately.

For example, visualize a plate with plain baked or broiled fish, sliced carrots and a pile of steamed cabbage. Acceptable, but plain. Unadorned. Unsauced. Now think about the carrots and cabbage simmering in a pot of broth.

After the vegetables bubble for ten or fifteen minutes, fish is dropped in the soup. The meal is ready to eat ten minutes after the simmering resumes. You can add salt, pepper, a bay leaf or a few pinches of compatible herbs to enhance the flavor even further. See Catfish Gumbo for this model—and then make up your own variations.

By combining water with foods you were going to eat anyway, and simmering them together, delightful and intriguing things can—and do—happen.

Dr. Crook, Soup Man At Heart

"My wife and I love soups of all kinds. So do our children and grandchildren when they come to visit us. We especially like vegetable soups and soups with rice in them.

"Soups possess many advantages. Here are some of them:

1. Most soups are easy to prepare.
2. Soups are an easy way to use vegetables— and vegetables promote good health. You can put one or two vegetables in a food processor or blender and use them as the main ingredient of the soup. Or you can load your soups with many different vegetables.
3. You can save and freeze meat juices and bones to use later in soup.

4. You can use chicken, turkey, lean beef, lamb, fish or seafood in soups. Experimenting is fun.
5. You can prepare just enough soup for a single meal or you can make a large pot full. When you make a large pot, you can put what's left in the refrigerator for the next day, or freeze it to use later—it's like money in the bank!"

Dr. Crook continues, "Although I usually recommend freshly prepared foods, there are times when you don't have the time, place, inclination or fresh ingredients needed to cook a meal 'from scratch.' Recently, when my wife was out of town for a week, on two different occasions I ate a 19-oz. can of Progresso Lentil Soup.

This soup is prepared by Progresso Quality Foods (Division of Ogden Food Products Corporation, Rochelle Park, NJ 07662). Here's a list of ingredients: water, lentils, celery, spinach, tomato paste, salt, soybean oil, dehydrated onions, olive oil and natural flavorings. It made satisfying meals."

Tips For Great Soups

- I'll share two "secrets" to help you make perfect soup.
  1. Learn to make flavorful stocks, and set aside time to do it.
  2. Always add an acid when simmering bones. It helps to extract both flavor and minerals from them. If you aren't allergic to yeast, add 2 tablespoons of vinegar to a pot of stock. Or use 2–3 tablespoons of lemon or lime juice or a teaspoon of unbuffered, corn-free vitamin C crystals (ascorbic acid).
- After long simmering, strain the stock and discard the vegetables (along with the bones). They've done their job by giving up their flavor to the stock. Chill or freeze the stock, or make your soup.
- When using stock for soup, add the fresh vegetables you choose and cook only until they're tender. When you follow these directions, it's easy to produce a delicious, nourishing soup full of fresh cooked (but not mushy) vegetables. The long-simmered broth, loaded with minerals, provides flavor and texture contrast to the recently added, crunchy vegetables. The aroma establishes your reputation as a cook!
- Adapt existing recipes to what you have in the house or what you want to eat.

- To thicken your soup, put about one-third of the vegetables in a blender or food processor and purée them with a little broth. Dried bean and pea soups work especially well, but you can use any fresh vegetables.
- Use a slow cooker (such as a crock pot) to simmer soups—either all day or overnight. This enables you to chop and assemble the ingredients when it's most convenient for you.
- Purchase a dozen *wide-mouth* pint canning jars at a hardware store or supermarket. They're perfect for freezing stock or soup. Remember two things—leave ¾ inch of empty space and lay the lids on *loosely* until the liquid is frozen solid. *Then*—the next day—screw the lids on tightly. To use, thaw 10 minutes in tepid water until the frozen block slides easily out of the jar into the pan to reheat. (Remember, use *pint* jars. 50% of my quarts cracked.) You can also thaw soups or stock in the microwave on the defrost cycle.
- If you wish to omit grains, and the recipe calls for rice or barley, substitute the same amount of whole buckwheat groats or washed quinoa. Add either of them half an hour or more before you serve.
- Use nut milks for cream soups instead of cow milk.
- Don't overcook your fish—it becomes tough and loses its flavor. Don't undercook it either. The average thin fillet is cooked properly in 10 minutes. To see if you've cooked fish long enough, remove it to a platter and flake it with a fork. If the fish flakes easily, it's done. Finish flaking into bite-sized pieces, return to the pot and serve at once. Delicious!

Rainbow Trout

Easy Asparagus Soup

Serves 2–4

On a day when I had "nothing in for lunch," I managed to find both asparagus and chicken stock in my freezer for a quick and satisfying meal. The soup was the main course for 2 hungry adults—and it disappeared. Thanks, Jan!

2 cups fresh asparagus, cut in 1-inch pieces
OR
1 package frozen asparagus pieces
1 cup chicken stock, fat removed
¼ teaspoon salt, or to taste
Pepper to taste, optional

Steam fresh asparagus until soft and tender, or cook frozen asparagus according to directions. Purée cooked asparagus in a blender or food processor with enough cooking water to make a medium thick purée. Add salt, pepper and stock to the purée and blend again to combine. Return soup to the pot to reheat.

Adapted from Jan Beima, R.N., from the office of
Gary Oberg, M.D., Crystal Lake, Illinois

Egg Drop Soup

Serves 1–2

You can make this soup as plain or fancy as you choose. Traditional oriental presentation calls for just the stock, egg and a pinch of minced chives or scallion tops floating on top. If you want to make it into a main course, add chopped vegetables—broccoli, cabbage, carrot—or even a few kernels of corn if you tolerate them.

2 cups homemade stock, skimmed
(chicken, turkey, beef, lamb, or pork—your choice)
1 egg, beaten
OPTIONAL ADDITIONS:
Salt and pepper, to taste
Pinch of minced chive or scallion top
Chopped vegetables, about ½ to 1 cup

Gradually pour the egg in a thin stream into the simmering stock, while stirring gently. Add salt, pepper and vegetables, if you want them. Simmer a few minutes until veggies are tender-crisp. Garnish each serving with floating chives or scallion top.

Adapted from Ken Gerdes, M.D., Denver, Colorado

Elizabeth's Tomato Soup

Yields 1 gallon

Dr. Crook's daughter contributed this delicious recipe. Their whole family enjoys it, and they make it in large batches to freeze. If your garden runneth over with tomatoes, you can make and freeze several batches of this soup—as much as you can store.

4 tablespoons olive oil
OR
2 tablespoons each of olive oil and butter
4 carrots, peeled and diced
4 stalks of celery, finely diced
3 medium onions, chopped
14 large, ripe tomatoes
OR
3 quarts of canned tomatoes, chopped, with juice
½ cup parsley, finely chopped
6 leaves of fresh basil
Salt
Freshly ground pepper, optional

Heat the oil (and butter, if you're using it) in a large kettle. Sauté the carrots, celery and onions for about 20 minutes or until very tender. Add the tomatoes and continue cooking over moderate heat for 25–30 minutes, or longer. Stir in the parsley and basil. Season with salt and pepper and cook a minute longer. Serve, or freeze.

Elizabeth Fontana, Nashville, Tennessee

Lentil-Rice Soup   Ⓛ

Serves 4–6

This recipe makes a hearty, nourishing soup. The legumes and grains complement each other to make high-quality protein. If you want to add another vegetable or two, don't hesitate. (I added a diced carrot for color.)

¹/₂	cup lentils	2	cloves garlic
³/₄	cup brown rice	¹/₂	teaspoon dill weed
7	cups water	1	bay leaf
³/₄	cup chopped onion	1	teaspoon salt

Rinse the lentils, checking for tiny stones or debris. Bring lentils, rice and water to a boil. Add onion, garlic, dill weed, bay leaf and salt. Reduce heat and simmer, covered, until the rice and lentils are tender—about one hour. Discard bay leaf and serve.

D. Vaughn Micklos, M.D., Buena Park, California

Kale-Lentil Soup   Ⓛ

Serves 6

Kale is a delicious, but little-known member of the cabbage family—well worth getting acquainted with. Tear the foliage off of the heavy center rib.

1   bunch of kale (12 ounces), coarsely chopped
1   onion, minced
3   garlic cloves, minced
1   can (14-ounce) tomatoes in juice
1   leafy stalk of celery, minced
1   cup lentils
4   cups water
Part of a fresh jalapeño pepper, minced, optional
¹/₂   teaspoon cumin powder
¹/₄   cup lemon juice

Rinse the lentils, checking for tiny stones and debris. Place everything except the lemon juice in a large pot. Bring to a boil, cover and simmer for 1 hour. Stir in the lemon juice.

Barbara Bassett, *Bestways*, June 1985

Oyster Soup   Ⓜ

Serves 2

Cauliflower purée takes the place of milk in this unusual soup. If you tolerate a little butter, though, use the real thing for flavor. If not, improvise with olive oil, or the "oil of the day" on your diet.

1   cup cauliflower, chopped
1 or 2 small containers of oysters
Broth from the oysters
1   cup water
1   tablespoon butter OR olive or other oil
Salt and pepper to taste
Parsley for garnish, optional
Optional vegetables for color—minced green onion, shredded carrot or red cabbage

Cook the cauliflower until tender. Purée in blender or food processor with the water and oyster broth. Transfer the purée to a saucepan, add the oysters and butter or oil. Cook until the edges of the oysters curl (about 3 minutes). Add parsley if desired or one of the vegetables suggested for color. Serve at once.

Adapted from Ken Gerdes, M.D., Denver, Colorado

Kasha and Cabbage Soup

Yields 10 cups

Nutritious, low calorie, yet filling. This soup is delicious! It also reheats well.

1   pound cabbage, chopped coarsely
1   medium onion, chopped
2   cups celery, chopped
3   cloves garlic, minced
¹/₂ cup parsley, chopped
1   8-ounce can tomato sauce
Juice of 1 lemon
¹/₄ to ¹/₂ teaspoon crushed red pepper
        OR
1 to 3 teaspoons fresh hot pepper, minced
¹/₂ cup kasha (buckwheat groats)
8   cups water

Put everything in a large pot. Cover and simmer 45 minutes. Add more water if needed.

Barbara Bassett, *Bestways*, June 1985

Cornish Hen Stock

Yields about 3–4 pints

Many people who react to chicken tolerate Cornish game hens. Part of the reason may be that the hens are used much less frequently than chicken. Yet, the flavor and texture of the meats are quite similar.

Here's the plan: Roast the hens when you want to have them for your meal. (See *Roast Cornish Hens*, page 277.) Make your stock (to enjoy a few days later) the day you serve the roasted game hens. Serve the breast meat for your meal, and allocate the rest to use for stock and soup.

Cut the legs and wings off. Strip the bits and pieces from the bones and freeze them. Put the bones of the legs, wings and carcasses in the stock pot.

Cornish game hen's bones, of 2 or more small hens
Water to cover
1/2 teaspoon unbuffered, corn-free vitamin C crystals
1 small onion, quartered
1–2 carrots, sliced
1–2 stalks of celery, with leaves
Handful of fresh parsley
1–2 bay leaves
1/2 teaspoon salt

Cover the bones with plenty of water and add the remaining ingredients. Simmer the bones, covered, for 2–3 hours—or overnight (in making stock, longer is better). After the hours of slow simmering, uncover the pot and increase the heat to reduce the stock (15–30 minutes). This concentrates the flavor and reduces the quantity you'll have to store.

Strain the stock through a colander into another pan or large bowl to retain the bones. Then strain it back into your stock pot through a fine strainer.

To freeze: Pour into wide-mouth pint jars to freeze, but leave ¾ inch headroom. *Refrigerate* the stock for a few hours. Fat separates and floats to the surface, forming a solid layer. Use both a fork and knife to lift the fat out of each jar. Put the flat disc of a two-piece lid loosely on top and place the jars in your freezer. The next day add the screw rings, and seal the jars tightly. Freeze and use within 3–6 months.

To refrigerate and use in 4 days: Put your whole pot in the refrigerator until you're ready to make soup. (See *Cornish Hen Soup*.) *Leave the solid layer of fat in place until you want to make soup.** Remove the solid fat from the top just before using.

Nell's Chicken Soup

Serves 2

Nell's soup tastes different with and without the yogurt—and both are good. Add a few vegetables if you wish.

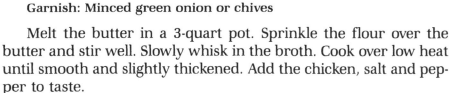

2	tablespoons butter (or oil)
¼	cup oat flour
	OR
2	tablespoons arrowroot
3	cups chicken broth, skimmed
½	cup chicken, cooked and shredded

Salt and pepper to taste
1   cup plain lowfat yogurt, optional
Garnish: Minced green onion or chives

Melt the butter in a 3-quart pot. Sprinkle the flour over the butter and stir well. Slowly whisk in the broth. Cook over low heat until smooth and slightly thickened. Add the chicken, salt and pepper to taste.

If you like and tolerate it, stir in the plain yogurt just before serving. Heat another minute or so, without boiling, until the soup is steamy. Garnish each serving with minced green onion or chives.

Nell Sellers, Jackson, Tennessee

---

*The long-simmered soup is sterile. When the fat forms the solid layer on top, it effectively seals out micro-organisms and protects the contents—just as paraffin seals jelly.

Catfish Gumbo

Serves 10

Delicious, and takes only about an hour to prepare.

¼ cup olive oil
1 cup chopped celery
1 cup chopped green pepper
1 cup chopped onion
2 cloves garlic, crushed
4 cups beef or other stock, skimmed
1 can (16 ounces) tomatoes, chopped
1 package (10 ounces) frozen okra
½ teaspoon thyme
1 bay leaf
½ teaspoon cayenne pepper
½ teaspoon oregano
1 teaspoon salt
4 farm-raised catfish fillets, cut in 1-inch cubes
5 cups cooked brown rice, optional

Heat the oil in a large stock pot. Sauté the celery, green pepper, onion and garlic. Add beef broth, tomatoes, okra, thyme, bay leaf, cayenne pepper, oregano and salt. Cover and simmer for 30 minutes. Add the catfish and simmer for another 15 minutes, or until the fish flakes easily. Remove the bay leaf. Serve over cooked brown rice (or millet, quinoa or buckwheat), if desired.

Fishing for Compliments:
Cooking with Catfish
The Catfish Institute

Cornish Hen Soup

Serves 2

The broth of this delicious soup will look murky rather than clear. Here's why: the acid in the stock pulled calcium and other minerals out of the bones during the long cooking.

1   pint of Cornish Hen Stock, page 183
3   slender carrots, sliced
1-2 stalks of celery, sliced
1   parsnip, optional
Handful of fresh parsley
Diced meat (from the legs and wings of your roasted hens)

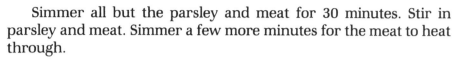

Simmer all but the parsley and meat for 30 minutes. Stir in parsley and meat. Simmer a few more minutes for the meat to heat through.

❖ VARIATIONS ❖

Add 1 or 2 small potatoes, diced, or ⅔ cup of *cooked* rice, millet, quinoa or buckwheat. If you prefer to use uncooked grain, add another pint of broth to the recipe.

Meal-In-A-Bowl

Serves 2

This recipe invites you to improvise. It's deliberately vague so you can use the ingredients you tolerate.

1   large or 2 small potatoes, diced
½-1 stalk celery, chopped
2   small green onions, chopped, (keep white and green parts separate)
½   teaspoon salt
2½   cups water
⅓   cup nuts of your choice
½-1 cup vegetable of your choice, diced (carrot, red or green pepper, fennel bulb, asparagus, kale, cabbage, etc.)
3-4 ounces cooked meat, poultry or fish

Simmer the potatoes, celery, white part of the onions and salt in water 12–15 minutes. If your other vegetable is raw, add it to the potatoes to cook, too. Grind the nuts in a blender.

When the potatoes are tender, measure the cooking water—there should be 2 cups. Add this to the nuts and blend into nut milk. Add the nut milk, green part of the onion and cooked meat, poultry or fish. Simmer a few minutes for flavors to mingle.

Adapted from Ken Gerdes, M.D., Denver, Colorado

Split Pea Soup   L

Yields about 10 cups

I used to think that making pea soup *required* a ham bone. But ham, even "honey-glazed" or sugared ham, contains preservatives that may bother some folks. But who said we couldn't substitute a fresh pork bone? Or lamb bones? Or turkey or Cornish hen bones? Or who said we absolutely *had* to include any bones or meat at all?

I never make my pea soup the same way twice. I've tried all of the above ideas, including vegetarian versions, and I've never produced one we failed to enjoy! So improvise to suit your own needs. Choose 2–4 options listed below, or use all—or none. Adapting is the name of our game.

1   pound dried split peas*
6–8 cups water
1   teaspoon salt
EVERYTHING else is optional:
2   bay leaves
1   cup, more or less, chopped onion**
2–4 cloves garlic,** minced or pressed
1   finely diced potato**
1/2–1 cup brown or wild rice
2–3 cups carrots,** sliced, diced or shredded
1–2 cups celery,** sliced
2   tablespoons lemon or lime juice,
     OR
3/4 teaspoon unbuffered vitamin C crystals
1/2 teaspoon toasted sesame oil
1/2 cup fresh parsley leaves, minced

Conventional Top-of-Stove Method: Simmer the peas, water and salt about 3 hours. Stir occasionally. Add any options you select, except the last three, and simmer another hour. If you want to include the citrus juice, sesame oil or parsley, stir them into the soup just before serving.

Crock-Pot Method: Combine the peas, water and salt in an elec-

---

*Sometimes a child rejects "green food" without even a taste. If so, he may accept it in a friendlier color—try using yellow split peas, instead.
**When making vegetarian versions of this soup, try sautéing the vegetables in 2–4 tablespoons of olive oil before adding them to the pot. A little fat enhances the flavor and makes the soup more satisfying.

tric slow cooker about 24 hours in advance. Add the options you want, except the last three, about 6–8 hours before serving time. When ready to serve, stir in the citrus juice, sesame oil or parsley. (You don't have to stir or watch the pot with this method.)

Garbanzo Potato Soup $\boxed{\text{L}}$

Yields 6 cups

This soup makes a delicious, hearty lunch or light supper. For a complete meal, add crisp Oat Waffles and a salad. As with any soup, you can vary the seasoning.

3   medium unpeeled potatoes, scrubbed and diced
1   red, green or yellow bell pepper, chopped
1–2 tablespoons oil
½   teaspoon fresh rosemary, crushed, optional
2   cups garbanzo beans, cooked,
    OR
1   can (1 pound) garbanzos, well rinsed
1   tablespoon lemon or lime juice
    OR
½   teaspoon unbuffered, corn-free vitamin C crystals
Salt to taste

Cover the potatoes with water; cook until soft. In a 3-quart saucepan, sauté pepper in oil. When tender, reserve 2 tablespoons for garnish. Stir in remaining ingredients, including the potatoes and their water. Simmer a few minutes for the flavors to mingle.

With a slotted spoon remove about a cup of vegetables. Purée the remaining soup in a blender or food processor. If needed, add water to get the consistency you like. Stir in the cup of vegetables and reheat. Garnish each bowl of soup with a bit of sautéed pepper.

❖ VARIATION ❖

For a spicier soup with a "kick," add about a teaspoon of fresh minced jalapeño pepper. (Use gloves, and never rub your eyes with your peppery hands.)

Elizabeth Pettus, Hurst, Texas

Save-The-Day-Soup

Serves 1 or more

Do you tire of plain, unadorned foods and baked or broiled foods that often dry out?

SOLUTION: Combine those foods that you were going to eat anyway in a pot with water. Voila! Soup!

This "recipe" first appeared in my newsletter, *Mastering Food Allergies*. It illustrates an unstructured approach to meal preparation rather than a hard-and-fast recipe. Like you, I'm sometimes too busy to fuss with a meal—even though my family is hungry. "STD" Soup has saved the day more than once at our house. I hope it does the same for you!

Meat or fowl, with bones OR fish*

Vegetables, your choice

Salt—go easy

Fresh herb of your choice

1 cup water per serving, approximately

Pinch of unbuffered, corn-free vitamin C crystals

Estimate the time your ingredients need to cook. Time is influenced not only by your choice of food, but by the size of the pieces. Experiment with large chunks, as well as with finely diced food.

Simmer your soup until everything is tender, probably 20 to 30 minutes. If one food takes more time to cook, start it first. Then, add the other ingredients. Taste. Adjust seasonings. Serve.

Examples: Cabbage, carrots, celery, catfish and dill. Onion, garlic, asparagus, any kind of poultry and basil. Broccoli, cauliflower, kale, lamb and rosemary.

Zucchini Soup

Serves 3–4

A good basic recipe that's even more delicious when you add your favorite fresh herb. My family flipped over this spiked with fresh basil from my garden.

---

*Note: Most fish cooks in 10–12 minutes. Only monkfish—or other thick fish—require 15 minutes or more. So fish might make the quickest soup—unless you start with precooked (leftover) meat or poultry. If you have the matching stock in your freezer, use it in place of water.

2   cups chicken or other stock, skimmed
1½ cups grated zucchini, unpeeled if small and tender
Salt and pepper to taste
1-2 teaspoons olive oil or butter
⅔   cup diced, cooked chicken or other meat, to match the
      stock used, optional
1   tablespoon chopped fresh basil, optional

Combine the stock, zucchini and seasonings and simmer 10–15 minutes. For thick, creamy texture: purée the soup. Add the oil or butter and the chicken or other meat. Heat through and serve.

❖ VARIATION ❖

Sauté ⅔ cup chopped onion and a clove of garlic in the oil or butter. When soft, proceed with the recipe above—but don't add oil again.

Adapted from Ken Gerdes, M.D., Denver, Colorado

Creamy Spinach-Chicken Soup

Yields 6–8 cups

If someone in your family is less than enthusiastic about spinach, try this soup. The puréed zucchini provides the creamy base that bathes the spinach. Assuming you use real homemade chicken stock, your soup will boast a fantastic flavor. If you happen to have fresh basil in your garden, so much the better!

You'll find this soup easier to assemble if you wash all of the vegetables before you start to cook.

1   large or 2 medium leeks, well washed
1-2 tablespoons olive oil
2   large zucchini or 3-4 small ones,
      washed and chopped
2   tablespoons chopped fresh basil
4   cups fresh spinach, washed and torn, divided
2   cups chicken stock, or same stock as fowl, divided
3-6 ounces cooked chicken, turkey, Cornish hen or duck,
      diced or minced

See Leeks, page 254, for cleaning hints. Drain the veggies.

Slice leeks thinly. Heat oil in a 3-quart saucepan. Add the leeks and sauté over medium heat until they're soft but not brown. Add 1 cup of the stock and simmer.

In separate pan, cook zucchini in the remaining cup of stock for 8–10 minutes. When it's tender-soft, purée it with the fresh basil leaves in a blender or food processor. Add to the leeks.

Put half the spinach into the bubbling pot, bring to boil again; add remaining spinach and diced chicken. Stir gently. Cover and simmer for 5–7 minutes. Serves four people as part of their lunch, or two or three for their whole meal. Freezes well.

❖ VARIATION ❖

Experiment using the fresh herbs you like and tolerate best, in place of the basil. If you prefer, use meat or fish (and stock) in place of the poultry.

Wild Rice Soup

Yields 4½ cups

This gourmet soup can easily fill the bill for a main course—especially if you add the chicken or turkey. Even though wild rice costs more, some folks who don't tolerate regular rice can eat it without problems.

1	tablespoon almond or olive oil
½	medium onion, finely chopped
¼	pound mushrooms, sliced, optional
¼	cup chopped celery
¼	cup barley or rice flour
3	cups chicken or turkey stock, skimmed
2	cups cooked wild rice
¼	teaspoon salt, if needed
1	cup Almond Milk, see Nut Milk, page 320
¼	teaspoon chervil
¼	teaspoon basil
¼	teaspoon marjoram
⅔	cup diced chicken or turkey, optional

Parsley or chives, minced, for garnish

In a 3-quart saucepan over medium heat, sauté the onion in the oil. Cook and stir about 5 minutes until the onion is golden. Add the mushrooms, if you're using them, and celery. Cook and stir for 2 minutes. Slowly mix in flour. Gradually add the stock, whisking constantly until the mixture is slightly thickened—5 to 8 minutes.

Stir in rice and salt, if you need it. Reduce heat to low. Stir in almond milk; add chervil, basil and marjoram. If you wish, add diced chicken or turkey. Simmer 5 minutes, stirring occasionally. Ladle the soup into bowls and garnish with parsley or chives.

Salads—More Than Lettuce

Lettuce May Spell Trouble

Lettuce belongs to the Composite Food Family. Other members include globe artichoke, chamomile, chicory, safflower, tarragon, dandelion, endive, escarole—and *ragweed*. When I first noticed that daily lettuce salads didn't agree with me, I jumped to the conclusion that I couldn't digest anything raw.

How surprised I was when coleslaw and a few other raw salads gave me no trouble. About the same time, I prepared a cup of chamomile tea. The minute I sipped it I knew it wasn't good for me. And yes, ragweed pollen wipes me out.

In spite of these problems with Composite Family foods, I can eat artichoke a few times a year and I occasionally season food with a pinch of tarragon without noticing any problem. After avoiding lettuce for a while, I now eat a little twice a month. Fortunately, because of my own experience, I searched beyond the lettuce leaf to discover other salad options.

Whole-meal Salads

You can make salads as complete and satisfying as you wish. Take, for example, the classic French Salade Niçoise. It contains tuna and potato salads, cooked (but still crisp) marinated green beans, tomato wedges, a hard-boiled egg and a few ripe olives. I stopped ordering it in restaurants long ago, though, because it's usually served floating in a puddle of oil and vinegar dressing. Still, Salade Niçoise provides us with a model of a hearty—and gourmet—salad to duplicate at home.

When you analyze the component parts of this salad, you can see that it contains both proteins and vegetables. With a leap of imagination, you can substitute turkey, rice and carrots; or duck, sweet potato and broccoli; or salmon, quinoa and peas, and so on. Let your imagination go! You can top your salad with a dressing of your choice, using as much or as little as you wish.

As you'll see, this whole-meal salad looks a lot like Next-Day Lunch Salad. However, the ingredients aren't necessarily left-overs—but then again, they could be. Versatility is salad's middle name. Read the introductory section to Lunches for proper precautions with leftovers.

Slaw in Many Guises

According to my dictionary, "slaw" means coleslaw, a salad made of chopped raw cabbage. But why not include other vegetables in our definition? Remember, most folks with candida experience food sensitivities. And you'll overcome them sooner by not eating *anything* repetitiously.

I've made successful slaw with jicama, carrots, white daikon radish (the one that's about a foot long) and red radishes. They're all different, all good. For mild, slightly sweet-tasting slaw, try jicama or carrots. For super-crisp, slightly fiery flavor, try either kind of radish. See the recipes in this chapter.

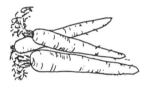 

Salad Bars—Plus or Minus?

When salad bars first appeared on the scene some years ago, almost all of the foods were displayed separately. The customer selected only those ingredients he wanted. However, the trends now seem to run toward an array of combination salads—potato salad, coleslaw, three to five pasta mixtures, bowls of marinating vegetables and so on. Often the only separate items are the torn lettuce and sliced or chopped onions.

Personally, I felt more secure partaking of the earlier version of salad bars, and I still favor the few restaurants in my area that retain the separate "fixin's." Combinations of unknown foods and additives add up to booby traps which may trigger your symptoms.

Slaw du Jour

Serves 4

In my quest for lettuce-free salads, I concocted a variety of slaws. I love their crunch, and their varied flavors. If you own a food processor, slaws are quick to make. I prefer the steel blade to the shredding disc, though both work.

2-4 cups shredded jicama, carrot, radishes, daikon radish, kohlrabi or cabbage (select one)

¹/₂-1 cup contrasting color vegetable:
shredded carrot, diced bell pepper (red, yellow or green), OR thinly sliced radishes

4 scallions, thinly sliced
OR

¹/₃ cup snipped fresh chives

¹/₃-²/₃ cup Nutty Mayo, page 208

OPTIONAL ADDITIONS:

¹/₂ cup minced parsley leaves, optional

1 tablespoon lime juice
OR

¹/₄ teaspoon unbuffered, corn-free vitamin C crystals

Dash of cayenne pepper

1 teaspoon chili powder

Salt to taste

Combine vegetables in a large bowl. Add parsley, if desired. In a small bowl, combine mayonnaise with any of the optional additions that you wish to include. Mix well; spoon dressing over the vegetables. Chill 30 minutes or more so the flavors can mingle.

Next-Day Lunch Salad

You may have been advised to avoid leftovers because of mold. But if you're careful in handling the food and use it in less than 24 hours, it should be okay (unless you're super-sensitive). Admittedly, this compromise falls short of perfection, but being human—and busy—you need a few time-saving short-cuts to help you "make it."

Prepare your lunch as part of cleaning up after the evening meal so it'll be ready the next day. Don't leave the food standing at room temperature. Here's why: Bacteria from the air doubles every twenty minutes in lukewarm foods. With this in mind, you might even package portions for lunch as soon as you cook the food, instead of waiting for it to sit around, cool and literally be "left."*

More strategies to reduce mold in refrigerated foods: Work with clean, fresh-scrubbed hands. Don't let anybody cough or sneeze over your food preparation area. Scald the glass jars you'll store the food in. By taking extra precautions, you can curtail bacterial and mold proliferation.

If you have enough food left for another meal, but won't be home to use it, freeze it for future lunches. Label it clearly. Some combinations of food are more receptive to freezing than others. You'll just have to experiment.

1   portion of protein food: lean meat, poultry, fish
     OR
     buckwheat, quinoa, amaranth, millet or rice
1   portion of one or more cooked vegetables
1   portion of a starchy food: white or sweet
     potatoes, beans, beets
     OR
     buckwheat, quinoa, amaranth, millet or rice
     Raw veggies to add crunch
     Salad Dressing to taste, see the Salad Dressing chapter

Combine the ingredients and toss to distribute the dressing. (This version carries well in your "brown bag.") Or chill the foods separately: at lunch time, arrange them on a plate and drizzle the dressing over all.

Sample combinations: you select the dressing

Slivered lamb, steamed brussels sprouts (quartered), brown rice and chopped radishes.

---

*Can you use this idea and still rotate your foods? Yes. Here's how: Count your day from 3 p.m. of one day to 3 p.m. of the next day. Purists will say, "Only eat a food once." And that's true, especially early in your treatment. But later, as you improve—and when time is short—you may think about "cheating" at your favorite fast food eatery. Don't. This idea is an infinitely better solution than abandoning your safe foods.

Diced turkey, sweet potato, cooked peas and raw celery.

Broiled orange roughy, quinoa, steamed broccoli and raw zucchini.

Poached salmon, white potato, green beans and scallions.

Buckwheat, lightly steamed broccoli and cauliflower, raw, shredded carrot and sliced radishes.

The possibilities are endless.

Tuna Salad

Serves 2

If you think onion, mayo and pickle relish "make" your tuna salad—and now need to omit them—you can experience a bad case of dietary "blahs." That's why I added the fiery radishes to spark the flavor. Only salt-free tuna is free of MSG.

2–3 tablespoons water

⅛ teaspoon unbuffered, corn-free vitamin C crystals

1 ripe avocado, divided

1 can (7 ounces) albacore tuna in spring water, salt-free

5–6 small radishes, minced

Salt to tast optional

Spinach leaves, optional

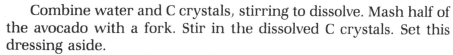

Combine water and C crystals, stirring to dissolve. Mash half of the avocado with a fork. Stir in the dissolved C crystals. Set this dressing aside.

Combine drained tuna and minced radishes. Add dressing and stir to mix. If you want a thinner dressing, just add another tablespoon or so of water. Taste and add salt, if needed.

Arrange torn spinach leaves on plates and divide the tuna between them. Cut the remaining half of avocado into strips. Arrange them attractively over and around the mound of tuna salad.

❖ VARIATIONS ❖

Add diced jicama for more crunch. Increase the amount of vitamin C crystals if you prefer more tang.

Spinach Salad   L̲ E̲ Y̲

This salad is a favorite at my house. I layer it on individual plates or in shallow bowls so I can juggle the ingredients to suit each person's needs or taste. For instance, I include the garbanzo beans as a source of protein for anyone who can't eat egg. And when I omit both egg and legumes, I add a little tuna or other cold fish for protein.

Spinach leaves, washed, patted dry
Carrot, shredded
Zucchini, diced or shredded
Beets, cold, steamed, sliced
Mushrooms, optional
Eggs, hard-boiled, 1 per person
Red onion slices
Garbanzo beans
Dressing of choice
Choice of seeds, raw or lightly toasted:
    sunflower
    pumpkin
    sesame

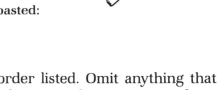

Assemble your salads in the order listed. Omit anything that doesn't agree with you. Add the dressing when you're ready to serve.

❖ VARIATION ❖

For more protein and starch, put a quinoa flatbread at the bottom of your salad. Proceed as above. Quinoa belongs to the same family as spinach and beets, so makes an appropriate addition to this salad.

Cucumber Relish

Serves 4–6

Do you miss dill pickles? This relish ought to help satisfy your taste buds. Eat it with a spoon, to top a tossed salad or slices of tomato, or use it to garnish any kind of burgers.

If you use fresh dill and forgo the pepper, this relish will contain little or no yeast or mold.

2   tablespoons water
¼   teaspoon unbuffered, corn-free vitamin C crystals
3   cucumbers
Salt
Freshly ground black pepper to taste, optional
2   tablespoons fresh dill, finely chopped
     OR
2   teaspoons dried dill

In a small cup, mix water and vitamin C crystals; set aside. Peel cucumbers and cut them in half lengthwise. Remove the seeds with a spoon or melon-baller, and discard. Shred the cucumbers in a food processor or by hand. Salt them lightly and place in a strainer for 10–15 minutes to drain.

Press lightly with your hand, then turn them into a bowl. When the crystals dissolve in water, add the mixture to the cucumbers. Add the dill and mix well. Cover and refrigerate at least 2 hours. Before serving, taste and add salt if needed.

Cauliflower and Broccoli Salad   Ⓜ

Serves 6

If you must avoid milk products, you'll have to improvise for the yogurt in this dressing. Select another dressing from the Salad Dressing chapter, page 204, as a substitute for Nutty Mayo if desired.

2   cups broccoli florets
2   cups cauliflower florets
½   cup sliced radishes
⅓   cup chopped red onion

Yogurt Dressing:
½   cup plain, low-fat yogurt
½   cup Nutty Mayonnaise (see page 208)
Fresh lime or lemon juice, to taste
Garlic powder to taste, optional

Mix broccoli, cauliflower, radishes and red onions in a large bowl. Combine ingredients for yogurt dressing; pour over vegetables and toss. Chill at least 3 hours before serving, so the flavors can mingle.

Adapted from Karen Dilatush, R.N., Coldwater, Mississippi

Lentil Salad [L]

Serves 4

A simple, classic salad—with the nutritional wallop of fresh, raw sprouts.

1   cup sprouted lentils
1   cup Romaine lettuce, torn into bite-size pieces
½   cup thinly sliced celery
½   cup shredded or chopped carrot
1   large or 2 medium tomatoes

Finely chop the sprouts. Mix them with the lettuce, celery and carrot. Slice the tomato and arrange the slices on 4 plates. Spoon the lentil mixture over the tomatoes. Serve with Tomato Dressing, page 206, or any vinaigrette.

Turkey-Vegetable Salad [E]

Serves 4

This main-course luncheon salad is easy to prepare and satisfying to eat. If you wish, try duck or Cornish hen instead of chicken or turkey. You can't go wrong.

½   cup broccoli or cauliflower florets (bite size)
1½   cups cooked brown rice
1   cup cooked turkey or chicken, diced
½   cup sliced or diced carrots
½   cup diced zucchini
Nutty Mayo to moisten, page 208
Lettuce leaves
Tomato wedges, optional

Blanch the cauliflower or broccoli for 2 minutes. Rinse immediately in cold water; drain well. Mix the brown rice and turkey with the vegetables. Moisten with dressing. (Chill an hour or so, if you can.) Arrange lettuce leaves on four plates, spoon the salad in the middle and surround with tomato wedges.

❖ VARIATION ❖

Any poultry salad benefits from a sprinkling of chopped, toasted almonds—½ cup almonds provides 2 tablespoons per serving.

Adapted from Barbara Boegel, R.N., Metairie, LA

Calico Salad

Serves 6

Unusual? Yes. But all salads can't consist of lettuce and tomatoes. Creativity and innovation help you break out of your rut and see foods differently. You won't know how you feel about this combination until you try it!

4   cups peeled and cubed butternut squash
1   green or red pepper, chopped
¼   cup chopped fresh parsley
1   tablespoon olive oil
1   tablespoon lemon or lime juice
½   teaspoon salt
1½ teaspoons fresh oregano
    OR
½   teaspoon dried oregano
¼   cup chopped nuts, optional

Steam or bake squash until tender but not mushy. Cool. Add peppers and parsley.

In a small bowl, combine the oil, juice, salt and oregano for the dressing. Pour over the vegetables and chill. Make several hours ahead and let marinate. Garnish with nuts, if desired, just before serving.

Adapted from *Nutrition Action Healthletter*,
Center for Science in the Public Interest

Chicken-Vegetable Salad ▢L

Serves 6

Colorful and complete, this salad makes a great luncheon main course. Substitute another dressing from the Salad Dressing chapter, if desired.

Start with chilled ingredients.

1½ cups diced cooked chicken
1½ cups cooked fresh peas
    OR frozen peas, thawed, not cooked
1¼ cups cooked brown rice
1½ cups finely diced celery
3-4 tablespoons diced red bell pepper
1   cup Nutty Mayonnaise, page 208
2   teaspoons lemon or lime juice
OPTIONAL GARNISHES:
    Lettuce leaves
    Parsley sprigs
    Tomato wedges

In a large mixing bowl combine the chicken, peas, rice, celery and red bell pepper.

In a small bowl combine the mayonnaise and lemon juice. Pour the dressing over the salad and toss lightly.

Serve in lettuce cups, garnished with parsley sprigs and tomato wedges, if desired.

❖ VARIATIONS ❖

Replace all or part of the chicken with cold turkey, duck or meat.

Adapted from R. H. McCrary, M.D., Hattiesburg, Mississippi

Tomato Cups

These cups make a festive presentation of even the most mundane filling. They're best when tomatoes are in season.

1   whole, large tomato per person

Unless skins are very tender, peel the tomatoes: Dip in boiling water briefly (count to 10), then dip in cool water. Skins slip off easily.

Cut a thin slice from the top of each tomato. Spoon out the seeds and some of the pulp. Salt the inside lightly. Turn upside down and chill.

Fill with your favorite seafood, chicken, or turkey salad. Serve on lettuce or other greens.

Snow Peas and Red Pepper Salad   [L]

Serves 2–4

A riot of color and flavor! To avoid using too many food families as you do in tossed salad, focus on one or two vegetables, as Marian does here. The results may surprise you!

¼   pound fresh snow peas
1   large red pepper, washed, cored, seeded, and cut into bite-sized pieces
½–1 small clove garlic, pressed
1   tablespoon oil
1   teaspoon dark sesame oil (Oriental type)
1–2 tablespoons lemon or lime juice
       OR
¼–½ teaspoon unbuffered vitamin C crystals dissolved in 1 tablespoon warm water
Freshly ground black pepper
1   tablespoon sesame seeds, toasted until golden

Prepare the snow peas: Wash, remove the tips and strings and cut in half. Steam until crisp-tender, 2–3 minutes. Rinse in cold water; drain.

In a serving bowl, whisk together a dressing of the garlic, oils and lemon or lime juice, or unbuffered, corn-free vitamin C crystals. Add the snow peas and pieces of red pepper; toss to mix. Season with freshly ground black pepper. If possible, chill the salad 10–30 minutes. Just before serving, sprinkle sesame seeds on top.

Adapted from Marian Burros, *You've Got It Made*

Sauces and Salad Dressings

Safe Sauces

Many folks on special diets just give up on sauces. Like salad dressings, commercial sauces and gravies may contain mystery ingredients that might trigger your symptoms—MSG, artificial colors or flavors, emulsifiers, flavor enhancers or preservatives. And that's before you consider how many sauces contain milk products—milk, cream, sour cream, buttermilk, and yogurt—that may contribute to your symptoms.

"Eat plain food, simply prepared." In the course of your recovery, how many times did you hear that? It's good advice. And in the first weeks or months of recovery, follow it. But down the road, when boredom sets in, consider this: You're probably better off devising simple sauces to add interest to your meals, than to get "fed up" and chuck the diet that's helping you get well.

After months, if not years, of plain-Jane eating, exploring this idea was a project I had to do—for myself. My challenge was to design a few non-grain, non-dairy sauces that taste wonderful—yet make them from plain food, simply prepared.

One way to prepare a sauce is to make cool Nut Milk, dissolve in it one to two tablespoons of arrowroot or tapioca starch, and cook a few minutes to thicken. This works well. (See "Creamy Nut-Milk Sauce.")

But the solution I like best evolved from puréed vegetables. (See "Velvet Sauce" and "Leek 'Cream' Sauce.") I hope these few, choice recipes make half as much difference in your enjoyment of meals as they did for mine.

Salad Dressings—With a Grain of Salt

Salad dressings can cause problems. Here's why. Almost all commercial dressings contain yeasty vinegar. Like sauces, many dressings are made with milk or sour cream, which may be a problem for some folks. Most contain MSG, various emulsifiers, flavor enhancers and preservatives, which cause problems for others.

What can you do in a restaurant? Use only oil from the offerings at the salad bar and request a few wedges of lemon or lime to squeeze to taste. Or carry your salad dressing from home. (I find a small vitamin bottle with a tight screw-lid works well. I put the bottle in a small plastic bag in case it leaks.)

Salad dressings at home are another thing entirely. Instead of citrus juice, you can use a pinch of unbuffered, corn-free vitamin C crystals dissolved in a little water or juice. This acid gives your dressing such a sharp tang that you won't even miss vinegar anymore! Once you learn to improvise, you can experiment with what's at hand, and create new "custom-designed" dressings yourself.

If using vitamin C as a seasoning is new to you, how can you tell if your powdered or crystalline product is unbuffered? Put a pinch in a little water, stir to dissolve, and taste it. The unbuffered kind (pure ascorbic acid) tastes sharp—like sucking a lemon.

Read the fine print of the label to find out about corn. If it doesn't specify "corn-free," assume that it's derived from corn. You'll be right 99% of the time! This may or may not be a problem for you, but most physicians recommend the sago-palm–derived products for their allergic patients.

Other ideas for dressings utilize fresh, raw tomatoes, grapefruit or other tangy foods to try to achieve the desired sharpness. The results are worthy, if not gourmet. Yet they lack the concentration of ascorbic acid necessary to give your salads an outstanding culinary "kick."

I've included "Avocado-Grapefruit Dressing" and "Tomato Dressing" as examples of this solution. Try the grapefruit dressing in the winter, when the citrus harvest is at its peak. Make the tomato dressing when fresh tomatoes are in season, about July through October. Don't bother with hard, tasteless winter tomatoes—you'll only be disappointed in anything you make with them.

Mayonnaise is a classic dressing and sandwich spread, usually made with egg. But because salmonella bacteria contaminate many eggs, I no longer recommend egg-containing homemade mayonnaise. Instead, I now use and recommend my "Nutty Mayo" (see page 208). It binds salads and spreads beautifully.

If you tolerate vinegar and want a fat-free, low calorie dressing, try one of the Pritikin No Oil Dressings—available in most food stores.

Italian Dressing

Yields ³/₄ cup

This makes an interesting no-vinegar, low oil dressing. The citrus fruit contributes the tang.

¼ cup olive or other oil
¼ cup lemon juice
¼ cup lime juice
¼ cup unsweetened apple (or pineapple) juice
½ teaspoon oregano
½ teaspoon dry mustard
½ teaspoon onion powder
½ teaspoon paprika
⅛ teaspoon thyme
⅛ teaspoon rosemary, optional

Combine all ingredients in a blender and "whiz." Chill well. Serve over any greens you like.

Tomato Dressing

Dresses 4 large salads

This simple dressing takes only a minute to whip up. It's especially good when your garden tomatoes are plentiful.

¼ cup olive (or other) oil
½ teaspoon unbuffered, corn-free vitamin C crystals (or more to taste)
    OR
3–4 tablespoons fresh lemon or lime juice
1 large tomato, peeled and cut up
1 red bell pepper (same size as the tomato), cored and cut up
¼ teaspoon salt

Blend all together. Refrigerate in a scalded glass jar. Shake well before serving. Use within a few days.

❖ VARIATIONS ❖

Tomato Dressing with Onion and Garlic: Sauté ⅓ cup chopped onion in 1 tablespoon of the olive oil. When soft, add the pressed or finely minced garlic and cook 2 minutes. Add to remaining ingredients and blend. (If you prefer to see the bits and pieces, stir the onion-garlic sauté into the blended dressing.) Top salads with a thinly sliced scallion, including the green top.

Tomato-Basil Salad Dressing: Add 8–12 large, fresh basil leaves to the other ingredients and blend well.

Adapted from Kendall Gerdes, M.D., Denver, CO

"C" Salad Dressing

Dresses 4 salads

My problem, like yours, was to find a salad dressing that had the gastronomic "kick" of vinegar—without the yeast. So I considered the simple classic dressing, oil and vinegar. If I substituted lemon or lime juice for the vinegar, I produced a tasty dressing. But many people can't eat citrus foods, so I wasn't satisfied.

If I subtracted the vinegar without putting anything in its place, I'd only have seasoned oil—hardly desirable in today's health-conscious culture. My solution was to use a puréed vegetable, seasoned with herbs or garlic, with only a little oil. I think it's as close as I've come to true inspiration.

1   medium zucchini, scrubbed but not peeled
¼   cup olive oil
2   tablespoons water
½   teaspoon vitamin C crystals, unbuffered
¼   teaspoon salt
OPTIONAL ADDITIONS: (choose one or two)
¼   cup chopped onion
1   clove garlic
6   fresh basil leaves, or to taste
1   tablespoon fresh tarragon leaves
2–3 tablespoons fresh dill

Cut the zucchini into 1-inch pieces. Combine ingredients in a blender and liquefy. If you want it thinner, add a bit more water. Use at once or chill for an hour or two. It will keep up to one week in the refrigerator.

Nutty "Mayo" (Egg-free)

Yields about 1½ cups

Think of this dressing as a seasoned, thickened Nut Milk. After you make it a time or two, you may want to adjust the seasonings to your taste. It tastes sharp and tangy. If you prefer a milder flavor, skimp on the mustard and vitamin C crystals.

How can you use it? Spread on bread or crackers, bind tuna, chicken, potato and other salads, season it with fresh dill weed or anything else you want to use as a dip for your raw veggies.

1¼   teaspoons dry mustard
2   tablespoons hot water
½   cup raw or dry-roasted cashews or other nuts
1   cup water
1   teaspoon vitamin C crystals, unbuffered
2   tablespoons oil
2   teaspoons starch*
½   teaspoon salt
OPTIONAL ADDITIONS:
    Fresh parsley
    Fresh chive
    Dash cayenne pepper

Combine mustard and hot water in a small cup; set aside to dissolve. Blend cashews until they are a fine powder. Add remaining ingredients, including the mustard mixture. Blend for one full minute, stopping once to scrape the bottom of the blender jar with a knife.

Pour the liquid into a small saucepan and cook a few minutes, whisking or stirring, until it just starts to thicken. Refrigerate in a scalded jar up to a week.

---

*Choose from arrowroot, kudzu, tapioca starch flour and potato starch.

Avocado-Grapefruit Dressing

Yields about 1¹/₄ cups

The avocado provides the oil and the grapefruit supplies the sharpness in place of vinegar. It may, in fact, be a bit too tart for some—the flavor varies with the fruit. I like it plain, with just the two ingredients. But if you prefer a milder taste, add the sweeter juice, too.

Use it on anything—assorted greens, fruit salads, tuna or other fish salads. Like a breath of fresh air, it brings a pleasant surprise to otherwise familiar fare.

1   ripe avocado
1   large juicy grapefruit
1-2 tablespoons apple, pineapple or orange juice, optional

Scrub avocado skin well. Cut and spoon fruit into a blender. Scrub skin of the grapefruit, pat dry, peel and cut into sections. Spoon half the sections and juice into blender. Process on high until smooth. Taste; add sweeter fruit juice, if necessary. Use remaining grapefruit sections in salad.

This dressing is best used the day it's made. If you must keep it, oil a piece of cellophane or plastic wrap and place it on the surface of the dressing. Refrigerate in a scalded bowl.

Basic "Vinaigrette" Dressing

Yields 1 serving

Salad dressings without vinegar often taste ho-hum. Not so with this pleasantly sharp dressing. And you'll find it quick and easy to make.

Use "Vinaigrette" on any salad that oil and vinegar would enhance. I even put it over boiled new potatoes! (See Potato, page 262.)

By mixing just the amount you want to use, you don't have to worry about using something stored in the refrigerator too long.

Use the following amounts *per person:*

1   tablespoon water
¼   teaspoon unbuffered, corn-free vitamin C crystals, slightly rounded
¼   clove garlic
Pinch of salt
Freshly ground pepper, optional
1   tablespoon olive oil*
Several fresh basil leaves or parsley sprigs
¼   teaspoon dry mustard, optional

Blend all ingredients in a blender for one minute. Pour over cooked or raw vegetables and toss.

Leek "Cream" Sauce

Leeks are the polite cousins of the onion. In this sauce, they ARE the sauce—yet the flavor is mild, the texture is creamy. Close your eyes to taste it and you'd swear you've broken your diet to enjoy "real" dairy cream sauce. Best of all, you control the richness of the sauce.

Leeks vary widely in size. Roughly, here's how I decide how many I need to prepare: One large leek serves two people, but not lavishly. If they are small, I buy one per person (sometimes with an extra one "for the pot"). If they're medium I might buy two leeks to serve three people.

But I also consider the use of the sauce. For example, I allow more sauce when I'm making "creamed" peas and new potatoes than I do if I just want to top fish or meatloaf with a dab of sauce as a garnish.

2-4 leeks
2-4 teaspoons olive oil
2-4 tablespoons water

*If you want to incorporate flax oil in your diet, try this recipe using 2 teaspoons of olive oil and 1 teaspoon of flax oil. When you're accustomed to the taste, use ½ tablespoon of each (1½ teaspoons).

OPTIONAL ADDITIONS:
4-6 leaves of fresh basil
Few sprigs of thyme
Few sprigs of parsley
Dash of salt or pepper

Cut off and discard the dark green part of the leeks. Please read "Leek," page 254, for tips on a thorough cleaning technique. When washed and drained, cut the leeks in ¼-inch slices. Use all of the white portion, possibly going into the *light* green area.

Steam the leeks for 10-12 minutes until quite soft. Scoop the leeks into a blender or food processor. Add 1 teaspoon olive oil and 1 tablespoon of water for each leek, and any seasonings you want to include.

Purée for one full minute (with a blender, stop once to scrape the bottom). Check consistency of the sauce and add a little more water if you want it thinner. Pour over cooked vegetables or fish—use as you would any cream sauce.

Nut-Milk White Sauce

1 Cup

The theory behind this sauce is simple—make Nut Milk, season it to resemble mayonnaise, add a starch to thicken it and bring to a boil. The sauce thickens quickly—about 10 seconds after boiling. It couldn't be simpler.

Two tips will assure a smooth sauce: Always mix any starch with cool liquid. And keep stirring those few minutes before it reaches boiling—preferably with a whisk. If you do those two things, your sauce will turn out smooth as silk.

This basic recipe is delightfully creamy, but may seem a little bland in taste, but it accepts the seasoning of your choice beautifully.

1   cup cool Nut Milk (use any nuts), page 320
1-2 tablespoons of arrowroot, potato, kudzu
     or tapioca starch*

---

* 1 tablespoon of starch makes a thin sauce, while 2 make a thick one. If you're undecided, use 1½ tablespoons.

OPTIONAL ADDITIONS:
Tiny pinch of salt
White pepper, to taste
Few sprigs of parsley, OR a few leaves of fresh basil
OR fresh tarragon, minced

Combine all ingredients in a saucepan. Stir to dissolve the starch. Cook over medium-high heat for a few minutes; reduce heat to medium low. Stir with a whisk almost constantly.

As it approaches the boiling point, the sauce will thicken rather abruptly—and if you're stirring then, it'll thicken smoothly. (Otherwise lumps occur.)

Velvet Sauce

Serves 2–4

One day I thought, "What would happen if I used a starchy food in place of a refined starch, when making a sauce? Might it lend additional flavor—as well as thicken it?"

I experimented with cooked sweet potato. The results tickled our tastebuds with such delight that I seldom make a starch-thickened sauce anymore.

I've learned to buy slightly larger sweet potatoes than I care to eat. As soon as they bake or steam I cut an end off, wrap and freeze it. When I want to make a sauce, I take a piece of sweet potato from the freezer, peel and dice it. No need to wait for it to thaw. It's so easy . . . and so good.

¹/₄ – ¹/₂ cup raw Brazil nuts*
2-inch piece of cooked sweet potato
Pinch of salt
1   cup water, vegetable cooking water or stock
Few sprigs of parsley OR leaves of fresh basil OR tarragon, minced, optional

Grind the nuts into meal in a blender. Scrape the packed nuts

---

*You can substitute other nuts, but almonds, pecans and walnuts all have such distinctive flavors they seem less appropriate for this sauce. Raw cashews, macadamias and pine nuts make good alternatives.

off the floor of the jar and add remaining ingredients. Blend on "high" for a full minute, to liquefy.

Transfer the mixture to a saucepan; cook, stirring, over medium high heat. The sauce thickens as it heats. By the time it boils, it's ready to use! Add fresh herbs just before serving, if desired. (From start to finish, this recipe takes less than 10 minutes.)

❖ SERVING SUGGESTIONS ❖

Scallops in Velvet Sauce—Keep the sauce warm over lowest heat. Poach tiny bay scallops 4–5 minutes and drain them (allow 4–5 ounces per person). Stir into the sauce. Serve over cooked rice, millet, quinoa or split sweet potatoes. Add a green vegetable and you'll have a banquet! What could be easier? Or quicker?

"Creamed" Tuna—Stir canned or fresh, cooked, flaked, tuna into Velvet Sauce. Eat "as is" or serve over anything.

"Creamed" Peas (or other vegetables)—Stir the cooked peas into Velvet Sauce.

Blueberry Sauce

Top your pancakes and waffles with this warm sauce. I make it when I have guests or more family to help eat it.

2   cups fresh or frozen blueberries
1   cup puréed sweet fruit—pears, pineapple, seedless grapes
    OR fresh-pressed apple cider
1   tablespoon starch—arrowroot, tapioca, potato or kudzu
2   tablespoons cool water
¹/₈   teaspoon unbuffered, corn-free vitamin C crystals,
    or to taste

In a saucepan, combine the blueberries with fruit purée of your choice. Simmer 10–15 minutes. Dissolve starch in the cool water. Stir it into the blueberries. Cook over medium-high heat just until the sauce boils again. Boil 1 minute; remove it from the heat. Stir in the vitamin C crystals.

Pour the sauce into a pretty bowl. Put a gravy ladle in the dish so guests may spoon it out easily. Serve warm.

❖ **NOTE:** For a sweeter sauce, simmer 2 cups puréed sweet fruit ❖ until reduced to 1 cup. Add the blueberries and proceed as above.

Real Applesauce

Real Applesauce is so easy to make I can't imagine why anyone wouldn't make his own. When you want the sauce to top pancakes or waffles, start the apples first. Then by the time you get everything else ready, the applesauce is ready, too.

1 apple *per person,* any kind except red delicious

¼ cup apple juice or fresh-pressed cider OR puréed ripe pears *per person* for the first four servings (add 2 tablespoons for each serving beyond that)

Dash of cinnamon, optional

Peel, core and dice the apples into a saucepan. Bring to a boil; reduce heat and simmer 15–30 minutes until the apples soften. Stir in cinnamon if you wish. Serve warm.

Cranberry Sauce

Cranberries aren't for holidays only. When they're in season, make this delightful sauce once a week to accompany a poultry meal. The sauce only takes 15 minutes. It freezes well, too. (See Strawberry-Pineapple Jam, page 318, for freezing suggestions.)

12- to 16-ounce bag of fresh cranberries

1 to 1½ cups fresh pineapple chunks and juice

Wash the cranberries in a colander. Remove any that appear shriveled or decayed. Pull off any stems that you see. Combine cranberries and pineapple in a 3-quart saucepan. Bring to a boil, reduce heat and simmer 15 minutes or until the cranberries have all "popped" and the sauce thickens. Serve warm or chilled.

Fish

During the past five years fish has been "in," while red meat has been "out." Here's why fish has received so many rave notices: Recent research studies show that people who eat fish are less apt to develop heart attacks, strokes, arthritis and other degenerative diseases.

The substances in fish generating the excitement are the Omega 3 fatty acids. They're especially abundant in salmon; they're also found in trout, tuna and mackerel and to a lesser extent in other seafood. Fish also is an excellent source of protein and B vitamins.

But in spite of its superior nutritional ingredients, you have to eat fish with discretion—even with caution, because today's fish are often contaminated with toxic chemicals (see pages 71-73).

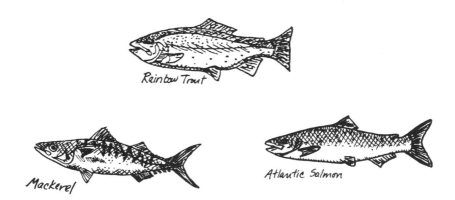

Rainbow Trout

Mackerel

Atlantic Salmon

Fish and Allergies

Thirty-two distinctly different families of fish and ten separate families of shellfish populate the waters of the world. You can, however, react to one kind of fish or seafood and not another.

For example: Most fish agrees with me, except those in the codfish family. Still, I eat a wide variety of fish including sole, flounder, monkfish, bluefish, catfish, turbot, butterfish, albacore tuna, pike, salmon, grouper, sea bass and black bass. With shellfish, the opposite is true. I react to most of them, but tolerate scallops twice a month with no problem. With so many kinds of fish and shellfish to select from, even if you react to one species, you may tolerate others.*

The point is that "fish" is just as general a term as "meat" or "poultry." To react to one kind of fish doesn't necessarily rule out others from different families.

Are you worried about eating fish from contaminated water? Your concerns are justified because mercury, PCBs and other chemicals have been found in alarming levels in some lake fish. Because of these findings, I choose ocean fish over lake fish every time. (Rationale: the bigger the "pond," the more diluted the pollutants.)

The great lakes have been particularly polluted in the past decade, although efforts are underway to correct the problem. An authority on Lake Michigan recently said, in effect, "In microscopic examination of a random sampling of fish, 100% had some form of cancer"! After elaborating on the sites and various organs affected, he added, "My family and I no longer eat Lake Michigan fish."

Should you avoid fish altogether? Hardly. No food is without its problems—meat, fowl, grains, fruits and vegetables, too! You need to be informed to make the best possible choices in selecting your food. After all, you have to eat *something*.

Cold-water ocean fish have earned a respected spot on my recommended list. The reason is they contain Omega-3s, low total-fat content, complete protein and many other valuable nutrients.

---

*If you've ever experienced a severe fish or shellfish reaction such as swelling or asthma, check with your physician before experimenting.

Cooking Methods

Steam, bake, broil, poach or oven-"fry" your fish. In this chapter you'll find recipes with specific directions for all health-promoting methods of cooking fish. Generally, you can expect a 1-inch thick fillet or steak to cook in 10–12 minutes. While not "instant," that's pretty speedy cooking (TV dinners take about 45 minutes to heat!).

How will you know when your fish is done? Most references say, "Fish is cooked properly when it flakes easily." But Julia Child says it's already "past perfection" when that happens. She teaches that fish is perfectly cooked when the appearance changes from translucent to opaque—just *before* it flakes.

On the other hand, noted nutritionist Beatrice Trum Hunter cautions us to avoid eating raw or undercooked fish because of the presence of microorganisms that may cause diseases in humans.

My advice: Err on the side of overcooking fish, at least until you learn to recognize the moment before it flakes. You won't ruin anything. Well-cooked fish is very good indeed. If you learn that moment just before it flakes, and you are certain from its appearance that it's cooked, congratulations! You will enjoy that fish, too.

I can't recommend the tasty breaded, deep-fried fish fillets. Here's why:

1. Super-heated fats break down into unhealthy, disease-producing substances called trans-fatty acids. They are hard to digest and may play a role in degenerative diseases.
2. When you bread fish, you probably use bread crumbs, wheat flour or corn meal, which contain yeast. All may cause symptoms because of yeast or grain allergies. They also encourage growth of yeast in your digestive tract.
3. Breading soaks up an excessive amount of fat, often doubling the calories in a serving.
4. An egg or milk dip is usually used to hold the breading in place. If you're sensitive to either, this method will provoke symptoms.

Steamed Fish

A super-simple method to prepare fish. A fish poacher, with a rack to hold the fish above water, is designed to do the job. But I use a steamer basket all the time. Also works well covered in a microwave.

Steam your fish alone or with vegetables. See The 20-Minute Meal below for an idea, and then make your own combinations.

1   small whole fish
    OR
Fish fillets, as many as your steamer accommodates in a single layer
Vegetables, optional

Start any vegetables that take longer than 10 minutes to steam. (See Vegetable chapter for steaming time.) Add the fish fillets 10 minutes before serving time. Thicker fish steaks may need 12 minutes, and a whole fish requires 15 minutes or more.

Steamed fish accepts a sauce well.

Steamed Fish and Veggies: The 20-Minute Meal

Serves 2

This recipe was born out of desperation on a day that just didn't have enough hours in it. Even with limited time you can cook fresh, whole foods "from scratch" by cutting them into uniform pieces that steam quickly.

4-6 small unpeeled potatoes, scrubbed
1½ to 2 cups zucchini, cut in ½-inch bite-sized slices
10-12 ounce black sea bass (or other) fish fillet, ½ to ¾ inch thick
Sprinkling of minced, fresh basil

Remove sprouted eyes from the potatoes. Leave the potatoes whole if they're not more than 2 inches across. If larger, cut in halves or quarters. Steam them in a 5-quart dutch oven with basket and ¾ inch of water in the bottom, for 10 minutes.

Meanwhile, scrub and slice zucchini. Add zucchini and fillets to steamer basket. Put basil on top. Cover tightly and steam another 10 minutes.

Carefully, using a pancake turner or wide spatula, remove the fish. Arrange the fish and vegetables attractively on two plates.

Poached Fish Fillets or Steaks

If poaching is new to you, don't worry. It's one of the easiest ways to prepare fish. It's quick—most fillets cook in 10 to 12 minutes. And the preparation is fat-free. Cold poached fish is a gormet's delight for fish salads.

Poaching differs from simmering only in the intensity of heat. Simmering keeps the liquid bubbling slower than a rolling boil. When poaching, the water "barely shudders."

Fish fillets or steaks at least ½ inch thick are the best candidates for poaching. If too thin, they are apt to fall apart.

My favorite is salmon tail pieces. True, they taper to ¼-inch thickness at the tip, but the heavy skin holds them intact nicely. Swordfish, halibut and many others work well, too—but expect a white (or light) end-product. If you must have brown, broil your fish instead.

Water to cover (about 1 quart)
1 or 2 fish fillets or steaks, ½ inch thick
OPTIONAL ADDITIONS:
1   bay leaf
2-4 tablespoons chopped onion
Few celery leaves
1   carrot, cut in sticks
Few sprigs parsley, tarragon or thyme
1   sliced lemon
(NO SALT)

In a 10-inch skillet (or poacher), heat water. Add any optional seasonings you choose. (Never salt the water—except for soup or stew—because it draws flavor into the water.)

Rinse the fillets under cold water. When the water boils, reduce the heat to medium and wait for the water to settle into a gentle roll. Add the fillets. (Avoid splashing by lowering each piece on a pancake turner.)

Adjust your heat up or down, as needed to make the water "barely shudder"—and hold it there. If you guessed wrong and the water doesn't cover the fish, do one of two things: Add boiling water until it does, or "baste" it—that is, spoon the boiling liquid continuously over the exposed surface of fish. It's easier to start with enough water.

Note the time the fish goes in the water. The rule is, "Allow 10 minutes per inch thickness." If your fish is thicker or thinner, figure the time accordingly.

When done, gently lift each fillet to a plate. Use a paring knife to separate the fish in the thickest place. If the fish is cooked through in that spot, it's done. If it's not cooked, return to the water another 1 or 2 minutes. If you wish, remove the skin. Serve at once. If you choose a tasty sauce from "ETC." chapter, make it in advance so the fish doesn't wait.

Broiled Fish

If you avoid this method of cooking because of the nasty job of cleaning your broiler pan, treat yourself to one of the new non-stick kind. They come in two sizes—and the smaller one fits most large toaster ovens. Having the right equipment is half the battle.

When broiling, use high heat for a short time. Coat the fish with a thin film of oil to prevent drying. Working on a piece of waxed paper facilitates oiling both sides of the fish—and I don't need to oil the broiler rack.

Fish fillets, steaks or shish kabobs* (fresh or thawed)
Oil, to coat
Boiling water

Adjust the top shelf of your oven so the fish (on top of your broiler pan) is 3–4 inches from the heat. Preheat broiler.

*See Fish Shish Kabobs, page 225.

Oil the fish on all surfaces. Arrange on a broiler rack.

When the broiler is hot (550°), pour ¼ to ½ inch of boiling water in the bottom of the broiler pan. Put the rack of fish on top. Broil 10 minutes per inch of fish thickness.

> ❖ **NOTE:** Do not turn any fish less than ¾ inch thick. From ¾ to ❖
> 1¼ inches, turn once after 6–8 minutes.

Baked Fish

Serves 1

Once you get a feeling for how quickly it cooks, it's easy to plan your meal around baked fish. I bake fish, usually plain, a few times every week. It's quick and easy to prepare, and delicious to eat.

If your fillets are extremely thin, place one on top of the other so they are less likely to dry out. If you wish, put whatever coating you choose between the fillets, sandwich-style.

4-6 ounces fish fillets or steaks ½-inch (or more) thick
Oil fish to coat

Preheat oven to 400°. Arrange the fish on an oiled baking sheet or in a glass pan. To prevent drying, coat the fish lightly with oil, or top it with any sauce.

Bake the fish 10–12 minutes. If fish is more than an inch thick, add a few extra minutes.

Serve "as is," or cradle the fish on a bed of sautéed spinach or shredded, lightly steamed carrots. Or create an interesting presentation with the vegetables already on your menu.

Baked Fresh Tuna

Serves 2–3

The nut butter protects the tuna from drying out—while adding its own delicate, gourmet flavor.

½ cup macadamia nuts, brazil nuts or almonds
Sea salt to taste
1 pound fresh albacore tuna steaks, 1 inch thick

Preheat oven to 450°. Grind the nuts with the salt in a blender. Process until the nuts become butter-like. Add a tablespoon of hot water if the mixture is too stiff.

Pat the tuna dry. Spread the nut butter over the tuna, covering top and sides. Bake for 15 minutes or until the thickest part of the fish is only faintly pink when cut.

Fillets of Sole Almondine

Serves 2–3

I'm still surprised when something so simple tastes so good. Maybe you'll enjoy this dish, too.

1   pound fillets of sole
Almond oil, to coat
½   cup toasted, slivered almonds
Sea salt to taste, optional

Preheat oven to 375°. Rinse the fish and pat dry. Rub lightly with oil and place in lightly oiled baking dish. Top with the almonds. Bake about 12 minutes until the fish flakes easily. Sprinkle with salt to taste, and serve.

Oven-Fried Cashew Fillets

Serves 1–2

Oven-fried fillets are for those who think delicious fish has to be breaded and fried. It doesn't. This recipe's baked ground-nut coating suggests a healthier alternative. And it's quick and easy too.

½   cup cashews, raw or dry roasted
Seasoning to taste (choose basil, dill, tarragon). Salt and
     pepper are optional
2 or 3 whitefish, or other, skinned fillets
½   teaspoon (per fillet) melted butter or oil

Preheat the oven to 500°. Grind the cashews and seasonings in a blender or food processor until they're a fine meal.

Rinse the fillets in cold water and roll them in nut meal. Place fillets on an oiled cookie sheet or one lined with parchment; drizzle with melted butter or oil.

Bake for 10–12 minutes, depending on their thickness. Remove the fillets to a plate carefully with a pancake turner.

Adapted from Sally Rockwell's *Allergy Recipes*

Stir-Fried Shrimp   L

Serves 4

Fillets of fish are just too delicate to stir-fry—but shrimp is perfect. If jumbo shrimp are too expensive, buy extra of the medium size and reduce the cooking time to about 5 or 6 minutes.

Patting raw food dry is an important part of stir-frying. When wet food hits hot oil it sizzles and splashes, causing a safety hazard. Just allow adequate time to prepare the raw food, drain and dry it, and you should have no problem.

16   raw jumbo shrimp
2   tablespoons sesame oil, divided
2   cups snow peas
Sea salt to taste, optional
3   tablespoons sesame seeds
1 1/3 cups brown rice, cooked and hot, optional

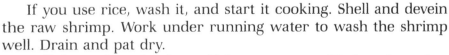

If you use rice, wash it, and start it cooking. Shell and devein the raw shrimp. Work under running water to wash the shrimp well. Drain and pat dry.

Pull the ends and strings off the snow peas. Wash and pat dry.

Heat wok or large, heavy skillet for a few minutes, then pour in 1 tablespoon of the oil. Wait several seconds for it to heat. Add the peas and stir-fry for 3–5 minutes until lightly cooked and bright in color. Remove from the wok; cover to keep warm.

Add the remaining tablespoon of oil and wait several seconds for it to heat. Add the shrimp and stir-fry for about 7 minutes, or until done. Return the peas to the wok, salt lightly if you wish, and add the sesame seeds. Toss lightly and serve "as is," or over the cooked brown rice.

❖ VARIATION ❖

Cut 1 red bell pepper into matchsticks and add it with the snow peas.

Fish Shish-Kabobs   L

Serves 1

Broil kabobs under the broiler of your stove, toaster oven or outside over very hot coals.

    4-6 ounces (per person) swordfish or other firm fish about an
        inch thick
    2-3 per person, of each of the following:
        cherry tomatoes
        green pepper chunks
        small whole onions (or ¼ of a thick slice of large onion)
OPTIONAL MARINADE:
Juice of 1-2 limes
1-2 tablespoons sesame or other oil
1-2 tablespoons wheat-free tamari (soy sauce)

Cut the fish into 1½ inch cubes.

Marinate 30 minutes if you want the extra flavor. If you omit soy, use the lime juice and oil alone.

Alternate fish and vegetables on skewers. They should touch, but don't crowd them even if you use two skewers per person. Roll the loaded skewers on paper towels to dry the fish. Oil all surfaces of the fish. Broil, turning several times, 10–12 minutes or until the fish is done.

Traditionally, shish kabobs are served with rice—but you can enjoy yours with a baked sweet potato or veggies of your choice.

Oven-Fried Pecan Catfish

Serves 4

This unusual flavor may surprise you. Mustard on fish? With pecans? You bet! Just try it and see.

2   tablespoons water
1   teaspoon dry mustard
4   8-ounce farm-raised catfish fillets
1   cup ground pecans

Preheat oven to 500°. Combine the water and mustard in a small bowl. Dip the fillets into the mustard mixture, then into the ground pecans. Shake off the excess.

Place fillets on an oiled cookie sheet or one lined with baking parchment. Bake 10–12 minutes or until they flake easily.

Adapted from *Fishing For Compliments:
Cooking with Catfish*, The Catfish Institute

Fish Skillet

Serves 4

Many classic dishes combine fish with tomatoes and herbs. I've made a chowder similar to this for years—but I added another 2–3 cups of liquid (half water, half tomato juice). If you tolerate multiple foods in combination, I know you'll love this one.

2   tablespoons oil
1   medium onion, chopped
1/2   green pepper, chopped
2   tablespoons chopped fresh parsley
2   medium tomatoes, coarsely chopped
1   teaspoon chopped, fresh basil
Dash of pepper, optional
1/2   cup water, tomato juice or chicken broth
1   pound flounder or sole fillets

Heat oil in a skillet. Add the onion, green pepper and parsley. Cook 3–4 minutes until the vegetables start to soften. Add the tomatoes, seasonings and liquid. Cook a few more minutes until the tomatoes are soft. Add the raw fish fillets. Cover and simmer over moderate heat until the fish flakes easily—about 10 minutes. Serve the fish with a generous topping of the vegetable sauce.

Nutrition Action Healthletter, Center for Science in the Public Interest

Stuffed Whole Fish

Serves 5–6

An impressive presentation to awe your guests—and you won't spend all day fixing it. Allow 30–40 minutes to chop and sauté the vegetables. Stuff the fish and refrigerate to bake later, or pop it in the oven. Now you're free to finish the rest of the meal—or visit with family and friends.

1   whole 3-pound fish—whitefish, trout, salmon, etc.*
Salt and pepper to taste
¹⁄₂   recipe vegetable stuffing (see page 309) or your favorite
     recipe for 3 cups of stuffing

Ask grocer to "butterfly" your fish (or you can remove the back bone, leaving the back, head and tail intact). When opened flat, the fish takes on a butterfly shape.

Preheat oven to 350°. Open the fish and remove any remaining bones. Season with salt and pepper, if desired. Place the open fish on an oiled oven-to-table baking dish—with edges, to catch juices.

Prepare stuffing. Pat it into a mound on one side of the fish, and into the head. Lift the other half of the fish over the stuffing, loosely closing the butterfly. Don't bother to fasten the fish closed with skewers—they aren't necessary.

Bake 45 minutes. After thirty minutes baste the fish with pan juices and cover it loosely with foil (shiny side down). To test for doneness poke the tip of a paring knife into the back, where the

*You can stuff any whole fish. But extremely bony varieties, such as walleyed pike are less desirable choices.

butterfly hinges. If it looks opaque, the fish is done. If translucent, it needs to bake a little longer.

Leave the fish on the platter where it baked and arrange extra, separately cooked vegetables or grain around it. You can use tiny new potatoes, quinoa, or any grain you can eat, cooked whole; or serve a mixture of rice and wild rice to round out your meal nicely. Garnish with lemon or lime wedges.

> ❖ **NOTE:** If you buy a smaller—or larger—fish, adapt the amount ❖
> of stuffing and baking time accordingly.

Vegetables

Vegetables are loaded with the good complex carbohydrates. Eating vegetables helps normalize your blood pressure, prevents heart disease, cancer and diabetes. Some of the earlier diets to control candida restricted all carbohydrates. However, most physicians now agree that eating less fat and protein and more complex carbohydrates helps a person overcome a candida-related illness.

However, you may still need to restrict the *high-sugar fruit* carbohydrates. Be sure to read Dr. Crook's discussion of this need to minimize fruits and maximize vegetables.

What's the best way to eat vegetables? Some say raw, others say lightly steamed or stir-fried. Since people with candida-related illness are often bothered by digestive problems, you have to answer that question for yourself.

How will you know what's best for you? If you eat a huge salad for lunch one day and notice undigested raw vegetables in your stool in the next day or two, your system isn't utilizing those foods in the raw form. And you're not getting those badly needed nutrients that you're eating.

Cooking Vegetables

Steam or stir-fry your vegetables only until tender-crisp. This reduces the loss of vitamins and other nutrients. However, when you cook vegetables in soup, you can cook them longer without losing many nutrients. Here's why: Although the nutrients leach out into the broth, they're not lost. You'll get most of them when you drink the soup.

For white potatoes, sweet potatoes, eggplant and many kinds of hard-shell squash, baking is an easy choice. In every case, puncture the vegetable with a fork a few times to permit steam to escape.

Yellow Light of Caution

A few vegetables need a word of caution. Corn is a grain, and many allergists rank it the number one "bad guy." *It also contains lots of readily available starches and natural sugars.* So even if you aren't allergic to corn, avoid it while you're fighting candida.

The legumes (peas and beans) may also spell trouble for many folks. They contain lots of protein and fiber. They also rank high on the recommended list of health-promoting foods—unless they don't agree with you. However, as a group they are one of the top 10 food allergens. Because they have so much going for them, legumes are included in this book, but are coded with an "L" to alert those who must avoid them.

Foods in the nightshade family disagree with many people. This family includes tomatoes, peppers of all kinds, white potato and eggplant. While symptoms vary, nightshades are reputed to trigger joint pains. Many arthritics swear that they experience less pain when they omit all of the nightshades.

Since mushrooms belong to the fungus family, people with yeast-connected health problems were once advised to avoid them because candida is a yeast-fungal organism, too. But reports from physicians and their patients show that about 50% of people with candida-related illnesses can eat yeast- and fungus-containing foods without developing symptoms. The other 50% show an allergic response.

Individual Responses

If you react to green beans, does this mean you need to avoid the whole legume family? Perhaps. Some physicians maintain that you must *avoid the whole family of any food that causes symptoms,* while others say, "Let's see what you tolerate."

For example, I get a "legume headache" only from green beans and alfalfa sprouts. I seem to tolerate dried peas and beans okay, and I haven't noticed symptoms when I occasionally use carob and guar gum. However, I *carefully* rotate all legumes. Having reacted to two of them, I try not to stretch my luck.

Similarly, an arthritic may discover that tomatoes make him uncomfortable, while he can tolerate other nightshades. Yet if a tomato-sensitive person eats a lot of potatoes, peppers or eggplant, his symptoms may flare.

You are unique. Listen to your body and learn to interpret its cues. The late Roger Williams, Ph.D., University of Texas, long ago developed the concept of *biochemical individuality.* Nowhere is it truer, or proved more often, than in the field of allergy.

All You Need to Know . . .

You may not be accustomed to selecting and preparing a wide variety of vegetables confidently. This chapter is designed to alleviate your anxiety about dealing with new—and old—vegetables. Since you'll probably use each vegetable by itself, I'm discussing them individually.

Artichoke, Globe

Composite Family

Selection: Look for tight petals; avoid loose, drooping ones. The touch of brown you commonly find on the tips is okay. It's probably caused by frost.

Preparation: Their irregular shape makes artichokes difficult to wash. So plunge them into water deep enough to cover completely. "Swish" vigorously, then invert to drain.

Steam: Put the artichokes on a rack in a deep pan—a stock pot or Dutch oven. Cover tightly in ½ to ¾ inches of water and steam 15 minutes for medium sizes or 20 minutes for large ones.

Serving: Here are two schools of thought about serving artichokes:

1. Julia Child says, "Cut away the top ⅔ and discard it. Then pull the remaining petals off, and discard them." This exposes the solid "meat" of the vegetable. Use a spoon to remove the hairy "choke." What remains is a shallow, cup-like disc that's tender and tasty. It's typically 2½ inches wide and 1½ inches thick, with a shallow hollow on top.

   You'll need one artichoke for each person when you stuff it with crab meat (or something), for a fancy luncheon. Or use it as a base for dinner salads. Or you can serve four to six people with one or two artichokes if you cut them up and marinate them in any salad dressing. Use them alone or tossed with other vegetables. (Perhaps because it's hard to find the edible portion, artichokes enjoy a rather inflated reputation as "gourmet" fare.)

2. Steam whole artichokes, as described above. Remove and discard tiny petals around the stalk. Pull the mature petals off one at a time. Hold the outer tip and dip the fatter, meaty end in any dressing or dip.

Instead of taking a bite, pull the meaty end through your teeth, getting a morsel of delicious artichoke "meat" (that is wasted in the method above). When you get to the middle, discard the flimsy petals. Use a spoon to remove the hairy "choke." Now . . . eat the artichoke cup that remains.

I do this occasionally when I want something different for lunch—and when I have plenty of time. Typically, I dip the petals in "C" Salad Dressing and have a small piece of fish with it, for my meal. It takes a while to consume a whole artichoke this way. For such a low-calorie food, it is surprisingly satisfying.

Artichoke, Jerusalem

Sunflower Family (not related to globe artichoke)

Many people avoid Jerusalem artichokes because they aren't sure what to do with them. They're irregularly shaped, bumpy little roots about the size of a golf ball. They are crunchy crisp with a pleasant, mild taste. Their biggest drawback is their appearance.

Selection: Choose firm roots. Avoid soft, withered specimens. Refrigerate until you use them.

Preparation: Scrub Jerusalem artichokes carefully, with a brush, because of their irregular shapes. Enjoy them raw or lightly cooked.

Raw: Dice or slice in salads. Or munch them like you'd eat radishes. Dip in a dressing, if you wish.

Cooked: Pat the washed and drained artichokes dry. Cut in thin slices and toss in a stir-fry for the last 2–3 minutes. Or stir-fry them alone, like fried potatoes.

Asparagus

Lily Family

Asparagus is at its best in the early spring. Some varieties are pencil-thin, others are fatter than the base of your thumb. Surprisingly, both are harvested at the same time and neither is "old and tough." Both varieties taste the same—although both have their fans who claim one or the other is "best." Buy the kind that looks freshest.

Selection: Look for tight, green and crisp tip ends. Avoid limp or shriveled asparagus stalks.

Preparation: Wash asparagus thoroughly. It grows in sandy soil, and nothing spoils a pleasant meal faster than biting into something that's gritty with sand.

Cut or break the bottom portion of the stalk to determine how much to discard. Try to snap it about one inch from the end with your hands. If it won't snap, move your fingers up a little and try again until the tough end snaps off. Then break or cut the ends of the other stalks at the same level. Occasionally, you may find *trimmed* asparagus, but that's unusual—and always more expensive. You'll find even more usable stems if you peel the lower portion.

Raw: Some tender asparagus tips can be eaten raw, but I usually cook them lightly.

Steam: Arrange whole stalks in a steamer basket in a Dutch oven. If the stalks are too long, cut two inches off the growing end and steam those ends for 2 minutes. Then add the remaining stalks. Steam for 10–12 minutes more. If you don't eat those ends, freeze them for Easy Asparagus Soup, page 178.

Equipment: You'll find a unique piece of cookware in specialty shops called an "asparagus cooker," a tall, narrow pot designed to cook asparagus in an upright position. It contains an inner basket for easy loading and unloading. Using only an inch of water, the thick bottoms can boil while the more tender upper stalks steam.

The special pot does a fine job, but it's strictly optional. I favor multipurpose equipment that fits many different foods. I especially like collapsible steamer baskets and use them for asparagus and most other vegetables.

Beans, Dried

[L]

Pinto, Kidney, Navy, Lima, Garbanzo, etc.—Legume Family

These are the nutritional "giants" that you've probably read about. They contain complex carbohydrates that candida folks need. They are also high in fiber, low in fat and very filling. Because many people hesitate to fix dried beans, I'm giving you explicit directions.

Selection: I recommend the organically grown dried beans, split peas and lentils that you'll find in health food stores.

Preparation: Pick over dry beans and discard any that look shriveled or moldy. Be on the alert for tiny stones about the size of the beans. Fill a large pan halfway with water and swish the beans vigorously with your hand to wash them. Drain and repeat until the rinse water stays clear. Discard any beans that float.

Cover the beans with fresh water two inches above the level of the beans. *Do not add salt at this point.* Cover loosely and set the pan aside for several hours (or overnight). Before cooking, *discard the soak water.* Rinse completely under running water; drain completely and cover again with fresh water. Simmer the beans until soft (see chart that follows).

This step is optional: If you experience trouble digesting beans, follow the steps above. Boil for 10 minutes, then pour into a colander to drain them *again.* Rinse, drain, cover with fresh water and resume cooking. Although some flavor and nutrients are lost, this extra step makes the beans more digestible. It virtually eliminates the problem of intestinal gas. Don't discard water after you start to cook lentils and split peas.

Cooking: Simmer the beans over low heat until tender—or even until quite soft, if you wish. Cooking time varies with the variety of beans, their maturity and moisture content. Here are approximate guidelines to help you time your meals:

	Pre-soak?	Simmering Time	Pressure Cooker
Soybeans	yes	3 hours	16–18 minutes
Garbanzo beans (chickpeas)	yes	2½ hours	18–20 minutes
Lentils	no		
Split Peas	no	45 minutes	not
Baby limas	optional		recommended
Pintos	optional		
Kidney	yes	1½ hours	10 minutes
Mung	yes		
White northern, large limas and most others	yes	1 hour, about	8–10 minutes

When the beans are tender, add salt. Add ½ teaspoon salt per pound of beans, or more to taste. Now you're ready to eat the beans or combine them with other foods—in soups, casseroles, spreads, etc.

> ❖ **Tip:** With the same time and energy you spend preparing one ❖ cup of dry beans you can easily fix one or two pounds, so you'll have several containers to freeze.
>
> **Bean magic:** To thicken the liquid of a bean dish into delicious gravy, mash a few beans with a potato masher to release the starch. Stir well and watch it thicken!

Beans, Green and Wax   Ⓛ

Legume Family

Selection: Choose fresh-looking beans. They should snap when bent in half. If they bend easily without snapping, find something else to buy.

Preparation: Remove the ends of the beans and snap them into convenient bite-sized pieces. Wash well. Steam them about 10 minutes. If you prefer to leave them whole, allow 12–15 minutes. Salt lightly after cooking, if you wish.

Though I prefer beans steamed, I learned that I can lessen my "legume reaction" by boiling the beans in water until they are tender. (I do this infrequently, perhaps half a dozen times a year.) Apparently, the portion that bothers *me* is water soluble. Try it if they give you a problem.

Green Beans Almondine: A simple, yet somehow fancy dish. While the beans cook, brown 1½ tablespoons of chopped or sliced almonds per person in a little almond oil. Take care that they don't burn. When the beans are tender, put them in a serving bowl. Stir in browned almonds, or sprinkle them on top to decorate your dish.

Check the Ingredients and Techniques chapter in Section 3 for details on freezing and blanching.

Beets; Beet Greens

Goosefoot Family

Selection: Look for beets with fresh-looking tops. Choose a bunch with beets about the same size—all small, medium or large—so they'll finish cooking at the same time.

Preparation, Beets: Twist the leaves off about two inches above the beets. Lay them aside. Leave a few inches of root on each beet, too. To wash beets, scrub with a brush. Pay particular attention to the grooves around the stem ends where soil may be imbedded. Don't slice or dice beets before cooking them, because any cut causes them to "bleed" their juices.

Steam, Beets: Put ¾ inch of water in a Dutch oven or similar big pot. Add beets in a steamer basket, cover tightly and steam. Cooking time varies with the size of the beets—30–50 minutes. (Huge beets might even need an hour, but I usually avoid purchasing them that big.)

Preparation, Beet Greens: While the beets are cooking, wash the "greens" (leaves) in large pan of water. Remove any parts that are damaged or decayed. Break a few inches off of the stems so they'll fit in your Dutch oven. Swish the leaves vigorously, then drain in a colander.

Steam, Beet Greens: When the beets are tender, remove them to a plate and place the greens in the same pot. Cover and steam the greens for 10 minutes. Use that 10 minutes to slip the beet skins off and slice or dice them.

Tangy Beets: If you like tangy food, such as Harvard Beets, try squeezing a little lime juice over both the beets and the greens. And you might like a dash of oil in place of butter, too.

> ❖ **NOTE:** Beet greens are a gold mine of vitamin A. Isn't it a ❖ shame that most people discard them?

Boniato

White Sweet Potato

Look in the specialty section of the produce department for these new tubers. Think of them as dry, light-colored sweet potatoes.

Although boniatos are related to our familiar yellow and orange sweet potatoes, they aren't *closely* related. So they're perfect to alternate with each other, a day apart, if you rotate your foods.

Selection: Select firm, dry specimens. Boniatos store poorly, so buy only what you plan to use within two days. Store them at room temperature, never in a refrigerator.

Preparation: Scrub and drain. Pierce the skin with a fork.

Bake: Place boniatos in a pie tin or on a cookie sheet. Bake about an hour, at 400°.

Boil: Cook peeled chunks in water for 45 minutes. This is one of the few vegetables not receptive to steaming. It discolors unless dropped promptly into boiling water.

Breadfruit

Artocarpus altilis

A starchy, bland Caribbean fruit that's used as a vegetable. Dry like bread, breadfruit is definitely an acquired taste. Natives use it in all stages of ripeness, from green, to half-ripe, to ripe. The texture of the breadfruit progresses as it ripens, from firm like raw potato to creamy like ripe avocado.

If you're allergic to grains, you may wish to experiment with breadfruit as an exotic alternative bread—if you can find it. Our markets don't carry breadfruit regularly—I've never had an adequate supply for recipe development.

Preparation: Scrub breadfruit and roast in the peel for 1 hour, at 375°. Slice, remove peel and serve as a bread-like side dish. Or cover the slice with your favorite sauce and return it to the oven while it absorbs the liquid, 10–15 minutes.

Broccoli

Crucifer (Mustard) Family

Selection: Look for dark green florets and firm, crisp stalks. If a stalk bends easily, or if the florets are yellowing, wait for a better selection.

Preparation: Wash broccoli in pan of water or hold it under running water. Pull the florets apart slightly as you wash the stalks. Drain.

Trim and discard half an inch from the bottom of each stalk. Cut more if they seem tough or peel the outer skin of the lower stalk. Cut the broccoli to suit your purpose.

Stir-fry: Cut into bite-sized pieces. Cut the tough skin off of the long stalks. Cut the tender center strip in ¼-inch slices. Add both the florets and stem slices to your stir-fry about 6–8 minutes before serving time. See Stir-Fry, in Section 3.

Steam: Stalks may be whole or halved. Thicker stalks need more time to cook.

Raw: Cut the broccoli as directed for the stir-fry. Munch it alone or add to a platter of raw vegetables.

Blanch: Necessary for freezing and often suggested before using raw. Submerge the broccoli stalks or pieces in boiling water or steam for 3 minutes. Immediately plunge into ice water to stop cooking.

Brussels Sprouts

Crucifer (Mustard) Family

Selection: Look for dark green or bright green, tight-headed specimens. Yellow leaves and a dark brown scar where the sprout was cut indicate that it was picked past prime.

Age is important in this vegetable because the flavor goes downhill soon after harvest. Brussels sprouts can go from sweet and tender when fresh, to downright bitter when they're old. They're not usually eaten raw.

Preparation: Swish the sprouts in cool water. Pull off one or two of the loose outer leaves to expose the tight sprout. Trim the cut end, but leave the sprout whole. Cut an "X" in the bottom of large ones so they will cook at the same rate.

Steam: Brussels sprouts for 8–12 minutes, depending on their size. Enjoy them "as is" or salt lightly. If you used to sprinkle vinegar over your sprouts, try lemon or lime juice, or Make-Believe Vinegar, page 325.

Cabbage; Nappa Cabbage; Chinese Cabbage

Crucifer (Mustard) Family

Selection: Look for fresh, healthy-looking, green cabbage. A few outer leaves may be loose and open, but inside you should feel a firm, heavy "head." Nappa and Chinese cabbages are elongated, almost stalk-like. Their coloring is paler green, with white ribs. Their flavors are clearly cabbage—but more delicate than head cabbage.

Storage and Preparation: Cabbage keeps well, especially if it's fresh when purchased. Wrap it, unwashed, in foil, cellophane or plastic and store it in your refrigerator. It'll stay fresh another ten days. To serve the cabbage, pull a few outer leaves off and discard—they're probably tough. Wash well and drain upside down.

Raw: The most common use for raw cabbage is coleslaw. Food processors make slaw quick and easy to prepare. Use the slicing blade or, for a finer texture, use the chopping blade. See "Slaw de Jour," page 195.

You can nibble raw cabbage by itself, just as you might eat carrot sticks for a snack. The cabbage takes a lot of chewing, and this helps you feel satisfied.

Steam: Cut in large cubes or slices. Steam 8–12 minutes, depending on the size and the maturity of the cabbage. Taste a bite raw to see if it's sweet to your tongue. Sweet usually means young and tender; check in 8 minutes.

Stir-fry: Dice cabbage into 1½-inch cubes. Or slice Chinese or nappa cabbage. Allow about 8 minutes, 10 if it's mature. See "Stir-Fry" in Section 3.

Carrots; Parsnips

Parsley Family

Selection: Like many root vegetables, carrots and parsnips store well. They may even have been stored quite a while before you buy them. The only way to assure freshness is to choose those with fresh-looking tops, instead of those packaged in plastic bags.

Try to bend a carrot or parsnip. If it bends easily, it's old and dehydrated. If firm, it's apt to be fresh.

Preparation: Cut off the tops. Scrub parsnips with a brush. Scrape carrots with a paring knife or vegetable peeler to remove the thin skin and dirt. If a carrot has a split side (where mold may dwell), cut it out carefully, under running water.

Raw Carrots: (Parsnips aren't eaten raw.) Raw carrot sticks are classic. So is "Sunshine Salad"—a mound of shredded carrots with a mayonnaise dressing. Forget raisins, though. If you want a hint of sweetness add halved fresh grapes or shredded apple or diced pear.

Raw carrots make great carrot juice, but go easy. Three or four carrots may go into a single glass of juice. That's a lot of simple carbohydrates, with no fiber to slow the absorption. You can compare naturally sweet carrot juice to fruit juices—so you may need to avoid it until you're nearly well.

Steam Carrots: Cut in ¼-inch slices and steam them about 10 minutes. Older or thicker cut carrots may take 1 or 2 minutes more.

Steam Parsnips: Steam scrubbed, whole parsnips about 25–30 minutes, until tender. Slit the skin down one side and remove it. Cut each parsnip in half lengthwise and remove the woody center core. To serve, purée like mashed potatoes or slice and stir-fry.

Stir-fry: Cut raw carrots or lightly steamed parsnips in ¼-inch slices or match sticks. Carrots take 7–10 minutes to cook tender-crisp, so add them early. Steamed parsnips need only 3–4 minutes. See "Stir-Fry" in Section 3.

Simmer in Soups, Stews and Casseroles: Carrots improve most combination dishes. You can add them early for soft (maybe mushy) texture. Or, for firmer body, add them 20 minutes before serving.

Less common, parsnips contribute their pleasant sweetness to mixed dishes, too. Scrape to clean, cut lengthwise to remove the core, then slice. Cook until soft, 40–60 minutes.

Cauliflower

Crucifer (Mustard) Family

Selection: Look for heavy, white heads of cauliflower. You may find occasional brown spots to trim, but the head should be firm.

Preparation: Pull the outer cup-like growth off to expose the cauliflower. Submerge whole head in water and swish it vigorously to clean. Drain.

Raw: Though many people eat it raw, candida folks should blanch their cauliflower to kill surface microorganisms. The florets should stay crisp.

Cut the florets into bite-sized pieces with a sharp knife. Munch alone or add to a vegetable platter. Chop raw cauliflower for salads, too. See Cauliflower Salad, page 199.

Steam: Cut florets, as above. Steam about 10 minutes. If you own a large stock pot, you can steam the whole vegetable. Use a steamer basket to keep the cauliflower out of the water. This makes a dramatic presentation.

If you miss cheese sauce, try this: Sauté a whole red pepper, chopped, in olive or other oil. Use medium-low heat so the pepper softens instead of browning. Just before serving, purée the pepper mixture into a beautiful red sauce. Add salt or pepper to taste. Pour over cauliflower.

Stir-fry: Halve or quarter the large florets so all pieces are about the same bite size. Cook them 7–10 minutes. See "Stir-Fry" in Section 3.

Celery

Parsley Family

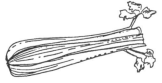

Selection: Look for fresh green foliage and a solid stalk. Avoid celery that feels spongy, exhibits yellowing leaves or has many splits in the ribs.

Preparation: Remove only as many stalks as you want to use. Scrub them vigorously with a vegetable brush. Wrap the rest and store it in the vegetable drawer of your refrigerator. Fresh celery, properly stored, lasts 2–3 weeks.

Raw: Cut into celery sticks. For a popular snack, spread any nut or seed butter in the hollow of the sticks. Use thinly sliced cut celery for salads or soups. Include the chopped leaves in soups and stews.

Steam: Cut cleaned and drained celery into slices from ¼ to 1 inch wide. Steam in a basket for 5–7 minutes.

Stir-fry: Clean, pat dry and slice as above. Cook ¼-inch slices about 5 minutes—they should still crunch. See "Stir-Fry" in Section 3.

Celery Root (Celeriac)

Parsley Family

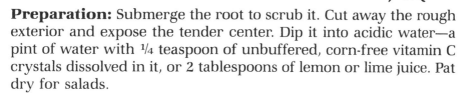

This kind of celery is cultivated for its root rather than for its stalks and leaves.

Selection: Look for a gnarled, stringy-looking root about the size of your fist. Despite the ugly facade, celery root is delicious.

Preparation: Submerge the root to scrub it. Cut away the rough exterior and expose the tender center. Dip it into acidic water—a pint of water with ¼ teaspoon of unbuffered, corn-free vitamin C crystals dissolved in it, or 2 tablespoons of lemon or lime juice. Pat dry for salads.

Raw: Shred or cut julienne strips for salads.

Cooked: Dice, shred or purée for soups and stews. Add it directly to the broth, or sauté the celery root in oil until it softens, purée, then add to soup or stew broth. Either way, celery root changes from firm to mushy rather quickly. If you prefer the firm texture, add it for only the last 10 minutes of cooking.

Chard, Swiss

Goosefoot Family

Selection: Choose bunches with crisp stalks and firm, bright leaves. It's fairly perishable, so only buy chard you plan to use within a few days. Some varieties have white stalks; others are red. Both taste the same—delicious. Chard is related to spinach and beets. If you like them, you'll love chard.

Preparation: To wash, swish vigorously in a sink full of water. Drain. Trim any bad spots from the leaves and stalks.

Raw: You can add a little chopped chard to a mixed-green salad, but don't overdo it. The chard quickly dominates. It's better cooked.

Sauté: Cut the leaves and stalks in half-inch strips and cook separately. Sauté the stalks 10–15 minutes, add the leaves and sauté briefly in 2 tablespoons of olive oil—perhaps another 5–10 minutes. Mediterranean cuisine would add a clove of garlic and a handful of pine nuts to the oil first, but that's optional. Toss a handful of chopped leaves into any stir-fry for the last 7 minutes or in soup or stew for the last 10–12 minutes.

Steam: In a Dutch oven or other large pot arrange *stalks* cut in half-inch strips in a steamer basket. Steam about 3 minutes. If necessary, bend, cut or tear the chard leaves to fit in your pot. Add them and steam another 2 minutes.

Boil: Add chopped or torn chard to soups or stews for the last 15 minutes.

Surprise Bundles: Use your favorite recipe for a grain or meat stuffing/filling. Slice the chard stalks, sauté as above, and add to the filling. Steam the whole leaves for 1–2 minutes. Rinse in cool water to halt cooking. Pat dry. Wrap a scoop of the stuffing in each leaf. Swiss chard leaves are quicker, and easier to handle—and more delicious—than filling smaller grape leaves.

Arrange the bundles in a baking dish, pour your favorite tomato or lemon sauce over them and bake 25–30 minutes in a moderate oven. The size of the portion determines whether Surprise Bundles constitute an appetizer or the main course.

Chayote

Gourd Family

Chayote is a distant cousin of pumpkin and zucchini—same family, but not close. Light to apple green in color, chayote is about the size and shape of a pear.

Selection: Chayote may be smooth or deeply ridged. It should feel firm and heavy, with no soft spots.

Depending on how well you like it, allow one vegetable for every one or two people. Buy extra, if you wish, because you can store chayote, lightly wrapped, in your refrigerator for three or four weeks.

Preparation: Peel under running water with rubber gloves. The raw "ooze" can irritate skin—so it's never eaten raw.

Sauté: Cut into chunks and sauté in oil. Use moderate to low heat to cook without browning, and stir often. The flavor is delicate, if not bland—somewhere between cucumber and zucchini. Eat chayote plain or season it as hot or spicy as you wish.

Steam: Prepare in chunks, as above, and steam for 25–30 minutes. If you'd rather not peel and cut it, steam the whole chayote, washed, for 40–45 minutes. The skin lifts away easily before serving. Add salt, pepper, butter or oil, or any seasoning you like.

Boil/Bake: Add diced chayote to soups, stews and casseroles.

> ❖ **NOTE:** The large seed, or pit, is also edible when cooked. The ❖ flavor is a cross between lima bean and almond. Steam the seed, or slice and sauté it.

Chicory; Endive; Escarole

Composite Family

Chicory, endive, and escarole belong to the large Composite Family. If you confuse them, you aren't alone—supermarkets often do, too. Don't worry about their botanical differences—market labels use the terms loosely, even interchangeably. Endive may say "Belgian endive," and chicory may say "curly chicory."

Before you decide to buy these vegetables, remember they're related to ragweed. So if you're bothered by late summer and early fall hayfever, eat them cautiously.

Selection: Choose crisp, tender heads. Slightly wilted produce often revives if you wrap and chill it after washing. If the outer edges show traces of yellow, however, don't buy. A pale yellow color at the heart is normal.

Preparation: Wash chicory, endive or escarole in a sink full of tepid water. Swish them vigorously to dislodge the sand. Turn them over to drain, or dry in a salad spinner.

Raw: These crisp greens have a slightly bitter flavor. They go best in multigreen salads. Use them for less than half of the greens or you'll face a disappointingly bitter salad. Think of them as seasonings, and use with a light touch.

Sauté, Bake, Steam: You can cook any of these greens just as you'd prepare spinach. Sauté in olive oil or steam briefly.

Casserole: Cover the bottom of a casserole with carefully washed greens. Season with salt and pepper if you wish. Dribble a tablespoon of oil over the top and add a few tablespoons of stock or water. Cover tightly; bake for 15–20 minutes at 350° until the greens are tender.

Corn

Grain (Cereal Grass) Family

Selection: If you tolerate corn, look for a source close to home so you'll know it's fresh. Many supermarkets advertise locally grown corn in season. To select, pull the silky ends apart to peek at the kernels of corn. They should look firm, rounded and full of juice. Dents in the kernels signal old corn. When you're satisfied that it's fresh, select the best full, well-shaped ears.

For best results, buy the corn the day you want to cook it. If you must store it, leave the husk in place, wrap and refrigerate it.

Preparation: Remove and discard the husk and silk. Leave the ears long or break them in half.

Steam: Put a steamer basket in your biggest stock pot and layer the ears of corn. The second layer should be at right angles to the first, so the ears will cook evenly. Steam 7–10 minutes and serve at once. They may toughen if you try to hold them.

Boil: Drop in a large pot of boiling water. Cook uncovered for 7–10 minutes. Remove the ears with tongs.

Daikon

Crucifer (Mustard) Family

Sometimes called an "oriental radish," the white daikon may be a foot long! It's carrot-shaped, with the tang of radish.

Selection: Choose one that's firm and free of blemishes. If you need a smaller size, ask your produce man to cut a large daikon into pieces.

Daikon becomes flabby in a matter of days, so purchase it only when you plan to use it within two days.

Preparation: Scrub with a stiff brush, drain and pat dry. Slice, dice, sliver or grate it.

Raw: Adds crunch to salads, relishes and vegetable trays. Use a slice as a "cracker" to scoop up a dip.

A small mound of grated daikon, spiked with lemon or lime juice, is an excellent garnish for many Japanese fish entrées.

Use the chopping blade of a food processor to chop a whole root for "slaw." See Slaw de Jour, page 195.

Stir-fry: Add slices, strips or cubes to any stir-fry during the last 2–3 minutes of cooking. The crisp texture takes the place of bamboo shoots and water chestnuts. See "Stir-Fry" in Section 3.

Soup and Stew: Toss small pieces into the pot for the last 10 minutes of simmering. Or cook briefly with potatoes or other root vegetables and purée for a delicious light soup.

❖ **TIP:** A little grated daikon adds moisture, flavor and texture to ❖ meatloaf or meatballs.

Dandelion

Composite Family

I don't need to describe dandelions, because they grow and thrive so many places. But have you thought of them as food? Gourmets discovered and popularized them in the past few years. They love the slightly bitter tang of dandelion greens. Fall hayfever sufferers may "pass" on this delicacy, however, because dandelions are kin to ragweed.

You'll find bundles of dandelion greens in the gourmet section of many produce departments. The flavor of commercial greens is usually less bitter than those from your yard. But the wild ones are nutritional equals. Use them alone in salads in April and May when they are quite palatable—tender and only mildly bitter. Later in the summer the bitterness intensifies in the mature foliage—so mix them with milder greens or cook them.

> ❖ **NOTE:** Avoid leaves with toxic spray residues. Forage only in ❖
> grassy areas that you know are never sprayed!

Selection: If you want to harvest your own, look for dandelions that stand straight and tall. Select healthy-looking greens, preferably small and immature. Avoid leaves that show tinges of yellow.

Preparation: Wash the greens well in a sink full of water. Drain. Pat dry for salads.

Raw: Use alone or in mixed green salads. Dandelions' pleasant bitterness is enhanced by assertive companions such as heated dressings that wilt the greens, creamy garlic dressing, walnuts and walnut oil, goat's cheese, olive oil, and beets.

Sauté: Toss tender, young greens in hot oil for 7–10 minutes—with or without garlic. For tougher greens, add 2 tablespoons of water and cover to steam another 3–5 minutes.

Soups, Sauces and Casseroles: Drop the greens into boiling water, boil until tender, drain, refresh in cool water and drain again. Now chop them and use as you would blanched spinach—in soups, sauces and casseroles.

Eggplant

Nightshade Family

Eggplants are usually dark purple and pear-shaped. Their sizes may vary from miniature to over a pound. You can bake, steam, or sauté them. People in Turkey, Greece and India cut eggplants into 1-inch cubes, parboil or steam briefly, then thread them onto skewers, alternating them with cubes of marinated lamb to broil over a fire.

If you're looking for a vegetable base for dips and spreads, puréed cooked eggplants may fill the bill.

Selection: Choose firm, heavy eggplants with uniformly dark coloring. Avoid them if they feel soft or look shriveled.

Preparation: Wash eggplants well. Many recipes suggest that you bake or steam the eggplants whole with the skin intact. Others direct you to remove the skin and slice or dice them to sauté or use in casseroles.

Bake: Put on a baking sheet or wrap loosely in foil and bake in a moderate oven for half an hour.

Steam: Place whole eggplant in steamer basket over ½ inch of water in a Dutch oven. Cover tightly and steam 12–18 minutes depending on size. Test often after 10 minutes so you don't overcook it. The shell appears to collapse if cooked too long.

Eggplant Dip or Spread: Bake or steam whole eggplant. Spoon the soft pulp into a bowl. Mash the pulp to make a dip or spread, or purée the pulp in a food processor. Make the texture either smooth or chunky. Season it to taste with salt, black or cayenne pepper, olive oil and herbs. Serves several as an appetizer or two for a light lunch. See the Breads chapter for flatbreads and crackers to accompany the dip.

A Mediterranean Touch: French, Italian and Greek cooks add to the above recipe two or more of the following optional ingredients:

2   garlic cloves
onions, chopped (generous)
mushrooms, sliced
tomatoes, coarsely chopped
finely minced basil, or oregano, or fresh parsley
salt, pepper and cayenne pepper, to taste

Sauté the vegetables in olive oil until soft. Add them to the mashed pulp.

For a dramatic presentation, handle the shells of the eggplant carefully when removing the pulp. Leave a ¼-inch shell intact. After mixing and seasoning the pulp, pile the dip back into the eggplant shells in high mounds.

Fennel

Parsley Family

Sometimes inaccurately called anise or sweet anise, fennel's faint licorice flavor is legend. Anise and fennel are similar—they're cousins in the great parsley family. But fennel is the subtle one to remember—and use.

Selection: Look for a firm head about the size of your fist with feathery foliage.

Preparation: Scrub with a brush under running water. Quarter the bulb, cut out the tough base and hard core parts. Slice thinly.

Raw: Cut slices into strips and add to salads. Dress with oil and lemon or lime juice or unbuffered, corn-free vitamin C crystals dissolved in a few tablespoons of water.

Sauté: Toss slices in oil over moderate heat for 10–12 minutes. Salt lightly. Optional enhancers include fresh-grated black pepper or a squeeze of lemon or lime juice. Add sliced fennel to any stir-fry.

Bake: Arrange the slices in a flat casserole, drizzle with a little olive oil, salt lightly and add 2 tablespoons of water. Cover tightly and bake in a moderate oven for 40 minutes. Remove the cover and bake another 20–30 minutes, until most of the liquid evaporates.

Soups and Stews: Sliced or diced fennel enhances most soups and stews. Its delicate flavor works magic in fish chowders.

Garlic

Lily Family

Eating substantial amounts of garlic helps curb candida in the digestive tract. Many physicians feel it's more effective in combating candida infection than the medication nystatin. (Go back and review what Dr. Crook says about garlic—see Index.)

But garlic doesn't help everyone—possibly because some folks react to it. For them, dosing up with garlic makes them feel worse, because they're aggravating their allergies. By experimenting, you can determine into which group you fall.

Garlic bulbs consist of several segments or cloves. Though tiny, they pack a powerful punch with their pungent flavor. Use them with discretion. If garlic irritates your skin, wear gloves to handle it.

Selection: Select solid bulbs. Examine them closely for mold before you pick one.

Preparation: Remove the hard membrane that covers each clove of garlic. Professional chefs do this by flattening the clove with the flat side of a chef's knife, causing the outer membrane to pop open.

Because of the intensity of its flavor, garlic is usually finely minced or forced through a garlic press. If you cook much, the garlic press is a handy tool for your kitchen. It makes quick work of garlic—especially when you're using several cloves.

Raw: Gourmets cut a clove of garlic in half and rub the inside of the salad bowl with the cut surface of garlic. Then they toss mixed greens with dressing in the bowl. Others prefer to incorporate garlic into salad dressing. Either way, the strategy is to avoid biting into the chunk of garlic.

Cooking: Recipes almost always direct us to sauté garlic. Often it's cooked with onions. But onions take 10–12 minutes to soften, and garlic needs only 2–3 minutes. Longer sautéing seems to embitter the garlic's flavor.

To avoid bitterness, let onions cook 7 to 9 minutes before adding the pressed garlic. After 3 minutes of cooking, add liquid to the sauté—for soups, stews, chili or spaghetti sauce. Long cooking in liquid after the brief sauté doesn't seem to cause any bitterness.

Jicama

Morning Glory Family

This strange-looking treasure first appeared in U.S. markets a few years ago. Jicama (HEE-ka-ma) looks like a huge turnip—except the tough outer skin is tan. The pure white center is crisp, sweet and mild. For me, it was love at first bite. Now when I serve a spread or dip with crackers and veggies, I use slices of jicama for my "cracker."

Selection: Look for a firm body. Check carefully for cuts or bruises that harbor mold. At home, store jicama in the vegetable drawer of your refrigerator. If you only use half, wrap the rest tightly. Before using again, slice that exposed surface off thinly and discard. Molds thrive on the cut surface.

Preparation: Peel the tough skin to expose the "meat" of the vegetable. A potato peeler will do, but it peels so thinly you may need to peel twice. I cut jicama in half, lay the cut side down on a board and slice the skin away, a method that is quicker but probably more wasteful. Rinse the white center and pat dry.

Raw: Slice, dice or shred—jicama's great just as it comes. Add it to vegetable trays or salads.

If you must "do something," sprinkle slices with lemon or lime juice, or make Jicama Slaw, see page 195.

Stir-fry: Cut jicama into matchsticks, cubes or slices—about the size you're cutting other veggies. Add them to the wok 4 minutes before serving. The idea is to toss them enough to warm them through, but they should still remain crisp.

Kale

Crucifer (Mustard) Family

Kale, a curly cabbage, contains 7,540 IU of vitamin A in one hearty serving—plus substantial amounts of calcium, iron and vitamin C. You'll recognize kale as the cabbage-clan member that doesn't form a head. The leaves are so curly they're all just a jumble.

Selection: Look for dark bluish-green color and crisp texture.

Preparation: Separate the leaves and plunge them into a sink full of tepid water. Drain. Strip the foliage from the tough center rib.

Steam: Use a Dutch oven or large stock pot to steam kale. Pile the leaves into a steamer basket, cover tightly and steam 5–8 minutes. If you wish to dress up your kale, salt it lightly, add butter or oil, or squeeze a bit of lemon or lime juice over it.

Kohlrabi

Crucifer (Mustard) Family

Small globes that may or may not be surrounded by foliage when you buy them in a supermarket. If present, you can steam the leaves like spinach and eat them, too. But primarily, kohlrabi is grown for its swollen, bulb-like stem.

Selection: For best flavor, select young, tender globes not over three inches in diameter. They should feel heavy and solid. The flavor may remind you of mild turnip.

Preparation: Pick the foliage off and scrub each kohlrabi well. Peel the tough outer skins off.

Raw: The solid centers can be julienned or diced for salads. But you don't need to "do something" with kohlrabi at all. They're fun to eat out of hand.

Steamed: Scrub small, unpeeled, tender globes. Steam them whole for 15–20 minutes. Briefly rinse in cool water; peel. Slice or quarter each globe, and serve.

If the globes are old or large, peel and cut them into ¼ inch slices or ¼ inch matchsticks. Steam 8–12 minutes.

Kohlrabi Salad: Marinate cooked matchsticks of kohlrabi in your favorite salad dressing. Flavor improves if you allow a few hours for it to chill and develop flavor. Serve alone or over torn greens of any kind.

Leek

Lily Family

Leeks are the aristocrats of the onion clan. While they possess similar flavors, the leek is more delicate. It looks like a huge, oversized scallion. The white body may be one to two inches wide. The green leaves are heavy and usually trimmed before the leeks appear in markets. But the root system is usually intact.

Selection: Choose fresh-looking, white-bodied leeks. Thin or fat, choose the size that meets your need. The tops, which contain most of the vitamins, are wonderful in soups. If you prefer to use only the white parts, buy about twice as much as you think you'll need.

Preparation: There's definitely a "knack" to cleaning leeks. The problem: sand and dirt hide between the many layers. Here's my game plan: Cut the leek in half lengthwise. Hold each half under a stream of running water. Gently separate the layers and let the water run through them. Do each side carefully.

You may need a small brush to scrub stubborn dirt stains from the outer layers. I suggest a new child's toothbrush for this purpose. If the outer layers feel flabby, discard them. When you're satisfied that the leeks are clean, turn the cut side down to drain.

Sauté: Cut the white portion in ¼-inch slices. Sauté them in olive (or other) oil for 10–15 minutes until they're soft, but not brown. Cook them with other vegetables or enjoy alone—they're that mild and pleasant.

Simmer: Add sliced leeks to soups, stews, or stock; simmer gently. They'll be done in 15–20 minutes, but longer is okay, too.

> ❖ **TIP:** Leeks are often puréed to make richly flavored broth or ❖
> sauce. See Leek "Cream Sauce," page 210.

Lettuce

Iceberg, Bibb, Romaine, Butter, Curly Leaf, Red Curly, etc.— Composite Family

Hayfever alert . . . All lettuces belong to the same family as ragweed! If you suffer with August-through-September hayfever and salads don't agree with you, try eliminating lettuce for a week to see if your symptoms improve. See the Salads chapter for ideas beyond the lettuce leaf.

Nutritionally, iceberg lettuce has little to offer. *Each* of the others has more nutrients. Here's a "rule" that usually holds true— The deeper the color of leafy produce the more nutrients it contains.

Selection: You'll easily spot freshness—or signs of aging—in these vegetables. Brown edges and limp leaves betray geriatric lettuce.

Preparation: Pull the lettuce leaves apart. Swish vigorously in a sink of deep water. Gently lift a handful at a time into a colander to drain. If you want to make a salad soon, pat the leaves dry with cotton towels, or dry them in a salad spinner.

To store unused lettuce, lay the leaves out on a dry cotton towel and roll them together. Slip the towel-roll into a plastic bag and refrigerate.

Raw: Despite what you see in restaurants, the best salads boast greens torn to bite size. Tearing is better than chopping or shredding lettuce. It prevents the edges from turning brown.

Mushrooms   Y

All Varieties—Fungi Family

Initially, doctors suggested that all candida folks avoid mushrooms. Yeast and fungi hail from the same family, so this seemed reasonable. But, Dr. Crook's questionnaire to several physicians indicated that *only half of their diagnosed candida patients reacted to mushrooms and other yeast- and mold-containing foods.* So if you aren't yeast sensitive, you can eat mushrooms, but don't overdo them.

Selection: When buying mushrooms, I select from a basket of loose mushrooms. For one thing, you can buy as little as you need for one meal. But most important, I think tightly wrapped packages compromise the quality of the mushrooms—and they may be a haven for mold and bacteria.

If you look carefully, you'll see a few drops of condensed moisture inside those packaged mushrooms. A damp environment, with no fresh, circulating air, spells trouble.

Use mushrooms as soon as possible after purchase. Store them briefly in the refrigerator in a brown paper bag.

Preparation: *Don't submerge or soak!* Brush gently with a small brush that doesn't tear the mushrooms, or wipe with a damp paper towel. If you're using them for a soup or stew, buy the large size instead of the tiny "buttons"—cleaning a few big mushrooms beats fussing with 25 little ones. Clean them only when ready to use.

Raw: Slice or chop. Add to salads and vegetable trays.

Sauté: Heat oil or butter before adding the mushrooms. Sauté about 10–12 minutes; stir once or twice as they cook. Mushrooms give up their juices and "cook down" or shrink. Keep this in mind when you buy.

Soups, Stews and Casseroles: You often sauté the mushrooms first, and then proceed with your recipe. You can add sliced mushrooms directly to a bubbling pot, without prebrowning, but most cooks agree the flavor is better the other way.

Okra

Mallow Family

Okra is an important ingredient in Creole cookery—it's the "gumbo" of many Louisiana regional dishes. Strangely, it's the seed pods of the plant that we eat as a vegetable. The pods range from 2 to 4 inches long and their diameter matches the size of your little finger. Cut crosswise, okra slices resemble little stars.

Selection: Choose clean, fresh-looking okra. Avoid pods that are dull and dry (too mature), or shriveled and withered (too long since harvest—starting to dehydrate). Because they're hollow, take care not to crush your fragile purchase on the way home from the store.

Preparation: Wash okra carefully, and drain well. Roll them gently on a cotton towel to dry. Cut off the stems and tips if not boiling. To cook, cut into ½-inch, round slices. (Okra is never eaten raw.)

Sauté: Heat 1–2 tablespoons of oil, add the okra and cook until tender. Stir and turn them often. In about 20 minutes, when lightly brown, check to see if they are tender. If not, add 2–4 tablespoons of water, cover and steam an additional 10 minutes.

Some people prefer to parboil the washed and trimmed pods for 3–8 minutes, drain well, then slice and sauté.

Boil: In a covered pan, boil whole okra about 10–15 minutes, or until tender. Cutting slices and tips will cause loss of inner juices which become "slimey" during cooking. Drain and serve. Salt and pepper to taste.

Soups, Stews and Casseroles: By far, the most common use for okra is in soups, stews and casseroles—but you often start those dishes by sautéing the okra alone or with other vegetables. Companion vegetables are usually onions, garlic and tomatoes. Others may include bell peppers, parsley, eggplant, bay leaf—and lots of pepper.

❖ **NOTE:** Avoid using copper, brass, iron or tin-lined cookware to ❖ cook okra. Those metals discolor it. While this isn't supposed to be harmful, esthetically, black vegetables aren't appetizing.

Onion, Scallion

Lily Family

Onions come in a wide range of sizes, from tiny pearls to the huge Spanish—with many varieties in between. Flavors range from hot to mildly sweet.

Selection: Look for solid specimens. Check them carefully for traces of mold between the layers of skin. Mold may appear as subtle gray blotches. Since onions can harbor mold, you should probably limit your purchase to the amount you'll use within the week. In choosing scallions, select those with the freshest green tops.

Preparation: Cut off the root ends of onions. In the large Spanish variety, use a paring knife to remove a cone-shaped core. Peel a layer or two of the thin skin away to expose the clean, solid onion.

Raw: Slice or dice Spanish or red onions to toss in salads or to top a burger. Scallions, the daintiest members of the clan, are often eaten out of hand. The medium-sized red onions are favored for salads—though there are no hard and fast rules on the many ways you can select, eat and enjoy raw onions.

Sauté: Use any onions you like—they all sauté beautifully, including sliced scallions with tops. Olive oil is the preferred, classic choice for sautéing onions, but folks who rotate their foods will find that any vegetable oil will do.

Sauté onions until they are soft, not brown, about 10–12 minutes over moderate heat. Reduce the heat if necessary to prevent browning. Stir them often.

If you can't hover over your onions, here's an alternate plan: Sauté and stir them for 2–3 minutes, add 2 tablespoons of water, cover tightly and steam until soft.

Bake: Wrap medium-sized onions individually in foil. Bake at 350° for 45 minutes or until tender.

Soups, Stews and Casseroles: Many, or even most, combination dishes call for onions and/or garlic in their recipes. These vegetables not only add their own taste, they also seem to enhance the other flavors present. The problem isn't how to use onions and garlic—the bigger problem is how to cook delicious dishes when we must omit them!

> ❖ **ROTATING TIP:** Two days after eating onions and garlic you ❖
> can use leeks or shallots. Though related, they are different
> enough that most people tolerate them at this interval. By rotat-
> ing, you can enjoy an onion-like flavor two days out of four.

Peas ☐L☐

Legume Family

Fresh Peas

Selection: Peas in the pod should look fresh and bright. They lose their sweetness as they mature—even more rapidly after they're picked. Because they enjoy such a brief season, you may decide to use frozen peas. Study labels carefully and select the package that contains nothing but peas—avoid sugar, wheat flour, corn starch or milk sauces.

Preparation: To shell, pull the tip off of each pod. Pull down the side to remove the string. Pull the pod apart and slide your thumb down the inside. The peas pop out easily. Rinse.

Steam: Pour the shelled peas into a steamer basket. Steam until tender, about 6–8 minutes.

Soups and Stews: Add fresh, raw peas 20–30 minutes before serving.

Casseroles: Add cooked peas or fresh peas, blanched for 3 minutes, or use frozen peas right from the bag, they're already blanched.

> ❖ **NOTE:** A pound of peas in the pod yields from 1 to 1⅛ cups. ❖

Dried Peas

You'll find dried peas easy to use. They only require water and time. If time is a problem, consider quickly combining the ingredients in a crock pot—at your convenience—to enjoy later.

Selection: Organically grown dried peas are available in most health food stores. True, the organic peas probably cost more than those in supermarkets, but I recommend them to help reduce the load of toxins your body has to handle.

Preparation: See "Split Pea Soup," page 187. For more information and cooking time, refer to the chart under "Beans, Dried" in this chapter.

Pepper, Bell

Green, Red, Yellow, Orange, White and Purple— Nightshade Family

Where will it stop? Agronomists develop a new color every few years, so it's no longer accurate just to say "green peppers." The color range gives you a chance to design the look you prefer in a dish. (I don't find the purple—which is almost black—as appealing as the others.) When you're on a limited diet, it's a great time to spend a little effort to create appetizing, attractive food.

Selection: Choose firm, bright-colored peppers. Buy only what you can use at one meal. A portion saved in the refrigerator tends to become contaminated with mold.

Preparation: Wash peppers under running water. Use a brush, if necessary. Drain or pat dry.

Raw: Slice, dice or cut into julienne strips. Add to any salad. Arrange on a vegetable platter.

Stir-fry: Dice. Add to any stir-fry for last 3–4 minutes of cooking.

Baked Stuffed Peppers: Leave the peppers whole. Remove the stem and core. Blanch peppers by dropping them into boiling water for 5 minutes. Remove and drain. Stuff any filling into opening. Or, even easier, cut the peppers in half lengthwise, blanch, drain and stuff with high mounds of filling.

Either way, arrange the stuffed peppers in a baking dish. Add a few tablespoons of water around the peppers, unless you're adding tomato sauce. Bake uncovered in a moderate oven 25–30 minutes, or longer if your filling requires it.

Ideas for stuffings include any meat loaf mixture, rice pilaf or other meat or grain combinations.

Soups, Stews and Casseroles: You can add diced peppers directly to these combination dishes. You may wish to sauté the peppers in a little olive oil, first.

Peppers, Hot

Jalapeño, Anaheim, Banana, Serrano, etc.—Nightshade Family

Caution: These peppers range from mildly hot to incredibly fiery! Even in minute amounts. Moreover, they contain a substance that burns skin. Your safest bet is to protect your hands with gloves. And never rub your eyes after handling these peppers!

With all of those cautions, why would anyone ever use hot peppers? The answer is simple. People love vivid taste experiences—even when the food brings tears to their eyes, clears clogged sinuses within seconds, and causes them to perspire profusely. You use hot peppers for seasoning—not to fill up on.

If you react to black pepper but want to put a little "zing" in your food, one of these peppers can fill the bill. See Garbanzo Potato Soup, page 188. I used *half* of a 2-inch Anaheim pepper to season about 2 quarts of soup. It suited our taste very well.

Selection: Look for firm, shiny peppers. Avoid any that are bruised or show signs of decay.

Preparation: Mince a bit of pepper—to your taste—and *put the minced pepper through a garlic press*. Pressing disperses the fire throughout the dish, so you won't bite into a chunk. The tiny green specks visible in the soup compare in size to black pepper.

Potato, White

Nightshade Family

Selection: Idaho bakers, red boiling potatoes or the new golden varieties—whatever your pleasure—select solid specimens. Avoid the bag with one or more broken potatoes, because mold sets up housekeeping on exposed raw surfaces.

Preparation: Scrub potatoes thoroughly with a brush. Use a paring knife to remove bad spots and sprouts. Peel or not.

Bake: Use the big baking variety. Puncture each potato twice with a fork to release steam, or one might explode in your oven! Lay them right on the oven rack and bake for an hour at 400°.

If you prefer a softer skin, here are two choices: 1) Oil each potato and bake them on a cookie sheet. 2) Bake as above, unoiled; remove from the oven and place them in a dry saucepan covered tightly for 10–20 minutes. The cold pan causes moisture to condense and soften the potato skins.

Steam: Most appropriate for small "new" red potatoes. Larger red potatoes require more time, or you can halve or quarter them. Steam small potatoes 15–20 minutes, and larger ones 25–30 minutes.

Boil and Mash: An American tradition. Even though mashed potatoes usually contain butter and milk, you can improvise. Boil peeled, diced potatoes in about half an inch of water. Add a little salt if you wish. Cook 20–25 minutes—most of the potatoes will steam-cook. When they are tender, remove from the heat, *but do not drain*. Add a splash of any oil and mash them as you would using milk and butter. You'll be glad you tried it!

Radish

Red Globe and White Icicle—Crucifer (Mustard) Family

Many varieties, from mild to hot. If you raise your own, stagger several small plantings, perhaps at weekly intervals, to assure a steady supply.

Selection: Choose firm globes or icicles. Bunches of radishes with fresh-looking foliage probably make a better buy than those stuffed in plastic bags.

Preparation: Scrub . . . scrub . . . scrub. Use a brush to do a good job. Drain. Trim the root and stem ends.

Raw: Eat out of hand. For more ideas see Tuna Salad, page 197, and Slaw de Jour, page 195.

Shallot

Lily Family

Shallots are the mild-mannered members of the onion family. Used alone, you might think that the food you're tasting contained modest amounts of both onion and garlic.

If you rotate your foods, shallots offer an onion-like seasoning you can use two days after eating onion and garlic.

Selection: Beware of moldy or soft specimens. Shallots may not "turn over" as quickly as other vegetables in the supermarket. Choose firm ones.

Preparation: Peel off thin, parchment-like coat. Chop or mince them.

Raw: You can mince shallots for a salad—though most shallot recipes call for cooking them lightly first.

Cooked: Sauté shallots 8–10 minutes, but take care not to brown or burn them. Add to soups, stews and casseroles in place of onions.

Snow Peas

Legume Family

Snow peas, or "pea pods," are flat, with a stem on one end, but usually no string along the side seam.

Selection: Because the whole pod is edible, select fresh, crisp snow peas. Avoid limp ones. Frozen ones are available, yet fresh ones are much better.

Preparation: Remove the stem ends. Swish in a sink full of water. Drain. Pat the snow peas dry on cotton towels so they don't spatter the hot oil when you cook them.

Stir-fry: Snow peas are at home in Oriental stir-fries. They're compatible with most other vegetables and add flavor, crunch and beautiful color. Cook them just until their green color intensifies—3–5 minutes. A minute too long means a dull, almost gray appearance. See "Stir-Fry."

Squash, Summer

Zucchini, Yellow Squash, Pattypan—Gourd Family

Delicately flavored, versatile, and inexpensive—no wonder these vegetables are so popular! Interestingly, in my work as a dietary consultant, I found few people who reacted to squash (I can't think of one!). I rank it second only to sweet potatoes in usefulness for allergy menus.

Selection: Look for small- to medium-sized specimens. They should feel smooth and firm.

Preparation: Scrub gently with a brush under running water. Set aside to drain. Do not peel zucchini if it's young and tender. Yellow summer squash is never peeled.

Raw: Add sliced or diced zucchini to salads, or cut into sticks for a vegetable tray.

Steam: Because of their delicate flavor, summer squashes respond best to steaming. Slice or dice zucchini and yellow summer squash. Steam them for 5–10 minutes. Steam pattypan squash whole for 15–18 minutes. Slice to serve.

Stir-fry: Pat any of the summer squashes dry. Slice or dice. Add to a stir-fry for the last 5 minutes.

Soups and Stews: You can add any of the summer squashes to a soup or stew during the last 10–15 minutes.

Steamed zucchini turns creamy when puréed. This trait makes it an ideal ingredient to use when you want a creamy, yet milk-free soup. See Creamy Spinach/Chicken Soup and Zucchini Soup, pages 189–190.

Squash, Winter

Butternut, Hubbard, Acorn, Buttercup, Crookneck, Kabocha, Spaghetti Squash, Sweet Dumpling, Golden Nugget, Delicata
—Gourd Family

The gourd family is really a "clan." Just when you think you're acquainted with all of the winter squashes, you'll discover another. You can do so much with them! I find they're almost universally well tolerated.

Selection: Look for firm specimens without blemishes. Pick the size and shape that appeals to you—they're all good.

Preparation: Scrub the shell with a brush. Drain or pat dry.

Steam: Cut large winter squashes in chunks. Some people peel them, but that's difficult to do and not necessary. Put the chunks of squash in a steamer basket and steam them until tender (probably 10–12 minutes). Serve the chunks just as they are, or drizzle a little oil over the surface. Let each diner eat his squash right out of its shell.

Steam small squashes whole, in a deep stockpot. Puncture them in several places and steam for 18–22 minutes. When tender, cut the stem end out and cut into two or three servings.

Bake: Puncture the hollow area several times with a long cooking fork. Bake whole, on a cookie sheet for 45–75 minutes, depending on size.

Huge squash may be cut into pieces. Arrange them in a 13x9-inch baking dish with a little water in the bottom. Bake at 350° for 45 minutes. Large squash may also be cut in half and placed shell side up, and cooked the same way.

Stuffed Squash: You can easily stuff any squash that's large enough. Prepare your favorite filling—cooked grain stuffings, such as buckwheat, quinoa or rice pilaf with bits of cooked meat or veggies, nuts, seeds or fruits. Bake whole squash as usual, slice off the top, clean out the seeds and strings, stuff and bake again for 30 minutes.

In this dish you're using the squash for your casserole. Note that everything is previously cooked for the stuffing. The half-hour baking time just heats the dish through. This makes a dramatic presentation! Practice on your family, then try it for company.

Sweet Potato

Morning Glory Family

Forget about the candied kind, and discover the delicious flavor of plain sweet potatoes. If you're searching for an almost universally hypoallergenic food, sweet potatoes come close to filling the bill.

Selection: Choose solid potatoes with no soft spots. The skin should be firm and tight. If they start to dehydrate, the skin shrivels. When you want to cook several potatoes together select all about the same size.

Preparation: Scrub the potatoes with a brush. Cut out any bad parts or deep folds or eyes.

Bake: Sweet potatoes leak juice when they bake, so put them on a cookie sheet or pie pan. Bake at 350° for an hour or 400° for 45 minutes. Slit and eat right out of their skins.

Steam: Arrange scrubbed whole unpeeled potatoes in a steamer basket. Steam them for about 25–30 minutes, depending on thickness. Or slice raw, unpeeled potatoes ¾ inch thick and arrange in the steamer basket and steam 15 minutes. Diners remove the skins as they eat.

Moist cooking encourages moist end results. If you avoid butter and eat your potatoes plain, the steamed potato comes out tastier and more moist than the baked potato every time.

Holiday Sweet Potatoes: Bake 8–10 sweet potatoes on a baking sheet. While they bake, cut and dice a fresh pineapple. Put all of the pineapple in a non-aluminum saucepan. Scrape the shells to extract all of the sweet juice. Simmer the pineapple 20 minutes.

When the potatoes are soft, slit the skins and scoop the meat into a large bowl. Add the pineapple. Use electric beaters and mash the mixture—just as you'd mash white potatoes. If you wish, add 1–2 tablespoons of walnut oil.

Pile the whipped mixture into an oiled 7x11-inch or 9x13-inch baking dish. Arrange pecan halves in an attractive pattern on top. Bake 20 minutes in a moderate oven. Alternative plan: Prepare dish in advance. Cover and refrigerate until 40 minutes before serving; then uncover and bake in a moderate oven.

❖ **NOTE:** Use this dish for special occasions—serve it to guests or ❖ carry it to holiday potlucks—it travels well.

Tomato

Nightshade Family

Tomatoes enjoy a unique status among vegetables—they're an important component of spaghetti sauce, lasagna, pizza, chili, all kinds of casseroles and countless other combination recipes. The magic of all those dishes is the tomato sauce.

Selection: You'll find no better tomatoes than those fresh from a nearby farmer's field, unless it's from your own organic garden! Vine-ripened tomatoes are vastly superior to hard, dry, often tasteless supermarket fare. Those shipped from distant states have to be picked underripe to ship well. Tomato handlers have learned how to obtain the red color to tempt us, but they haven't mastered natural flavor yet.

Sometimes in winter the best-tasting specimens are little cherry tomatoes. Though targeted for salads, I quarter them for open-faced sandwiches on a variety of Flatbreads, page 158.

Preparation: Wash well. Slice or dice, as you prefer.

Raw: Slice, chop or stuff tomatoes for salads. Or garnish sandwiches. To prevent a watery tossed salad, Julia Child recommends that you seed and juice the tomatoes before chopping their "meat."

Sauce: See Tomato Dressing, page 206. Consider making and canning enough tomato sauce for the year when tomatoes are in peak season.

Soups, Stews and Combination Dishes: Tomatoes seem to improve anything with a saucy consistency. Basil and other herbs combine with tomatoes to create different taste sensations. See Elizabeth's Tomato Soup, page 180, and Catfish Gumbo, page 185.

Turnip, Rutabaga

Crucifer (Mustard) Family

These old-fashioned root vegetables seem to have slipped from popularity, yet both are delicious and nutritious. Turnips are small globular roots with white flesh.

Rutabagas, sometimes called "yellow turnips," are larger roots with yellow flesh. They're usually heavily treated with white wax to keep the air away from the vegetable. The wax is non-toxic, so not objectionable. You discard the wax when you peel the rutabaga.

Selection: Choose firm, heavy turnips. Small, young turnips are almost always sweeter and more tender than large, mature ones. If the tops are intact, it's easy to distinguish between old and fresh turnips.

Like many root vegetables, turnips store well without their tops. Although I prefer them fresh, properly stored small- to medium-sized turnips are quite acceptable. One medium rutabaga serves 3 to 4 people.

Preparation: Peel both vegetables with a potato peeler, and dice them. The following cooking times assume you cut your vegetables in ½-inch dice.

Steam: Steam young, diced turnips about 6–10 minutes. Or steam small ones, about the size of a golf ball, whole and unpeeled for 20–25 minutes. The skins slip off easily after cooking. Slice or dice and serve.

Steam diced, young rutabagas, which are apt to taste mild, for 15–25 minutes.

Boil: Cook large, diced mature turnips, and most rutabagas, in water to cover. This seems to tame their stronger flavors better than steaming. Drain and serve.

Mashed Turnips and Rutabaga: Use your mixer to mash either turnips or rutabaga—the same technique as for making mashed potatoes. Instead of draining all of the cooking liquid, pour off, but reserve, all but ½ inch of the water. Add a splash of oil and whip until smooth and light. Add small amounts of the reserved liquid if you need it to obtain the consistency you want.

Yam

Yam Family

True yams are rarely if ever, found in North American markets. The vegetables that Americans buy labeled "yams" are usually the darker varieties of sweet potato.

Yams have higher moisture and sugar content than sweet potatoes, making them highly perishable. They're African tubers that grow and are used locally like our sweet potatoes. However, they belong to a different food family.

Main Dishes: Meat, Poultry and Vegetarian

Meats

Don't expect to find 101 ways to fix beef in this chapter. Perhaps in the past, you felt you were giving your family a variety of foods when you served hamburgers one day, beef stew another day, pot roast of beef another, steaks for a special treat, and on and on. You aren't alone. Before I learned about food families and the importance of rotating foods, I did just that.

Now the word "variety" has new meaning. We know we must avoid eating *anything* repetitiously. Consequently, you'll find little beef in this chapter. Another reason beef isn't my first choice: It's related to milk, one of the "big three" food allergens, along with wheat and corn. Not surprisingly, beef is a relatively common allergen, too. (Anyway, beef recipes abound elsewhere.)

Interestingly, even though beef and lamb belong to the bovine family, many milk/beef sensitive people eat lamb with no problem. Many allergists consider lamb "hypoallergenic" (less likely to cause allergic reactions), so you may want to eat it occasionally.

Pork belongs to an altogether different food family (swine) and agrees with many people who must avoid beef. Yet, some people dislike pork for religious reasons; others avoid it because it may be contaminated with parasites.

Nevertheless, pork possesses certain good qualities. For one thing, it's an excellent source of B vitamins and proteins. Pigs are also bred leaner than they used to be, and I've found that eating pork tenderloin, or well-trimmed chops occasionally, helps me vary my diet.

Avoid smoked pork products, sausages, ham and bacon. They contain excessive amounts of the wrong kind of fat—plus nitrates and unknown quantities of mystery additives.

If you react to all supermarket meats, you may be sensitive to the meats, the chemicals or other additives in the meats, or to the plastic they're wrapped in. In solving your problem you have two options—both expensive:

1. Buy samples of organic meat and test yourself with them. Sometimes it's the antibiotics, hormones or other additives in supermarket meats that cause symptoms.
2. Order exotic meats by mail from the resources listed in Section 3. They are shipped in dry ice. Hippos, lions, beavers, giraffes and other wild animals contain more muscle and less fat than domestic livestock. Experiment with them in stews that require slow, moist cooking. See Lean-Meat Stew, page 283, and Slow-Cooked Pork Pot, page 282.

Poultry

"Here a chick, there a chick, everywhere a chick, chick . . . . Old MacDonald had a chick . . ." What's the most common and over-used poultry on American tables? No contest. Chicken. Turkey runs a strong second, increasing as year-round availability makes it feasible to eat it any day of the year. But when is the last time you ate duck? Cornish game hen? Goose? Quail? Pheasant? If you search, you can find birds other than chicken. And you may enjoy the change!

If you live near a poultry shop or farm, you may be able to purchase organic birds fed unsprayed grains and raised without chemicals and hormones. Many health food stores carry a few selections, usually frozen, or they can order them for you.

Please . . . cook poultry properly. Here's why: Most commercially produced chickens are contaminated with salmonella and other bacteria. Fortunately, those organisms are destroyed by cooking. You can also reduce the degree of bacterial contamination by refrigerating poultry and rinsing it before cooking. Chill or freeze leftovers immediately to keep the chicken safe to eat again.

Avoid leaving poultry in a hot car after purchase. If you run numerous errands when you shop, take an iced picnic cooler in the car. (Use the extra space in it for meat, fish or frozen foods.) Thaw frozen poultry slowly in your refrigerator or quickly in your microwave oven, rather than gradually at room temperature.

Vegetarian Main Dishes

In 1977 the Select Committee on Nutrition and Human Needs of the U.S. Senate published new *Dietary Guidelines*. They say, in effect, "Reduce your intake of red meat, and eat more fish, poultry and complex carbohydrates—especially vegetables and whole grains." Since the guidelines came out, many health-oriented people started to eat less meat, using it as a condiment and flavoring, rather than the main attraction at every meal.

Numerous studies show that vegetarians enjoy exceptionally good health, usually better than the general population. They experience fewer heart attacks, strokes, less hypertension 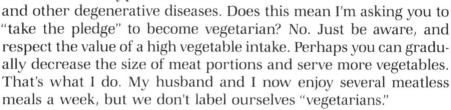 and other degenerative diseases. Does this mean I'm asking you to "take the pledge" to become vegetarian? No. Just be aware, and respect the value of a high vegetable intake. Perhaps you can gradually decrease the size of meat portions and serve more vegetables. That's what I do. My husband and I now enjoy several meatless meals a week, but we don't label ourselves "vegetarians."

Labels aside—go ahead. Try a few meatless meals. And don't worry about "vegetarianism." I'm sharing our favorite Three-Bean Stew with you. It's tasty, satisfying—and so simple. When I start with cooked beans, it only takes 30 minutes to get a meal ready.

Where will you find the best fresh vegetables? You have to shop around. Start by looking for a good natural foods co-op that carries organic grains and vegetables. While they cost more than a supermarket, co-ops try to hold down the cost of quality produce.

If you grow your own vegetables, learn about organic gardening. Through reading and studying, you can find out how to re-build your soil as you re-build your health. And you can enjoy your harvest all year long by freezing and canning your excess produce.

Since my husband and I learned that we should eat more vegetables and less meat and other high-protein foods, we changed the way we order in restaurants. Rather than each ordering a huge portion of chicken or fish, we devised this game plan: We go to our favorite Chinese restaurant (where we trust them when they say "No MSG") and divide two entrées. We order one entrée with chicken or duck (perhaps cashew chicken) and one entrée of Buddha's Delight or some other all-vegetable dish. We divide both orders, and effectively reduce by half the amount of animal protein—and double our intake of vegetables in that meal. For more on the health implications of too much protein, read Dr. Crook's discussion in the first part of this book.

Why "Organic"?

Why do I urge you to buy expensive "organic" vegetables—and to eat more of them? When you're rebuilding your health and that of your family, you need to use the purest foods you can find. And scientific studies published in *Pesticides Monitoring Journal* 2, show that meat, fish and poultry contain 40 times more pesticides than root vegetables, 35 times more pesticides than cereal grains and 5 to 10 times more pesticides than legumes, fruits and leafy vegetables. So why burden your body with the antibiotics, hormones and pesticides found in typical supermarket food?

Consider your battered immune system, reeling from yeast overgrowth, trying to cope with the constant influx of problem substances it can't metabolize. In a second scenario, visualize your compromised immune system receiving only pure food for nourishment, enhancing its ability to heal your body.

Which scenario is most conducive to your recovery?

I rest my case.

Mix 'N Match Stir-Fry

Stir-fry, I discovered, takes longer to explain than to do! It's an ancient Oriental method of quick cooking. If it's new to you, take it step-by-step. If you want to experiment but don't own a wok, try a small stir-fry, for 1–3 people, in you largest skillet.

When you recognize the merits of stir-frying, treat yourself to a tempered steel, not stainless, wok. Follow directions for its care. A wok is the ideal pot in which to stir-fry. Bowl shaped, the food slides to the bottom, where it meets the heat. And the wok cooks a lot of food with a minimum of oil.

Versatility is the name of the stir-fry game. My "recipes" tend to consist of what I find in my refrigerator. They aren't the same twice. You can stir-fry with or without meat. Cook all-vegetable combinations or add slivers of chicken, turkey or any poultry, beef, lamb or pork. Vegetarians who tolerate soy can work with cubed tofu in the same way. You may include a wide variety of vegetables or use just one or two, as in a meat-broccoli combination, accented with scallions or red peppers.

As the name implies, stirring is essential to the success of stir-frying. Keep turning the food over with two wooden spoons. The motion is similar to tossing a salad—you hold a utensil in each hand, scoop under the food until the spoons meet, and flip. Even though the heat is intense, the food won't burn if you keep it moving. The quick cooking retains most nutrients, too.

To plan your time, allow 10–12 minutes to cook—but 45–50 minutes to thoroughly wash, drain, pat dry and dice the vegetables. And if you want to marinate meat or poultry, sliver it first to marinate while you prepare the vegetables.

Here's how I organize the meal: If I'm making rice or baked sweet potatoes, I start them first. To give the stir-fry my undivided attention for the several minutes of cooking, I do all washing, drying, cutting and chopping in advance. The vegetables must be cut into sizes that will cook quickly and tender-crisp. Meats need to be cut in the same small sizes.

I arrange the ingredients in order, by the amount of cooking time needed. Meats first; then 10-minute vegetables; 7–8-minute vegetables next; 4–6-minute vegetables; and the 2–3-minute vegetables last. I line up bowls or saucers of prepared items on the counter where I can reach them easily during cooking.

Always preheat the wok, then add a small amount of oil. If using meat, cook it first, then remove and set aside until later. You will probably need additional oil or other liquid for the vegetables. Now, toss and stir in the vegetables. Longest-cooking first, medium-cooking next and shortest-cooking last. If two vegetables go in about the same time, add them separately, 30–60 seconds apart, so the first food can start to warm.

Never add several cups of chopped food in a stir-fry all at once. The cold items cool down the oil and halt cooking. By the time the wok is hot enough to cook again, you end up with soft vegetable stew.

When vegetables are done, return the meat, add desired sauce, and heat briefly.

Meat or poultry: Use slivers of tender meat, not stew cuts. Cooking time will vary with size. If meat has been marinated, drain well before cooking. Most recipes specify raw meat or poultry, however, cooked items can work well too.

One last stir-frying tip—don't forget to have fun!

Sample Combinations

Marinating food means soaking it in an acidic tenderizing solution. The most elementary marinade is lemon or lime juice sprinkled or patted on all surfaces. Let it soak 30 to 45 minutes. Marinating is always optional, but, unquestionably, it improves the results. See the "ETC." chapter for more marinade ideas.

If you're unfamiliar with any of the vegetables, see the Vegetables chapter for selection and preparation tips. Note: Scallions are the preferred form of onions. Large onions, no matter how they're sliced or diced, tend to burn.

I offer the following suggestions only to get you started. Feel free to "mix 'n match," making up your own combinations.

Beef

red bell pepper, 1-inch cubes
scallions, ½-inch slices
broccoli—florets and peeled stalks, in ¼-inch slices
cauliflower florets

Lamb

carrot, thin slices
celery, medium slices
spinach or chard leaves, torn or whole
jicama, diced or in sticks

Pork

cabbage, 1½-inch cubes
yellow bell peppers, in 1-inch cubes
scallions, ½-inch slices
kohlrabi or daikon radish, cut in matchsticks

Chicken/Turkey/Duck/Cornish Game Hen

snow peas
mushrooms, sliced
red bell peppers, in 1-inch cubes
Jerusalem artichokes, sliced

Preheat the wok or skillet over high, or medium-high, heat. Pour 1–2 tablespoons of oil in a thin trickle around the outer edges of the wok, so the side surfaces get oiled, too. Wait a few seconds (I count to ten) and add the first food.

See additional explanation of stir-fry in the Ingredients and Techniques chapter of Section 3. Serve over brown rice, quinoa or baked sweet potatoes.

Sweet 'N Sour Stir-Fry Sauce

Serves 3–4

I save this delight for rare and festive occasions. It's enough to "sauce" any stir-fry that serves 3–4 people. Mix it before you start cooking.

1   cup of crushed fresh pineapple, with all of the natural juices you can scrape out of the shell

1   tablespoon starch—arrowroot, tapioca, kudzu

½   teaspoon salt*

1   teaspoon dark sesame oil

2   tablespoons sesame seeds, lightly toasted

Combine pineapple with the starch, soy sauce and sesame oil. Stir to dissolve the starch and set aside.

One minute before the food is done, stir the pineapple mixture again and pour into the stir-fry. Stir. The sauce boils and thickens in seconds.

Serve the stir-fry over cooked rice, quinoa, or a baked sweet potato—or not over anything at all. Top each portion with a sprinkling of toasted sesame seeds.

---

*I use the salt in place of 1 tablespoon of wheat-free soy sauce or tamari. When you're better, you can try one of them in this sauce.

Roast Cornish Hens

Serves 2–4

I serve Cornish hens a couple times a month. They're widely available, not too expensive—and not as much trouble as bigger birds. Plus, they're different enough that many people who react to chicken tolerate them.

As long as you're heating the oven, why not bake sweet potatoes or hardshell squash at the same time? The combination makes an easy meal to prepare.

If you're concerned about consuming animal fat, notice that the skin is retained during roasting (to help keep the lean breast meat from drying out) and discarded before serving. The basting fat is minimal—it trickles across the breast skin into the roasting pan.

All of my references suggest one hen per person. But when I roast two, we share one and dice the meat of the other to make soup. (Or you can prepare more—line up 4–6 hens on a cookie sheet with edges, to catch the juices.)

Right after dinner I cut the meat off of the other hen and freeze it. I toss the bones of both hens in a stock pot of water to make Cornish Hen Stock (page 183), which can be frozen. Four to eight days later I add vegetables to the stock and diced meat for a great soup. That's a lot of mileage out of two little hens!

2   Cornish hens
½   teaspoon oil

Preheat oven to 450°. If frozen, thaw the hens in the refrigerator 24–48 hours.

One-and-one-quarter hours* before you want to eat, remove the package of giblets from each cavity. Rinse each hen under running water. Shake the water off and pat them dry. Lay the hens on a wire rack on a baking sheet or in a 9x13-inch glass pan.

Remove the fat pads that you usually find at the entry to the cavity or around the neck. Stretch the fat pads across the breast to baste the bird while it's roasting. Pour the oil into a teaspoon and

---

*I like to offer a time frame for preparations so that foods will finish cooking at the same time. I plan 15 minutes to wash and dry the birds, place the fat pads and apply the oil—50 minutes roasting time—and 10 minutes to carve and get my meal on the table. Not bad for a nice dinner!

dribble it along the legs. Use the back of the spoon to spread the oil in a thin film over the legs and the sides of the birds, if you wish. Leave the cavities unstuffed. Tie the legs together.

Pop the hens in the oven. Immediately reduce the heat to 350°. Roast until tender, about 50 minutes. No need to baste during roasting—the fat pads do it for you. To serve, discard the skin from across the breast and carve. Let each diner remove skin from the legs.

❖ VARIATION ❖

Stuff the birds, but don't pack tightly. Add 15 minutes to the roasting time. See "ETC." chapter for stuffings.

Roast Turkey or Turkey Breast

Because turkey is traditional for Thanksgiving and other holidays, you may overlook its year-round convenience. You can choose from whole turkeys, breasts, thighs, legs, wings and ground turkey.

Buying ground turkey or specific parts wins for convenience—but for better economy, buy the whole bird.

Shop around for organic turkeys in your area—or the least chemically contaminated you can find. Health food stores often stock excellent frozen organic turkeys.

Stuffing, optional (See "ETC." chapter)
1   whole turkey or turkey breast, fresh or thawed in
     refrigerator 2–3 days or longer, depending on size of bird
Oil, if needed

Preheat oven to 450°. If you want stuffing, prepare it first. Immediately reduce temperature to 325° when turkey is placed in oven.

Remove the giblets from the cavity. Simmer them for your gravy or discard. Rinse the turkey and pat dry. Pull off the fat pads that are usually found beside the cavity or around the neck. Stretch them out so they'll lay flat and place along the breast bone.

As the fat melts it'll baste the turkey. If you have enough fat, drape the legs, too. If not, apply a thin film of oil over the legs. If you wish, lay 3–4 layers of cheesecloth loosely over all. This holds oil around the breast meat and helps prevent drying.

Unstuffed Breast or Whole Turkey: Put the bird in a roaster, on an oiled rack, and roast uncovered. See following chart for timing.

Stuffed: Stuffing is always optional. Spoon stuffing loosely (not packed) into the cavity of a whole turkey. To stuff the *turkey breast*, turn it over on a long piece of cheesecloth. Fill the hollow with stuffing. Close the cheesecloth to hold the stuffing in place. Turn the breast skin-side up on an oiled rack. Roast uncovered until tender.

To Roast: After 30–45 minutes, baste your bird with pan drippings. (I recommend using a baster. If you use a spoon, take care not to burn yourself.) If you laid plenty of fat across your bird, you don't need to baste again. If your bird didn't have much fat, baste every 30–45 minutes. Roast until the meat is tender and reaches an internal temperature of 185°. Remove from the oven 15 minutes before serving time. Let it rest undisturbed for 10 minutes. Then carve and serve.

Timetable	Unstuffed	Stuffed
3–5 pounds	1½–2 hours	Add 15–25 minutes
5–7 pounds	2–2½ hours	Add 25–35 minutes
7–9 pounds	2½–3¼ hours	Add 35–45 minutes
10–15 pounds	3½–4½ hours	Add 45–60 minutes
Over 16 pounds	More than 5 hours (14 minutes/pound)	Add 5 minutes/pound

Oven-Fried Chicken: Strip 'N Shake   E

Serves 2–4

This version with the egg bath is the real thing. Crispy on the outside, moist and tender on the inside—and it's not too tough to double or triple the recipe for a crowd.

1   fryer chicken, cut up, or 2 breasts, split and skinned
1   large egg
1   tablespoon water
½   cup flour—buckwheat, amaranth, quinoa, oat
½   teaspoon salt
Several grindings of fresh pepper
½   teaspoon paprika, optional
½   teaspoon dry sage or poultry seasoning, optional

Preheat oven to 450°. Rinse chicken well and pat dry.

In pie plate, whip the egg and water together with a fork. Dip each piece of chicken in the egg. Lay dipped chicken on a wire rack to dry for 5–10 minutes.

Combine the flour and seasonings in a paper or plastic bag; add chicken, one piece at a time, and shake until evenly coated.

Arrange chicken pieces, bone-side down, on a jelly roll pan, Pyrex dish or in two piepans. Put them in the oven and immediately reduce the temperature to 400°. Bake 35–40 minutes.

Oven-Fried Chicken: Strip 'N Dip

Serves 2–4

When you bake chicken without skin, the coating becomes a substitute "skin," keeping the inside moist and tender while the outside gets crispy. This batter technique solves the problem of improvising a "skin" for adequate protection—without the usual egg bath.

1   fryer chicken, cut up, or 2 breasts split, and skinned
1/2   cup flour—buckwheat, amaranth, quinoa, oat, rice
1/2   teaspoon salt
Several grindings of pepper
1/2   teaspoon paprika, optional
1/2   teaspoon poultry seasoning, optional
1/4   cup of water
1   tablespoon oil

Preheat oven to 450°. Rinse chicken pieces and pat thoroughly dry.

Combine the flour and seasonings in a small bowl. Stir in the water and oil to make a thick batter.

Dip each piece of chicken in batter and place it bone-side down on a jelly roll pan, Pyrex dish or in two piepans. Put the chicken in the oven and immediately reduce the temperature to 400°. Bake 35–40 minutes.

Busy-Day Banquet

Serves 2

This dish evolved on one of those *I-don't-have-time-to-cook* days. I just tossed everything together in a pot and put my feet up for 25 minutes. A steamer basket was the magic ingredient. I didn't mind a bit only having one pot to wash.

2   sweet potatoes, scrubbed
2   apples, thin slice removed from the top ·
2   lamb or pork chops, well trimmed
12   asparagus stalks, tough ends removed,
      OR
2   cups chopped cabbage, or broccoli (for 2 people)

Place a collapsible steamer basket in a 5-quart Dutch oven with 3/4 inch of water in the bottom. Arrange scrubbed sweet potatoes and apples in the basket. Put the chops on top, cover tightly and steam 25 minutes.

Add the vegetable of your choice and steam another 10 minutes, or until everything is tender. Use tongs and a slotted spoon to transfer the food to dinner plates. Arrange the foods separately—this isn't a stew!

Slow-Cooked Pork Pot

Serves 4

Sometimes I like to start dinner at breakfast time—and a slow-cooking electric pot makes that possible. The food cooks in the time specified. But if you're not home from work or not ready to eat, another hour or two doesn't hurt. The temperature of electric slow-cook pots (185–200°) is low enough not to destroy many nutrients—yet hot enough to kill bacteria.

Tips for successful slow-cooking: Use the specified amount of liquid. If you adapt another recipe with lots of liquid in which the juices "cook away," reduce the amount you use (usually ½ cup or less, unless you want stew). Always cover tightly. Cut vegetables bite-sized. Trim fat from the meat.

¼   cup water
1   large onion, thin-sliced
3–4 carrots, thin-sliced
1–2 stalks of celery, sliced
¼   cup minced fresh parsley, divided
Salt to taste
1-1¼ pound pork tenderloin, trimmed and sliced
Optional: Herbs or spices, to taste*

Put the water in the bottom of slow-cooker. Add vegetables and half the parsley. Add salt and the herbs or spices. Mix the vegetables with your hand; remove ½ cup of the vegetables.

Arrange pork tenderloin slices on the top of the vegetables. Scatter the reserved ½ cup vegetables and remaining parsley on top of the meat. Cover tightly and cook on "Low" for 8–10 hours.

❖ VARIATIONS ❖

• Add peeled and sliced white or sweet potatoes.

• Substitute any other lean meat or poultry for the pork. Experiment with wild game—it responds well to slow, moist cooking.

---

*Determine seasonings by discovering which herbs and spices agree with you. Start by adding a few thin slices of fresh ginger to the pot (discard them when you serve). Or add fresh tarragon, basil, thyme, oregano or sage. Start with one herb, to determine tolerance.

When you're better, add a diced apple or tomato and 1–2 teaspoons of curry powder—a dried blend of many herbs and spices. Curries are usually thickened, as in the variation for All-Day Stew.

• For All-Day Stew—Quarter each slice of pork tenderloin or dice your choice of meat. Use ¾ cup of water. An hour before serving, stir 2 tablespoons of tapioca starch flour into ¼ cup of cool water. When dissolved, stir into the stew.

Lean-Meat Stew

Serves 4

Here's the dilemma: You want to reduce the animal fat in your diet—but lean meat often means tough meat. Extremely lean (ground) patties or burgers even taste dry and tough.

Solution: Combine the lean-ground meat with vegetables and water or stock for this stew!

Further purée part of the vegetables to thicken the broth into delicious gravy.

1   pound lean ground pork, lamb, turkey or chicken*
½ – 1 tablespoon olive or other vegetable oil
1   cup coarsely chopped onion
2   teaspoons fresh herbs,** minced
12 – 14 small new potatoes, unpeeled, scrubbed
6   large carrots, pared, sliced ½ inch thick
3   large or 4 smaller ribs of celery, cut in ¾-inch chunks
1 – 2 medium parsnips, cut in ½-inch pieces
Water, stock, or half water and half fresh-cooked
      stewed tomatoes to cover
½   teaspoon salt

On waxed paper, pat the meat flat, to ½-inch thick. Cut it into ¾-inch cubes. Heat the oil in a Dutch oven, add the meat cubes and brown lightly.

Add onions and fresh herbs. Cook for 5 minutes, stirring twice. Unless the potatoes are less than 2 inches across, cut them in halves

---

*If you have wild game, soak it in marinade for 2 hours. Cut the meat into 2-inch cubes and grind it in a meat grinder or food processor. Use the ground meat to make this recipe.
**Herbs add a lot to this or any stew. Try fresh sage, thyme or tarragon with poultry; rosemary with lamb; basil or oregano with pork. Fresh parsley or dill complement any meat.
  If you substitute dried herbs, reduce the amount to half or less—and realize that the dried herbs usually contain molds and yeast.

or quarters. Add the potatoes, carrots, celery and parsnips. Cover the vegetables with liquid.

Cover tightly and simmer until the vegetables are tender—about 20 minutes. Measure 1½ cups mixed vegetables with a little broth, and purée in a blender. Stir the purée back into the stew. Simmer and stir for 3–5 minutes until the stew bubbles and thickens.

Three-Bean Stew   L

Serves 4–6

The fresh herbs, onions and garlic lend a classic flavor to this stew. When I use quick-cooking basmati rice, I call it my thirty-minute "quickie" meal—and I've even served it to health-conscious guests.

1¼ cups brown or white basmati rice
2 cups water
½ teaspoon salt
2 tablespoons olive oil
1½ cups Spanish onion, coarsely chopped
3–4 cloves of garlic, pressed or minced
Fresh minced basil and oregano to taste*
2 cups cooked pinto beans, in cooking liquid
2 cups cooked garbanzo beans, in cooking liquid
10 ounces frozen lima beans
¼ teaspoon salt (if beans are salt-free)
Generous grinding of fresh black pepper, optional

Rinse the rice two or three times in cold water. Combine rice, water and salt in saucepan. Simmer the brown rice about 40 minutes, or white basmati rice for 20 minutes.

In a 3-quart saucepan, sauté the onions in olive oil until they start to soften, 7 or 8 minutes. Add garlic and herbs. Cook and stir 2 minutes.

---

*Customize this recipe to your taste. Start with 1–2 tablespoons each of fresh basil and oregano, or choose one, if you limit your condiments. Then record the amount you use—and whether you prefer a bit more or less of that herb's flavor. The next time you make this recipe, adjust it accordingly.

Add the pinto and garbanzo beans with their cooking broth. Add water if the liquid doesn't cover the beans by ½ inch. When the beans boil, add frozen limas. When it boils again, cover and simmer 5–10 minutes.

Serve over rice. Add a salad or fruit dessert.

❖ VARIATION ❖

Grain-free: If you don't tolerate grains, try one of these substitutes for the rice: Cooked oriental bean thread noodles (made from mung beans), quinoa or buckwheat. (See Index for Cooked Quinoa or Buckwheat.)

To prepare bean thread noodles, pour boiling water over dry noodles. Let them soak (rather than boil) for 10–15 minutes; drain and serve.

Lamb Patties in Fresh Tomato Sauce

Serves 4

If you must forgo hamburgers with sweetened catsup, perhaps you'll savor lamb "burgers" in this fresh tomato sauce. They don't take long to prepare.

1   cup fresh tomatoes, diced, cooked
2   teaspoons olive oil
¼   teaspoon salt
Pinch of rosemary, crushed
2–4 tablespoons green pepper, minced
6–12 fresh oregano leaves, optional
4   lamb patties

In a saucepan combine tomatoes, olive oil, salt, rosemary, green pepper and the oregano. Bring to a boil, reduce heat and simmer until the sauce thickens.

While the sauce simmers, broil the lamb patties.

To serve, pour the sauce over the patties.

> ❖ **NOTE:** To limit fats in this recipe, ask your butcher to cut away ❖
> the visible fat before he grinds your lamb.

Adapted from Ken Gerdes, M.D., Denver, CO

Brazil Burgers

Your food processor or grinder can earn its keep preparing this nut 'n veggie burger—everything in it gets ground. Allow yourself half an hour besides the baking time, to assemble them.

What can you do with Brazil Burgers? I like to top them with sautéed, sliced Vidalia or Spanish onion. Steamed carrots and baked potato round out the meal.

For a more casual meal, I serve Brazil Burgers on any flatbread—as an open-faced sandwich. I serve mustard, sliced tomato, sliced onion and alfalfa sprouts on top. These burgers are even good cold, in a lunch box!

Egg Substitute: 1/3 cup water

     4 teaspoons flax seeds

1 cup raw Brazil nuts

2/3 cup celery chunks

2/3 cup carrot chunks

2/3 cup onion chunks

1/2 cup parsley leaves

1/2 cup green pepper chunks

1/3 cup sesame flour or sesame (or other) seeds

1 1/2 teaspoons whole cumin seeds

Handful of fresh dill, foliage only

1 teaspoon whole fennel seeds

1/4 teaspoon salt

Freshly ground pepper, to taste

Combine the water and flax seeds in a small saucepan. Bring to a full boil, then turn off heat. Let them soak until needed. Preheat the oven to 375°.

Grind nuts and transfer them to a large bowl. Combine the remaining ingredients in a food processor, or put them through a grinder. Grind into meal—not a purée. Add this mixture to the ground nuts.

Scrape the flax seed mixture (it's the consistency of egg white) into the bowl with everything else. Toss and stir several minutes to mix well.

Line a cookie sheet with parchment, or oil it, and drop scoops of the mixture on it. Using a rubber spatula, pat the mounds into flat patties.

Bake for 40–45 minutes until golden and crisp around the edges. Use a pancake turner to lift the burgers.

Desserts and Treats

Can you eat dessert on your candida-control diet? No . . . and yes. While physicians often differ in the exact details of what they permit, most agree that it's necessary to avoid sweets, especially refined super-sweet, "gooey" desserts. Readily available sugars, including honey and maple syrup, feed your yeast—just when you're declaring war.

As you probably know, even the natural sugar of fruit may cause problems. This is why Dr. Crook and many other physicians advise you to avoid fruits entirely during the first three weeks of your diet. After that, you can experiment and reintroduce small amounts of fruit gradually. In that way, you can determine how much fruit you can handle without provoking symptoms. After omitting fruit for a while, you'll welcome even those small portions—and they'll taste incredibly sweet and delicious.

You may find that you develop symptoms to fruit that you eat between meals, yet you may tolerate a little bit after a meal, as a dessert. Here's why: The rapid assimilation of natural fruit sugar dumps a load of sugar into your bloodstream (almost like when you eat sugar or honey) and may trigger your symptoms. The fruits that you eat after a meal assimilate more slowly and may not bother you. The recently ingested fats and proteins in the stomach impede that rapid assimilation and prevent the sudden surge of sugar.

If you aren't sure why all of this is so, review Section 1. It is important to *really understand why* the strategy of eliminating sweets is crucial to your recovery. Hopefully, when you understand the reason, you can implement the diet without feeling deprived.

Why then does a candida cookbook even include desserts? Because as you recover and go on a maintenance diet, you'll find that you tolerate small—and then larger—amounts of fruit. When that time arrives, you can use your fruit allowance to make a minimally sweetened dessert *that you may tolerate.* Recipes from newspapers and magazines, and in your "Big Fat Cookbook" (that you used to depend on) tempt you with sugary-sweet desserts. Don't fall for them or your symptoms will really flare!

"Minimally Sweetened"

The recipes in this chapter have been specially developed to satisfy your sweet tooth without causing your candida to flourish. But you have to determine your own tolerance for them. Maybe at first you'll only tolerate two bites of a dessert, then maybe a small serving once a week. I doubt that any of us can really go back to desserts every day.

Yet, like everyone else, you'll want to celebrate special occasions—birthdays, graduations, weddings, anniversaries and holidays. You'll want to mark those events with "something special" to eat. Without a chapter of minimally sweetened desserts, you'd be tempted to go "whole hog" and buy *sweet* sweets in a bakery or order sugar-laden pie or cake in a restaurant.

So . . . the ideas are here. It's up to you to use them wisely, and with restraint.

All-Fruit Sorbet #1

The consistency of this sorbet will remind you of soft-serve ice cream. Since the sorbet consists entirely of fruit, select sweet, ripe specimens to obtain the best flavor.

Making this delightful treat may tax your patience. Still, if you want an all-fruit frozen dessert—like ice cream—badly enough, you'll learn how to do it. And you'll persist until the mixture is smooth . . . and tantalizing. Experiment with different combinations like banana with sweet berries or pineapple, grapes with apricot, etc.

I favor the soft consistency, but if you prefer a firmer texture, prepare the sorbet just before you eat dinner. Put in individual serving dishes and pop them into the freezer for half an hour. To serve, stir each dish a bit to break up possible ice crystals.

1-2 cups frozen fruit chunks*: bananas,** peaches, nectarines, apricots, strawberries, raspberries, blueberries, seedless grapes, mango, pineapple

1-2 tablespoons water or lime juice

OPTIONAL ADDITIONS:

1-3 teaspoons oil

½ teaspoon vanilla (best with banana mixtures)

Pinch of unbuffered vitamin C crystals (for a tang similar to lemon juice)

Put dessert dishes in your freezer. Combine 1 tablespoon of water and 1-3 teaspoons of oil in a blender, OR 2 tablespoons water and no oil. (Oil adds a smoothness, called "mouthfeel," that makes the sorbet more like ice cream.) Add any other options you want.

Add 3-4 chunks of frozen fruit and blend until smooth. Gradually add more fruit, blending after each addition. Stop often to push fruit down into blades. Be patient. Serve in chilled bowls.

> ❖ **NOTE:** Do not double this recipe. If you want more sorbet, ❖ scrape the first batch into dishes and put them in a freezer. Then prepare another batch.

All-Fruit Sorbet #2

This frozen treat is similar to Sorbet #1, except it requires special equipment: The Donvier Ice Cream Maker. It costs $20–$30, depending on the size you choose. I cook for two, so I bought the pint size. But you can also find it in a larger "family" size.

Simple and ingenious, this piece of equipment fascinates me. It has an outer plastic container, paddle, handle and lid—plus the

---

*To freeze your own fruit (like nectarines, grapes, various berries, etc.) wash well, drain and arrange on a plate or cookie sheet. Leave seedless grapes whole, but halve nectarines, apricots and peaches and remove pits. Cut into pieces about the size of a grape or cherry. Freeze uncovered several hours until the fruit is solid. Make the sorbet or wrap the fruit tightly and store in freezer to use within a few days.

**To freeze bananas: Peel ripe, freckled bananas. Wrap each whole banana in plastic wrap, like a thin "skin," or brush them lightly with lime juice (or water with vitamin C dissolved in it). Place on cookie sheet to freeze. To puree in blender, cut into ¾-inch pieces.

magic: an inner, metal container that you store (empty) in your freezer. That inner cylinder contains a super-cold liquid between its walls. When frozen, it's so super-chilled that it'll freeze anything you put in it!

Place your freezer control at the coldest setting.

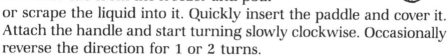

2   cups of cold puréed fruit
Pinch of vitamin C crystals, optional (for tang)

Prepare the purée from refrigerated fruit, or chill it one half hour. Remove the inner tub from the freezer and pour or scrape the liquid into it. Quickly insert the paddle and cover it. Attach the handle and start turning slowly clockwise. Occasionally reverse the direction for 1 or 2 turns.

If mixture is watery, as with orange juice or puréed honeydew, freezing takes about 15 minutes. But if you start with a thick, thoroughly chilled purée, of say, peaches and raspberries, you'll achieve the soft-serve frozen consistency in 10 minutes or less.

Serve at once or divide into individual chilled dishes and put in the freezer while you eat dinner. In about half an hour, when you serve the sorbet, stir each dish lightly to break up any crystal formation.

❖ VARIATION ❖

Add ¼ teaspoon of guar gum to the purée in the blender and blend well. This promotes a smooth texture and prevents crystalline formation if you store the sorbet in your freezer before serving. It doesn't affect the taste.

Raspberry Delight

Serves 6–8

This lovely dessert is possible any time of the year as long as you can find frozen raspberries and fresh pears or grapes.

Note that this recipe is all fruit. So save it for later in your recovery, when you tolerate a whole dish of fruit. It's still less sweet than desserts made with honey, maple syrup or even the frozen fruit juice concentrates. It's just fruit plus tapioca. I love it.

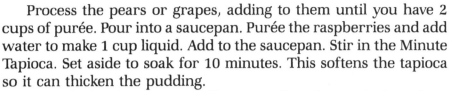

2   cups puréed ripe pears (peeled) or seedless grapes
1   cup raspberries, puréed (strain if you wish)
Water
¼   cup Minute Tapioca*
1   cup of whole raspberries

Process the pears or grapes, adding to them until you have 2 cups of purée. Pour into a saucepan. Purée the raspberries and add water to make 1 cup liquid. Add to the saucepan. Stir in the Minute Tapioca. Set aside to soak for 10 minutes. This softens the tapioca so it can thicken the pudding.

Bring fruit mixture to a boil over medium heat, stirring often. When it bubbles up in a full boil, remove from the heat.

Allow the mixture to cool undisturbed for 20 minutes. (It thickens as it cools.) Stir hard, about 5 strokes, then gently fold in whole raspberries. Chill.

❖ VARIATIONS ❖

Raspberry Parfaits—Make 1 recipe of Creamy Nut Topping, page 325, and chill. In sherbet or parfait glasses, spoon a layer of Raspberry-Tapioca Delight, a layer of Nut Cream, another layer of Delight, topped with a dollop of Nut Cream. Elegant for special occasions!

Pineapple Pudding—Purée a whole fresh pineapple for all of the liquid. Work over a plate to catch as much pineapple juice as you can. Add water if needed to make the 3 cups. Optional—After cooling, stir in whole raspberries or sliced strawberries.

No-Flour Fudge Brownies   Ⓨ Ⓔ Ⓛ

16 Small Squares

The structure for these amazing brownies comes from the ground pumpkin seeds, carob powder and eggs. The brownies are minimally sweet, light as a feather—and delicious. I think they'll satisfy youngsters of all ages who must skip birthday cakes and holiday goodies.

---

*This makes a soft pudding. If you prefer a stiff consistency add another tablespoon of Minute Tapioca.

I designed the brownies so you control the sweetness. See the Note for how to increase and decrease it. Make the brownies so you and your family can safely enjoy them.

2   eggs, separated
¹/₃   cup unsweetened apple or grape juice or concentrate
     (See Note)
1 ¹/₂ teaspoons vanilla
¹/₈   teaspoon salt
¹/₄   teaspoon unbuffered, corn-free vitamin C crystals
¹/₄   cup carob powder, sifted (don't pack it)
1   cup pumpkin seeds, ground into meal
³/₄   cup walnuts, coarsely chopped
1   teaspoon baking soda

Read the Note and decide how much sweetener you want to use. If you need to simmer the juice, do it first.

Preheat oven to 350°. Oil an 8x8-inch pan. Cut a square of parchment or waxed paper to fit the bottom of the pan. Put the paper in place and oil it, too.

Grind the seeds into fine meal in a blender, and save.

Put yolks in a medium mixing bowl; add vanilla, salt and vitamin C crystals. Whisk a few minutes until light. While whisking the yolk mixture, gradually add the fruit juice or concentrate, then the carob powder.

Combine ground seeds, walnuts and baking soda and mix well. Beat the egg whites with an electric mixer on "low," for 1 minute, on "medium" for 1 minute, then on "high" for 2 minutes. They should hold a stiff peak and look shiny. Set aside. Working quickly, stir the seed meal into the carob–egg yolk mixture.

Gently but quickly fold the egg whites into the batter with a rubber spatula.

Scrape the batter into the prepared pan and bake for 25 minutes, or until a toothpick thrust in the center comes out dry. Cool for 10–15 minutes, then loosen around the edges with a knife and flip it over on a wire rack to cool. Peel the paper off. When cool, cut into 16 squares.

❖ **NOTE:** The brownies require ¹/₃ cup of liquid, but you have ❖
options:

1. Use ¹/₃ cup of apple juice, or white or dark grape juice (Not very sweet; each brownie contains 1 teaspoon of juice)

2. Start with ⅔ cup of juice and *reduce it to ⅓ cup by boiling* (each contains 2 teaspoons of juice)

3. Start with 1 cup of juice and *reduce it to ⅓ cup by boiling* (each contains 3 teaspoons of juice)

4. Use commercial, unsweetened juice concentrate (each brownie contains 4 teaspoons of juice)

Banana Oat Cookies

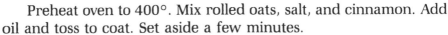

12 large cookies

Sweetened only with bananas, chewy oat cookies are delicious the day you bake them. They're not great "keepers" though—but who cares? They tend to disappear quickly.

These cookies look like those large ones you see in shopping centers. Yet they're different, barely sweet—and quite chewy. The combination of nuts and grain complement each other, yielding high-quality (complete) protein.

Use sweet, fully ripened (freckled) bananas. Hard, green-tinged specimens won't produce enough sweetness to make good cookies.

3   cups rolled oats
½   teaspoon salt
½-1 teaspoon cinnamon
        OR
¼   teaspoon allspice
¼   cup walnut oil*
¾   cup chopped pecans or walnuts
2¼ cups sliced bananas, lightly packed

Preheat oven to 400°. Mix rolled oats, salt, and cinnamon. Add oil and toss to coat. Set aside a few minutes.

Mash bananas with a fork or liquefy in a blender. Add nuts and bananas to the oat mixture and mix well.

Using a ¼ measuring cup, scoop 6 mounds of dough (slightly rounded) onto each of 2 unoiled cookie sheets.

Flatten cookies to about 5 inches across with a fork or spatula. Bake on a high rack for 10 minutes. Remove from the oven and

---

*You can make this recipe with as little as 2 tablespoons of oil. But since the cookies aren't very sweet, the added richness enhances the flavor and texture.

press each cookie flatter with a fork. Return cookies to the oven and bake another 8–10 minutes.

❖ VARIATION ❖

Banana-Peanut Oat Cookies—Instead of the ¼ cup of oil in Banana Oat Cookies, use 2 tablespoons of peanut oil plus 2 tablespoons of peanut butter. Toss the oil with the oats as directed above. Combine the peanut butter with the mashed or puréed bananas, and proceed with the recipe.

Adapted from *Allergy Cooking, Tricks and Treasures*
With permission from the author, Nancy Burrows
(526 Belmont Road, Grand Forks, ND 58201)

Strawberry Shortcake

Serves 4–6

I couldn't make it through June without improvising a strawberry shortcake. When the berries are in season, there's nothing better!

Although you find this in "Desserts," I don't use it that way. I make shortcake for the "main event" (breakfast or lunch)—it's the whole meal.

To understand the function of the banana or other fruit, think about a shortcake in which the berries are sweetened and topped with whipped cream. The other fruit sweetens the berries and makes them creamy (like whipped cream that's mixed into the berries, not a garnish on top).

1   recipe of Country "Corn" Bread, page 165, any flour
3-4 cups fresh strawberries
2   ripe bananas or pears,
        OR
1½ cups seedless grapes
½   cup cashews, Brazil or other nuts, optional

Bake the bread. While it's baking, clean the strawberries. Quarter or slice them into a large bowl.

Purée the bananas, pears or grapes in a blender one minute or until liquefied. For a richer "cream," add nuts to the puréed fruit and blend again. Pour the creamy mixture over the berries and mix.

Remove "Corn" Bread from oven, and immediately cut it into portions (I use ¼ of the recipe when it's my meal). Split the bread in half using serrated knife. Handle the bread gently—it's hot and crumbly, like good biscuits.

To assemble: Arrange the split halves on individual plates. Spoon the berries over the shortcakes. Enjoy!

> ❖ **NOTE:** If your berries aren't very juicy, mash them with a po- ❖
> tato masher twice or just enough to release the juice.

Magic Apple Pie

1 10-inch pie

When I browsed through Nancy Burrows' *Allergy Cooking, Tricks and Treasures,* I was fascinated by this recipe. Was this a real pie? Where's the crust? She called for honey, which is taboo for candida folks. Could I improvise satisfactorily? I had to try.

Surprise! My husband and I were delighted with my minimally sweetened version. And I found Nancy's way of putting it together quicker and easier than making a separate crust.

1½ to 2 cups puréed ripe pears or seedless grapes
1   cup brown rice flour
¼ to ½ teaspoon salt
¼   teaspoon nutmeg, freshly grated, optional
1   teaspoon cinnamon
4   cups raw cooking apples, thinly sliced
⅓   cup oil
¼   teaspoon unbuffered, corn-free vitamin C crystals
     OR
1   teaspoon cream of tartar
1   teaspoon baking soda
2   tablespoons boiling water

Make sweetener first: Wash fruit well and put in blender to the 3 cup level. Liquefy. Add additional fruit to bring purée to between

1½ and 2 cups. Transfer to a saucepan and boil 20–25 minutes—until it measures ⅔ cup.

Meanwhile, oil and dust with flour a 10-inch pie pan. Combine flour, salt, nutmeg and cinnamon and mix well. Peel and slice the apples. Preheat oven to 350°.

Stir vitamin C crystals into cooked purée. (If you're using cream of tartar, combine it with the flour.) Add the oil.

> ❖ **E-Z MIX TIP:** Pour the oil right into the measuring cup where ❖ you're measuring ⅔ cup of purée. Fill it to the 1 cup level.

Pour fruit mixture over the flour mixture and mix well with electric beaters or a whisk. Combine the baking soda and boiling water, stir to dissolve and add to the batter. *Quickly fold in the apples.* Scrape batter into the prepared pan and place in oven. Bake 45–55 minutes, or until pie is brown and apples are tender.

❖ VARIATIONS ❖

Apple-Walnut Pie—Add ½ cup coarsely chopped walnuts to the flour mixture. Use walnut oil in the recipe.

Peach-Almond Pie—Use fresh ripe peaches (or frozen peaches, thawed) in place of the apples. Add 1 teaspoon of pure almond extract to the purée just before pouring it over the dry ingredients. Stir ½ cup of chopped, toasted almonds into the flour mixture if you want them.

Adapted from *Allergy Cooking, Tricks and Treasures*
By permission of the author, Nancy Burrows

Fresh Pineapple Upside Down Cake

1 9-inch cake

Cake without sugar, honey or maple syrup? Yes! I'm not pretending that it's equally sweet. It's not. However, if you've omitted sweets for a long time, you'll delight in the subtle sweetness the pineapple provides.

Isn't this cake a lot of trouble, starting with fresh pineapple? There's nothing hard about it, but you'll need to allow about an hour for preparation—plus the baking time.

Please understand, I'm not suggesting you make desserts—even specially adapted ones—a daily or weekly event. Part of the game plan for recovering your health is to "unhook" from the idea of needing frequent desserts. I offer this fruit-sweetened recipe for a treat—to help you celebrate a special occasion in your life.

1	fresh pineapple
1	tablespoon oil
8 – 12	pecan halves, optional
1 1/2	cups white buckwheat flour
1/3	cup tapioca or arrowroot starch
2	teaspoons baking soda
1/4	teaspoon salt

OPTIONAL ADDITIONS—choose *one* (or none):

> 1 teaspoon ground ginger OR cinnamon
>
> 1/2 teaspoon freshly grated nutmeg
>
> 1/4 teaspoon ground cloves

1/3 cup walnut or other oil
1 tablespoon vanilla, optional

Cut the pineapple in quarters. Use a serrated knife to cut out the core. To loosen the fruit, cut 1/2 inch parallel to the rind. Work over a plate or bowl to catch the juices. Leave the loosened fruit in place; make two cuts lengthwise. Then cut across the fruit several times, dicing the pineapple into chunks. Scoop diced pineapple into a blender or food processor. Scrape across the shell with a spoon to get all of the juices.

Purée the pineapple. Pour into a saucepan and simmer over medium heat 20–25 minutes, or until it becomes syrupy and measures 1 2/3 cups.

> ❖ **E-Z MIX TIP:** While the fruit simmers, wash the blender jar, ❖ dry thoroughly and grind your buckwheat groats into flour— or do this first, before you use your blender to purée the fruit.
>
> Use a 2-cup glass measuring cup to see how much pineapple you have. If necessary, return the purée to the pan to simmer again. If the level is less than 1 2/3 cups, add a little water and stir well.

Oil a 9-inch pie plate and arrange the pecan halves, rounded sides down, like spokes of a wheel. Blend 1/3 cup pineapple purée with 1 tablespoon of oil. Process 15–20 seconds. Use a teaspoon to distribute this mixture evenly around the pecans.

Preheat oven to 400°. In a mixing bowl, whisk together the

flour, starch, baking soda and salt. Combine the remaining pineapple purée (1⅓ cups) with the ⅓ cup of oil and vanilla.

Make a well in the flour; add the pineapple mixture. Mix with a rubber spatula until all dry ingredients disappear. Immediately scrape the batter into the pie plate, over the pineapple and pecans.

Bake 20–22 minutes, or until a toothpick thrust into the center comes out dry. Remove from the oven.

Invert a plate or wire rack over the pie plate. Best when cooled 20–30 minutes before cutting.

Amaranth Alegría

The Mexican people originated alegría. It's a confection with a slightly sweet coating similar to Cracker Jacks. Instead of coating popped corn, you coat puffed amaranth.

Puffed amaranth isn't available in most health food stores, but you can order it direct from Nu-World Amaranth. (See Section 3 for Food Resources.)

Even though this snack confection is in the chapter with desserts, I must confess to eating it for breakfast.

1 tablespoon oil (or butter)
1 tablespoon aguamiel (See "Sweeteners," page 329.)
1¼ cups puffed amaranth

Combine oil and aguamiel in a 2- to 3-quart saucepan. Warm it gently just until the aguamiel melts and disperses throughout the oil, about 2 minutes. Stir in the puffed amaranth and continue to stir for several strokes until the amaranth is evenly coated. Eat with a spoon.

❖ VARIATIONS ❖

- Make 3 times the recipe. Press it firmly into an oiled 9x9-inch or 7x11-inch baking dish. Chill. Cut into bars.

- Add ¼ cup chopped pecans and stir well to coat. (I do this when the Alegría is my whole breakfast.)

Carob-Sesame Fudge

Dark, chewy and rich, this fudge is a winner. Make a batch with honey for guests and another batch with "fruit sweetener" for you and your family (they'll look identical). The fruit-sweetened one is minimally sweet, but really quite good. The difference in the two kinds is comparable to milk chocolate versus semisweet.

- ½ cup peanut, almond or cashew butter, at room temperature (soft)
- ½ cup peanuts (roasted), almonds or cashews (Use same kind of nut as your nut butter)
- ½ cup pumpkin seeds
- ½ cup sesame seeds, divided
- ½ cup carob powder
- ½ coconut, optional

Pinch of salt, optional

- ½ cup Fruit Sweetener (when you're well, use honey)

If your nut butter is refrigerated, remove it, measure a half cup and set aside to soften. Grind the peanuts (or other nuts) into fine meal. Put in a bowl. Grind the pumpkin seeds only briefly (small pieces are OK) and add to the bowl. Stir in all but 2 tablespoons of the sesame seeds, the carob, coconut and salt. Mix well.

Gently toast the 2 tablespoons of sesame seeds in a dry fry pan over moderate heat, then set aside. Combine the nut butter and Fruit Sweetener (when the fruit purée measures ½ cup, remove from heat, stir in the nut butter and combine well). Pour this thick liquid over the mixture in the bowl. Mix well—it will be thick. Press into an 8x8-inch pan, pressing with a flat spatula. Scatter the toasted sesame seeds on top. Pat them into the fudge and chill. Cut into 1-inch squares. Fudge freezes well.

❖ VARIATION ❖

Substitute walnuts or pecans for the sesame seeds, and use more of them (up to ⅔ cup). Reserve 2–3 tablespoons, chopped, for the top. Use the rest in the fudge, coarsely chopped.

Nut 'N Seed Crust

I've reworked this recipe and eliminated grain flour altogether. I consider it a great improvement! The quantity is exactly right for a 9-inch pie. No rolling, no leftover scraps.

³/₄ cup Brazil nuts or cashews*
¹/₄ cup sesame seeds*
¹/₄ cup tapioca or arrowroot starch
¹/₂ teaspoon cinnamon, optional
Pinch of salt, optional
3 tablespoons boiling water

Grind the nuts, half at a time, in a blender. Put the nut meal in a small bowl. Grind the sesame seeds and add to the bowl. Add the starch and optional seasonings if you want them. Stir mixture well. Add the boiling water and stir with a fork until it comes together into a ball.

Oil a 9-inch pie plate. Press the ball of dough into the center, flattening it with wet fingers or a wet rubber spatula. When it fills the bottom, use your fingers to mold the mixture up the sides. Go back to the center often to pat it thinner, so you can move the dough out toward the edges. Smooth the top edge. Bake at 350° for 20 minutes. Cool while you make the filling.

Squash Pudding

One day when I baked a large squash for dinner, I wondered what to do with the leftover portion. We hadn't eaten a dessert in weeks, so I decided to experiment with what I had on hand. My husband and I loved the results!

I cut off the rounded end, halved it, removed the seeds and

---

*These nuts and seeds make a crust with great flavor. But if you wish, substitute all pumpkin seeds. Also works well.

strings, and stuffed the halves for our main course. I used the solid squash in the long, skinny neck for an improvised pudding. The pudding baked while we ate dinner.

1 small to medium butternut squash, baked, page 265 (or the neck only of a larger squash)

4-6 cubes of Fruit Sweetener, page 322, thawed
OR
1-1 ½ cups puréed fresh pineapple, ripe pears (peeled), seedless grapes or bananas

2-4 tablespoons oil

Dash of cinnamon or nutmeg, optional

¼ cup pecans, in halves or pieces, optional

Split squash. Discard seeds and strings. Scoop hot squash out of shells. Add the remaining ingredients, except pecans, and purée with an electric mixer or food processor (consistency similar to mashed potatoes).

Scrape into an oiled casserole. Sprinkle with the pecans, if you wish. Bake at 350°, 30 minutes. Serve warm or cold.

Sesame-Oat Squares

A wonderful nutty, chewy dessert or snack treat. With no egg and no leavening, these squares may remind you of granola bars. They're easy to make—and delicious.

2 cups rolled oats

½ cup chopped peanuts, almonds or cashews

¼ cup oat bran

¼ cup sesame seeds

Pinch of salt, optional

⅔ cup Fruit Sweetener (when you're well, use honey)

⅔ cup peanut, almond or cashew butter, room temperature (Use same kind as the chopped nuts, above)

Combine the oats, chopped nuts, oat bran, sesame seeds and salt in a large bowl. In a small bowl, cream the Fruit Sweetener or honey with the nut butter until thoroughly blended. Scrape the creamed mixture over the oats, nuts and seeds, and mix well. (The dough will be thick.) Pat into an 11x7-inch baking dish. Bake at 300° for 35 minutes. Score deeply with a knife while warm. Cut into squares when cool.

❖ VARIATION ❖

Substitute another rolled grain for the oats—rye, barley or rice (grain flakes for hot cereal, like oatmeal). In place of the oat bran, use ¼ cup of the same kind of flour (rye, barley or rice). Or blenderize puffed rice or amaranth to make ¼ cup of very light "flour."

Nutty Pumpkin Pie

This no-bake version is the easiest pumpkin pie you'll ever make! And it's free of eggs and milk, too. It's perfect for holidays.

1   Nut 'N Seed Crust, baked
½   cup Brazil nuts or cashews*
1¼   cups boiling water
1   pound of pumpkin purée (1⅔ cups)
⅔   cup Fruit Sweetener** (when you're well, use honey)
½   teaspoon cinnamon
⅛ to ¼ teaspoon ginger
3   tablespoons arrowroot or tapioca starch
2   tablespoons cool water

Prepare the crust first and set aside to cool. Make nut milk by grinding the nuts in a blender to a fine powder. Add the boiling water and process for 2 minutes. Add the pumpkin, Fruit Sweetener or honey and spices. Blend well.

In a 3-quart saucepan dissolve the arrowroot in the cool water. Stir in the pumpkin mixture. Bring to a boil over medium heat, stirring often. Allow to boil for 3 minutes. Remove from heat and

---

*May substitute pumpkin seeds for the nuts, if you prefer.
**Start with about 2 cups of fresh grape purée. Reduce slowly, stirring often. Or use a double boiler.

cool until filling is lukewarm. Pour the filling into the pie shell, cover and chill.

❖ VARIATION ❖

For even spicier pie, add ¼ teaspoon of grated nutmeg or ground cloves or both, if they agree with you.

"Etc."

Dips, Stuffings and Miscellany

Earlier in this book you read, "The best recipes [for controlling candida] are no recipes at all"—meaning, eat whole food, plain. This holds true for the early weeks, even months, of your diet to control candida.

As the weeks pass and you improve, you'll find yourself longing for a few "extras"—the bells and whistles that make meals more fun. Here they are—ideas for simple but interesting ways to vary the way you eat—without doing yourself in.

Your recovery may be slow, and the diet may be long-term. You're more apt to stick with a diet that includes delicious "trimmings" to jazz up your plain meals. By providing you with this chapter of specially adapted recipes, I hope to satisfy your yearning for "something"—lovely sauces (not thickened with flour), dips for veggies, Ho-made Baking Powder, Better-Butter Spread, and more.

You'll find suggestions for non-bread stuffings for poultry (Oatmeal Stuffing, Waldorf Stuffing, and Waffle Stuffing), dairy-free "cream" sauces (Leek "Cream" Sauce, Velvet Sauce and Nut-Milk White Sauce), an improvised egg-free Nutty Mayo, Make-Believe Vinegar, a no-vinegar Tenderizing Flavorizing Marinade, and on and on.

Amazingly, all of those things and more, are possible—*within* the guidelines of your maintenance diet.

You don't need this chapter early on, and you don't need it every day, even on maintenance. But the ideas are here. You decide when—and how often—you can use them.

Pasta Improvisations

If you don't tolerate wheat products, perhaps you miss traditional pasta (I did). Yet we can easily improvise something to put our favorite sauce over.

"Pasta" #1—Spaghetti Squash

Bake, boil or steam a spaghetti squash, page 265. An average one that weighs 3¼ to 3¾ pounds cooks in about 45 minutes. It's done when the shell yields to the gentle pressure of your finger—and a dent remains.

To bake, *puncture with a fork three or more times* and put on a baking sheet. Bake at 375°. Turn the squash over after 25 minutes and bake 20 minutes more.

Cut the cooked squash in half lengthwise. Remove and discard the seeds. Use two forks to loosen the strands of squash—they look just like spaghetti! Pile the "pasta" on plates. Top with a tomato-based spaghetti sauce or with a basil- and oregano-seasoned "cream" sauce. Sauce may contain cooked ground meat, flaked tuna or diced poultry. Or enjoy the dish vegetarian style.

"Pasta" #2—Rice Elbow Macaroni, by "Food For Life"

Ask your health food store to order this product for you. Like any pasta, it's bland by itself. You can do great things with it—macaroni salads, pasta primavera or use as a base with "creamed" anything over it (for example, cooked chicken, turkey, or tuna with peas and celery). For the salads, moisten with half a recipe of Nutty Mayo. For a hot dish, choose Leek "Cream" Sauce, Nut-Milk White Sauce or Velvet Sauce, pages 208, 210, 211 and 212.

"Pasta" #3—Bean Thread Noodles (made from mung beans)

Look for these in the Oriental section of your supermarket. The thin noodles are white and usually appear in clear cellophane packages. Pour boiling water over them in a large pan. Let soak 10–15 minutes. (Don't boil them.) Drain. I often use two knives to chop the softened noodles a bit before serving.

Top noodles with any flavorful sauce—my favorite seasoning is ginger. Or toss the noodles with assorted raw vegetables and Nutty Mayo, page 208, for a salad. For a delicious hot dish, toss the noodles with lightly steamed veggies and about half a recipe of Nutty Mayo (freshly made, still warm).

"Pasta" #4—Other Vegetables

Let's get creative! Use a mound of French-cut green beans under your pasta sauce. Or use the shredding disc of a food processor to make long strands of zucchini. Use them raw or lightly steamed and drained. These are especially good when topped with a sauce that features basil or oregano, or both.

Waffle Poultry Stuffing

For a 3-pound bird

Now isn't this a creative idea? Nancy Burrows of Grand Forks, ND, dried a couple sections of leftover waffle—added seasonings—and produced delicious, wheat-free (even grain-free) poultry stuffing. I hope you love it as much as I do!

2	4-inch waffle sections, dried crisp in low oven
2–3	green onions, sliced thin
1	large celery rib, finely diced
1/4	teaspoon salt, optional
	Pinch of dried sage*
2	tablespoons almond (or other) oil
2	tablespoons (or more) boiling water

Cut or tear waffles into small pieces. Toss with onion, celery, salt and sage. Drizzle oil and mix gently. Sprinkle with enough boiling water to moisten.

Put the stuffing in a 3-pound chicken, or other bird.** Bake it in a covered roasting pan at 350° for 1½ hours. Remove the cover for the last 30 minutes to brown your bird.

---

*If you use *fresh* sage (to avoid the yeast and mold of the dried), you need more than a pinch. Start with 8–10 leaves, minced. Decide if you want more or less sage the next time you make this recipe and jot a note in the margins of your book.
**For a larger bird multiply proportionally. For example, 1½ times this recipe stuffs a 5-pound bird.

If you have some stuffing left after filling the cavity, put it in a small, oiled baking dish. Refrigerate it until 30 minutes before dinner. Bake it for the last half hour the bird is roasting.

Adapted from *Allergy Cooking, Tricks and Treasures*
By permission of the author, Nancy Burrows

Waldorf Stuffing

About 6 cups

This stuffing has been a personal favorite for many years. I vary it from time to time, but this is the version I start with—and keep coming back to.

2   cups cooked quinoa, buckwheat, brown rice, wild rice, whole oat groats, hulled barley or whole rye
1   recipe Nutty Mayo, page 208
1–2 unsprayed apples, cored and chopped
2   large ribs of celery
1   cup walnut pieces
10–15 large, fresh sage leaves, minced
OPTIONAL ADDITIONS:
Additional unbuffered, corn-free vitamin C crystals, to taste
Salt to taste
½   cup chopped onion, sautéed until soft
½   teaspoon celery seeds
Black pepper, to taste (generously)
6   sprigs of fresh thyme, stems removed
Few leaves of fresh savory or marjoram, minced
Apple juice or water, if needed to mix

Cook the grain first. Start with ¾ dry measure. Use 2¼ cups water for quinoa, buckwheat or wild rice; OR 1½ cups water for brown rice, oats, barley or rye.

Make Nutty Mayo and set aside to cool. Combine apples, celery, walnuts, sage and any other seasonings in a big bowl.

When the grain is tender, add it to the stuffing. Add the Nutty Mayo and toss to mix. If you need additional liquid, add a little water or apple juice. Stuff a 12–14 pound turkey and roast according to the weight of your bird.

Esther's Favorite Stuffing

Stuffs a 9-pound bird

I don't know Esther, but I think she's onto something with this all-vegetable recipe for stuffing. You can make it early on, when the sage and other traditional ingredients might disagree with you.

2   small onions
2   ribs celery, thinly sliced
1   tablespoon oil (or butter)
2   carrots, peeled and coarsely shredded
2   yams (sweet potatoes), peeled and coarsely shredded
½   cup minced fresh parsley

In a 3-quart saucepan, sauté the onions and celery in oil until golden. Remove from heat and add the carrots, yams and parsley. Toss well, to mix.

Spoon the stuffing into a 9-pound turkey. Or stir in 2 tablespoons of water and put the mixture in an oiled casserole. Bake, covered, in a 350° oven, 45–60 minutes.

Adapted from Esther Tenebaum, *The Allergy Gourmet*, by Carol Rudoff

Oatmeal Stuffing

Serves 6

Oatmeal Stuffing tastes just like old-fashioned bread stuffing! Since you cook everything in preparation, you can serve this stuffing as a side dish to go with broiled chicken or left-over roast turkey.

2   cups rolled oats
2   eggs
2   tablespoons oil
1   clove garlic, pressed
½   cup finely chopped onion
½   cup finely minced celery
Salt and pepper, to taste
2   tablespoons minced fresh parsley
1   teaspoon poultry seasoning
¼–½ teaspoon dried sage, rubbed in your palms
2   cups (or more) chicken broth, skimmed of fat

In a medium-sized bowl, combine the oats and eggs. Stir together until the oats are coated with egg. Set aside to soak for 5 minutes.

In a large skillet, heat the oil until it's hot enough to sauté, and add oats. Toast oats in the oil. Stir and toss often until they are golden brown and in small clumps like ground beef.

Add garlic, onion, celery and seasonings. Cook slowly until the vegetables begin to soften, about 3–5 minutes. Add the chicken broth and simmer until the liquid is absorbed, about 5 minutes.

The dressing should remain moist even when the liquid disappears. Add a little more broth or water if needed. Serve hot.

Adapted from Carol Kremin, *BESTWAYS* Magazine, March 1986

Tenderizing Flavorizing Marinade

You can enhance any meat or poultry by marinating it. With fish though, we usually marinate only the steaks of swordfish, halibut, tuna, shark and other large fish.

Timing varies with tenderness. If you're marinating wild game, it may benefit from 24 hours of soaking. If you're marinating fish, 20 minutes may be enough to enhance it. Experiment, to discover what marinating can do for you. Refrigerate any food that marinates more than half an hour.

1/3   cup fresh lime juice or Make-Believe Vinegar, page 325
2   tablespoons olive or other oil
2   teaspoons dark sesame oil (oriental type)
OPTIONAL ADDITIONS: (choose 1-3)
Freshly ground pepper
1/2 to 1 inch of fresh ginger, peeled, minced and forced
      through a garlic press
1/2 to 1 clove of fresh garlic, pressed
1/4 to 1/2 cup chopped onion
1/16 teaspoon cayenne pepper
6   fresh basil or tarragon leaves, minced

Combine the ingredients in a large bowl that will hold the meat. Usually, you cut the meat and poultry into cubes or strips. But leave fish steaks whole. Turn pieces over several times to coat. Set aside to soak. Refrigerate if needed.

To cook meat or poultry with vegetables in a slow cooker or stove-top for stew, add half of the marinade, and enough water to cover.

To stir-fry meat or poultry, drain it and reserve the marinade. (See Stir-Fry, page 274.)

Broil or grill marinated fish steaks or chicken breasts.

If you want a sweet and sour sauce for your meal, add 3/4 cup of unsweetened (but sweet-tasting) fruit juice to the marinade. Stir in 1 1/2 tablespoons any starch until it dissolves. Heat in a small saucepan. Let it boil 5 minutes. Serve with the food that marinated in it.

Baked "French Fries"

If you have the French-fry cutting disc for your food processor, these "fries" are quick and easy to prepare. While they bake unattended, you can fix the rest of your meal.

Compared to top-of-the-stove deep frying, these are much more carefree—and better for you, too!

3-4 medium baking potatoes
2   tablespoons oil
Salt to taste

Preheat your oven to 400°. Peel and cut the potatoes into French-fry strips. Put the potatoes in your largest mixing bowl (or use a Dutch oven) and dribble the oil over them. Using two spoons or rubber spatulas, toss the potatoes to coat with oil.

Scatter potatoes on a lightly oiled baking sheet in a single layer. Bake 35–45 minutes. Remove from the oven to turn the potatoes with a pancake turner once or twice while baking. Sprinkle lightly with salt as soon as you remove the "fries" from the oven. Use a pancake turner to lift the potatoes to a platter.

Adapted from *Rotational Bon Appetite!*

Potato Pancakes   E

I never had enough patience to shred or grate potatoes to make pancakes until a few years ago when I bought a food processor. Now I can make potato pancakes quickly and easily.

3–4 large potatoes
1   egg
2   tablespoons potato starch
OPTIONAL ADDITIONS:
Pinch of salt
1   small onion, grated
¼   cup chopped bell pepper (green, red, golden)
Handful parsley leaves, minced

Peel and grate or shred potatoes. Beat egg lightly with a fork and add to the potatoes. Stir in starch and mix well.

Preheat a griddle over medium heat. Oil the surface lightly and drop the potato mixture by a tablespoon into mounds. Flatten the cakes with the spoon. Cook until the edges turn brown. Turn once with a spatula.

Adapted from *Rotational Bon Appetite* by Stephanie Hayes, R.D., and Barbara Maynard, R.D. (Published by WJR & Associates, The Environmental Health Center, 8345 Walnut Hill Lane, Suite 205, Dallas, Texas 75231)

Sesame No-Grain "Breading"

Breads about 1 pound

You can make oven-"fried" anything—fish fillets, pieces of chicken, or tofu "cutlets." Prepare enough of the "breading" for one meal, or several. If you multiply the recipe, just use the amount you need to coat your food. Store the rest in the refrigerator. Discard any leftover "breading" that touched your raw meat, fish or poultry.

¹/₄   cup sesame flour*
1   tablespoon sesame seeds
1   tablespoon starch—arrowroot, tapioca, potato or kudzu
¹/₄   teaspoon salt
¹/₈   teaspoon cayenne, optional
2   teaspoons paprika
1-2 teaspoons oil

Combine ingredients in a flat dish and mix well. Rinse the food to be breaded and shake off the excess water, but don't pat dry. Turn the food over several times in the sesame mixture until it's well coated.

Put the coated food on a baking sheet. Dribble oil across the top of the coating. Bake in a hot oven the time needed for your food to cook.

❖ **Here's a guideline to help your timing of fish:** In a 400° ❖
oven, bake fillets 10–15 minutes, depending on the thickness of your fish. Check thin sole and halibut in ten minutes. Ocean perch, which seems to swell in the heat, requires 15 minutes. Snapper and other fillets ¹/₂ inch thick or more require 15 minutes or more.

If you're baking something else in a hotter oven, subtract a little baking time, and put the fish in toward the end of baking. But if you're baking something else in a less-hot oven, wait for the first food to finish, turn up the heat and quickly bake your fish. Prolonged, slower cooking tends to dry out fish.

---

*You can buy sesame flour in most health food stores. Or substitute ground sesame seeds if you wish. I prefer the flour because the manufacturers have removed much of the oil—yielding a product lower in fat.

Garbanzo Bean Spread   L

About 2½ cups

This delightful spread did wonders for a lunch of Snow Pea and Red Pepper Salad, page 203, and Amaranth Crackers, page 170. It's easy to make and satisfying to eat. Think of it as sort of a non-dairy, low-fat "cheese."

Because the beans need to soak overnight, you need to plan your timing. I start the soak at bedtime one evening. Then I make the recipe before or after breakfast, let it simmer unattended until about mid-morning, and chill it until lunch. Leftovers go in the freezer for future lunches or munches.

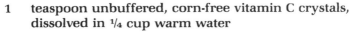

1	cup dry garbanzo beans
½	cup Brazil or other nuts
1	small red pepper
1	teaspoon salt
¼	cup lemon or lime juice
	OR
1	teaspoon unbuffered, corn-free vitamin C crystals, dissolved in ¼ cup warm water
1	cup water

Fresh chives or other herbs of your choice
2–4 tablespoons olive or other oil

Sort the dry beans carefully—*discard* shriveled or moldy-looking beans and the loose halves and fragments of beans. Wash the beans several times in fresh water. Cover them with water two inches above the beans. Boil 5 minutes, then turn the heat off. Let the beans soak overnight.

Drain the soak water and rinse the beans with fresh water. Drain again. Combine all ingredients except the herbs and oil, in a blender or food processor. Process about a minute.

Oil the top pan of a double boiler. Scrape the bean mixture into it and cook, covered, for 1 hour. Stir the spread once or twice. After an hour, remove from heat and stir in the herbs and oil. Taste and adjust seasonings. Pour mixture into a wet bowl and chill.

> ❖ **NOTE:** If you know this is more than you can use, fill a few ❖ small containers (perhaps clean baby food jars) and freeze them as soon as the spread is cooked to prevent mold. It's money in the bank for future quick meals.

❖ VARIATION ❖

Fifteen minutes before the spread will finish cooking, sauté ¹/₂ to 1 cup of onions in the olive oil, until soft but not brown. Stir in 1 clove of garlic, mashed or minced, for the last 3–4 minutes. Mix into the spread very well, to blend the flavors.

Invent new combinations to suit your taste. Improvise with anything you used to add to cream cheese or sour cream.

Adapted from Ken Gerdes, M.D., Denver, Colorado

Spinach Dip

2 ¹/₂ Cups

Serve this dip at a party, where many people will nibble at it—or serve it as a luncheon main course for two. In either case, accompany it with raw vegetables and your choice of homemade crackers or tortillas.

The original recipe called for ¹/₂ cup of mayonnaise—that's ¹/₂ cup of pure fat! And 1¹/₂ cups of low-fat yogurt—a problem if you avoid milk and all dairy products. Substituting "Nutty Mayo" eliminates the dairy problem and cuts the fat in half, too.

1   10-ounce package of frozen chopped spinach, thawed
1   Recipe of "Nutty Mayo," page 208
¹/₂   cup chopped parsley
1   green onion, finely chopped
     OR
3-4 tablespoons fresh chive
OPTIONAL SEASONINGS:
2-3 teaspoons fresh, or ¹/₂ teaspoon dried, oregano or basil
2   tablespoons fresh, or 1¹/₂ tablespoons dried, dill weed

Drain spinach in a strainer. Prepare "Nutty Mayo." Just before mixing, squeeze the liquid out of the spinach. Mix everything together. Cover and refrigerate 30 minutes or more.* Serve the dip with a platter of fresh vegetables or homemade crackers.

Adapted from Janet Lorimer, *BESTWAYS* Magazine

---

*Interestingly, you can enjoy this dip warm, too. I learned this when I made the Nutty Mayo (which was hot) and moved right along into "Spinach Dip." I can imagine the warm dip making a big hit at a winter party.

Fruit Butter

About 7 cups, or 3¹/₂ pints

The water content of fruit varies from one variety of fruit to another and from year to year. So simmering time for fruit butters will vary, too. I either start this project in the morning, when I'll be home to stir occasionally and test when it thickens, or I start it in the evening in a slow-cooking electric pot and let it cook on "low" all night, covered. In the morning I remove the cover, and cook another few hours to thicken, stirring every hour or so.

Don't try fruit butter until you're feeling better and tolerate fresh fruit well. Clearly, as the fruit cooks down and the moisture evaporates, the sweetness of the fruit becomes more concentrated. So go easy! Just figure that 1–2 tablespoons of fruit butter equals a whole fresh apple, peach or pear (or 2–3 plums, a cup of cherries, etc.).

4	quarts peeled apple, peach or pear chunks
4	cups apple or pear juice, or apple cider
1–2	teaspoons cinnamon (to taste)
1	teaspoon allspice
¹/₂	teaspoon powdered cloves
1–3	teaspoons lemon juice
	OR
¹/₄	teaspoon vitamin C crystals, optional

METHOD 1: Combine the fruit and juice in a heavy pot. Cook uncovered, over low heat. Stir, scraping often to prevent scorching. When the fruit is soft, add spices and stir well. If the mixture seems too dry (or starts to stick and scorch on the bottom), add another cup or two of juice or cider. Continue simmering gently, uncovered, until thick enough to spread. See "Note" for test. Taste it. If you want a little more tang (depends on the sweetness of your fruit), stir in the lemon juice.

METHOD 2: Combine the fruit, juice or cider and spices in a slow-cooking electric pot. After a few hours (time isn't critical in slow-cooking) when the fruit is soft, remove the lid. Stir about once an hour for a few hours. When thick, test it as described in the following "Note." Add lemon juice if desired.

> ❖ **NOTES: 1.** An old-fashioned test for doneness: Drop a tea- ❖
> spoon of hot fruit onto a cold plate. Wait one minute. If a ring of

water separates and surrounds the fruit, cook it longer. Stir often to prevent scorching. Retest. It's done when no watery puddle develops in a minute. **2.** To freeze: Ladle the hot fruit into containers. If plastic, secure lids and put in the freezer at once. If glass, place lids on lightly, slightly tipped, and freeze. In 24 hours, screw lids on tightly. **3.** To can: Bring to a boil a teakettle of water and a deep canning kettle, with a rack in the bottom, *half* full of water. Ladle boiling fruit into 3 scalded pint jars and cap tightly with (new) 2-piece, ring-and-disc lids. Place the sealed jars on the rack in the canning kettle. Add boiling water from the teakettle to cover the lids by 1–2 inches. Simmer for 10 minutes. Using tongs, lift jars to a rack to cool. Store at room temperature. **4.** When you can or freeze 3 pints of Fruit Butter, expect to have about another cup left over. Scrape into a small scalded jar and refrigerate. Use within a week to 10 days.

Fresh Fruit Jam

Make only as much of this "jam" as you will use at one meal. (You can't make a lot and preserve it.)

It's a great way to top your bread with fruit—and know how much you're getting. (All-fruit jams in the health food stores are cooked down, concentrated and sweetened with either apple or grape juice concentrate. A few tablespoons may be the equivalent of 10 pieces of fruit!)

CHOOSE ONE:

1   ripe pear, apple, peach or small banana
     OR
2   nectarines, plums or kiwi
     OR
3   small apricots
     OR
½   cup berries, pineapple, mango, pitted bing cherries or
     seedless grapes
Pinch of unbuffered, corn-free vitamin C crystals (omit for
     berries, plums, kiwi, pineapple and cherries)

Clean and prepare the fruit (peel the pear, apple, banana, kiwi, pineapple and mango). Put it in a blender and sprinkle it with vitamin C crystals, except as noted above.

Process with quick on-off technique *once or twice*—STOP! Check the consistency. If should be like applesauce. Over-processing liquefies the fruit, and you end up with a sauce that's too runny for jam.

> ❖ **NOTE:** If you prefer, you can mash ripe banana with a fork and ❖ not use the blender.
> The only fruits I found unsuitable are those with very high water content, such as melons and citrus fruits, or some berries or plums that taste too tart.

Strawberry-Pineapple Jam

This is a "real" jam that you cook, but too low in sugar to can or seal with paraffin. I suggest freezing in small jars.

2   cups strawberries, washed, drained and capped

½ to 1 cup fresh pineapple cut into small pieces or puréed

1   tablespoon starch: arrowroot, tapioca, potato or kudzu

2   tablespoons cool water or pineapple juice

Slice the strawberries thinly into a saucepan. If they're large berries, cut them crosswise, too, to make small pieces. Add the pineapple (see Note). Bring to a boil, reduce heat and simmer uncovered, for about ½ hour.

While the fruit cooks, bring a kettle of water to a boil. Arrange the jars and lids in sink, and pour the boiling water over them. Let them stand full of hot water until you're ready to use.

The fruit mixture thickens slightly as some of the liquid evaporates. Stir it occasionally. Three minutes before it's done, combine the starch and cool water, and add to the boiling fruit, stirring constantly for 3 minutes, as the jam thickens.

Carefully pour the hot water out of the jars (use rubber gloves if you have them, to protect your hands). Immediately spoon the hot jam into the hot jars. Leave ½ inch space in each jar. Place the lids on loosely and let them cool up to an hour.

Put the jars of jam in a freezer. The next day (or 6 hours later) tighten the lids. To use, move a jar into the refrigerator the evening before you want the jam for breakfast.

> ❖ **NOTE:** Pineapple's strong flavor tends to dominate. You need at least ½ cup to sweeten the jam adequately. For a more pronounced pineapple flavor and a little sweeter jam, use up to a cup of it. If you use more than ¾ cup of pineapple, add 1 more teaspoon of starch. ❖

Nut and Seed Butters

Easy—though messy—to prepare, I find the blender does a better job with nut and seed butters than a food processor. By doing the job yourself the variety is limited only to the kinds of nuts and seeds you can find.

- ½ cup raw or roasted nuts (cashews, almonds, Brazil nuts, pine nuts, hazelnuts, pecans, walnuts) or pumpkin or sunflower seeds, unsalted.
- 1–4 teaspoons oil (see Oils, Ingredients and Techniques in Section 3).

Grind the nuts or seeds into a fine meal in blender. Stop to scrape the bottom once or twice. Add 1–2 teaspoons of oil, and continue blending 2 minutes. Check the consistency of your "butter." Add a bit more oil if you want it thinner. (I've even used a little hot water when I didn't want to add any more oil. It was fine.)

Better Butter   Ⓜ

Linseed oil contains an ideal ratio of essential fatty acids—higher in Omega-3s and lower in Omega-6s. Many physicians ask their patients to take some oil each day to help in their recovery.

Too often, however, patients find it distasteful and stop taking it.

This recipe incorporates the flaxseed oil into a buttery spread that is quite pleasant to use. The catch is that butter is a milk product, so this won't be suitable for everyone.

$^1/_4$ - $^1/_2$ cup flaxseed oil, food grade (from a health food store)
$^1/_2$ cup butter, softened

In a small bowl combine the oil and butter with a whisk; refrigerate. Use as a spread or to season cooked vegetables.

DO NOT COOK WITH THIS BETTER BUTTER. Heat destroys the effectiveness of those Omega-3 essential fatty acids.

> ❖ **NOTE:** Start by adding $^1/_4$ cup of flaxseed oil to your butter. ❖
> The next time, make Better Butter with $^1/_3$ cup of oil. Finally, use
> the $^1/_2$ cup of oil. This gives you and your family a chance to get
> used to the flavor of the oil gradually.

Nut Milk

Quick and easy to whip up, you'll find many ways to use this creamy liquid over cereal or in making sauces, soups, "shakes," etc. Nutritionally, nut milk contains fat and lacks the high calcium and protein levels of dairy milk. I don't suggest it for drinking.

Even though the nuts bring a fair amount of fat into Nut Milk, you can adjust the amount of fat it contains by varying the quantity of nuts you use—to make a leaner or richer mixture. Think about the wide range of fat you can select in dairy products—from skim milk to whipping cream. Similarly, I suggest a range for the amount of nuts.

2 tablespoons to $^1/_2$ cup raw nuts—almonds, Brazil nuts,
    cashews, or pine nuts
1   cup water
OPTIONAL ADDITIONS:
$^1/_4$ - $^1/_2$ teaspoon pure vanilla
$^1/_2$ banana or pear, 1 nectarine, or a handful of seedless
    grapes to add sweetness and body

Grind nuts to a fine meal. Add the water and vanilla or a little fruit, if you wish. Blend for one full minute. Stop twice to scrape the packed nuts off the bottom of your blender jar. Store any unused Nut Milk in a scalded glass jar and use within two days.

> ❖ **E-Z SERVE TIP:** If you're making Nut Milk to pour on your ❖
> hot cereal, use hot water—like magic you have warm milk!

Roasted Nuts or Seeds

When you roast your own nuts and seeds, you know what you're getting. Commercial ones are tossed with unspecified oil before roasting—and nuts and seeds are already high-fat foods.

$\frac{1}{2}$ to 1 pound raw nuts or sunflower or pumpkin seeds

Spread nuts or seeds on a cookie sheet and bake at 300° for 12–20 minutes. Smaller nuts, like pine nuts, need less time than giant cashews. They're done when they smell toasty and fragrant, and are lightly tanned—but not burned.

Pineapple-Banana "Milk"

I classify this as a "quickie" item in my bag of tricks. Use it over cereals, puddings or to top plain cake that's become a little dry.

1   ripe banana (with freckles)
2   cups pineapple chunks*
$\frac{1}{4}$ - $\frac{1}{2}$ cup water, or to taste

Break banana into 1-inch pieces. Combine with pineapple in a blender or food processor. Process until liquefied. Add water to make the "milk" as thin or thick as you want it. Refrigerate.

---

*If raw pineapple burns your mouth and tongue, boil the pineapple for 5 minutes. Cool quickly in your freezer. Then proceed as above. It won't burn!

Fruit Sweetener

If you're troubled by molds so much you can't use frozen fruit juice concentrates as sweeteners, you'll treasure this recipe. Start with fresh, well-washed fruit and cook it down to a slightly concentrated, thickened sauce. Freeze promptly in small amounts. No standing around at room temperature, no accumulation of air-borne molds, fungi or yeast.

CHOOSE ONE:

1   fresh, ripe pineapple
    OR
6   sweet, ripe pears
    OR
6   Golden Delicious apples
    OR
1½ pounds sweet, seedless grapes
    OR
2   ripe, fragrant mangoes

Prepare the Fruit:

PINEAPPLE—Quarter the pineapple, lengthwise. Cut parallel to the rough outer edge, leaving about ½ inch of the rind. Leaving the fruit in place, dice it by making 2 lengthwise cuts, then several crosswise cuts about ½ inch apart.

PEARS or APPLES—Peel the pears or apples, core and dice.

GRAPES—Wash well. Discard any grapes with broken skin.

MANGOES—Quarter the mangoes and pull the skin off. Work over a bowl to catch the juices and cut the fruit off the stones. Use a spoon to scrape pulp from the skins.

Purée the diced fruit until it's nearly smooth. Add a pinch of vitamin C crystals to all fruit except pineapple. Transfer to a saucepan. Boil, reduce heat and simmer about half an hour, stirring occasionally, until slightly thickened (like applesauce or honey). Cool for 10 minutes.

Freeze the Fruit in Cubes:

Measure 2 tablespoons into each space of an ice-cube tray. Freeze quickly with freezer turned to coldest setting. When solid, transfer cubes of Fruit Sweetener to container with a tight fitting lid. Store in the coldest corner of your freezer.

> ❖ **NOTES:** Fruit Sweetener is too concentrated to *eat. Use it to* ❖ *sweeten foods,* especially when a recipe calls for fruit concentrate or purée. And experiment!
> Freckled, ripe bananas make a great sweetener, too. Just mash with a fork, or for a more liquid state, purée in a blender—no need to cook them.
> Two cubes = ¼ cup; Four cubes = ½ cup of sweetener.
> Thaw in seconds in a microwave or over low heat in a small pan. See Dessert Chapter for recipes.

Egg Substitutes

Eggs have more than one function—they bind, lighten and raise a product.

Egg substitutes, on the other hand, bind. That means they hold things together, but they don't lighten or raise anything. I don't want you to entertain unrealistic expectations about what you can do with these substitutes.

#1—Use in Place of One Egg

    1   tablespoon flax seeds, whole or ground
    ⅓   cup water

Combine the seeds and water in a small saucepan. Bring to a rolling boil, then remove from heat and allow the seeds to soak until you need them. This mixture thickens and looks like egg white.

Usually, you add this to other liquids in a recipe. If you're using a blender, put Egg Substitute #1 in it, too. Otherwise, whip with a fork to loosen it slightly before mixing into a batter.

#2—Use in Place of One Egg

    ⅓   cup cool water
    1   teaspoon starch—arrowroot, tapioca, potato or kudzu

Combine ingredients in a small saucepan and stir until smooth. Bring to boiling while you stir. As soon as it bubbles and thickens, remove from heat and set aside to cool.

Follow recipe instructions, adding Egg Substitute #2 in place of the egg(s) called for.

#3—Use in Place of One Egg

¼ cup fruit purée

1–3 teaspoons oil

Add both the purée and oil to a recipe instead of an egg.

> ❖ **NOTE:** Neither Egg Substitute #1 or #2 affects flavor. But Egg ❖ Substitute #3 sweetens your end-product slightly. It is most appropriate for muffins, pancakes or other quickbreads.

Ho-Made Baking Powder

Why include this baking powder when I always add the alkaline and acid substances directly into my recipes? Because I want you to have the tools to convert your family's favorite recipes by yourself.

Ho-Made Baking Powder is a single-acting kind. That means it starts acting as soon as you mix the liquid and dry ingredients. So you must have the oven preheated and the pan prepared BEFORE you take that last step—combining the wet and dry ingredients. Then waste no time in popping it into the oven!

1 tablespoon potassium bicarbonate (available from pharmacy)
OR
sodium bicarbonate (baking soda)

2 tablespoons cream of tartar

2 tablespoons starch—arrowroot, tapioca, potato or kudzu*

Mix ingredients very well—either with a whisk or by sifting the mixture a few times. Store in a small, airtight container.

---

*Most kudzu starch that you'll find in health food stores comes in little chunks. Put it in a blender and process for a few seconds before using it in this recipe.

❖ **NOTE:** You may need to use a little more Ho-Made Baking Pow- ❖
der than is called for in a recipe, especially if it's an old recipe
that was designed for double-acting baking powder. Use about
1½ teaspoons per cup of flour.

Adapted from *Cooking For The Health Of It*,
Published by Nutrition For Optimal Health Association,
(Box 380, Winnetka, Illinois 60093)

Creamy Nut Topping

Think of this as a non-dairy "whipped cream"—and use it in any
of the ways you'd use the real thing. It's faintly sweet, smooth and
very creamy. It does wonders for a plain fruit dessert.

½ cup raw cashews or Brazil nuts
½ cup (more or less) puréed seedless grapes,
peeled pear or banana
½ teaspoon pure vanilla

Grind nuts to fine meal in a blender. Add fruit and blend again.
Scrape the bottom with a knife to loosen packed nuts. Process
again for 1 minute. Chill ½ hour or more. Spoon onto any plain
dessert.

Make-Believe Vinegar

Vinegar develops its sharp bite while it's aging. Of course that
means it contains yeasts and molds. While you're fighting candida,
your doctor probably wants you to avoid aged foods—like vinegar.
Try this instead.

I include this recipe to help you adapt some of your own favorite recipes.

½ cup water, room temperature or warm

1 teaspoon unbuffered, corn-free vitamin C crystals

Combine the water and vitamin C crystals in a small jar. Shake or stir to dissolve. Store in a refrigerator and use within a week.

> ❖ **NOTE:** Although all pure ascorbic acid crystals contribute the ❖ same degree of flavor sharpness, I've found a product that dissolves almost instantly. It's "Dull-C" by Freeda Vitamins. Other crystals take a long time, 12–15 minutes, to dissolve, or longer in cold water. See Resources for more information.

Homestyle Baby Food: Cubes of Convenience

First we used grinders, then blenders, now food processors. The equipment may change, but the idea of pureeing food for our babies has been around a long time.

In an overview of mankind, commercially prepared baby food on supermarket shelves is a relatively recent convenience for parents. With that vast selection of readily available baby food, you may choose to buy yours. If so, that's fine. But read those labels and select jars of pure food, with nothing added except water.

When I spent 15 minutes reading baby food labels recently, I was appalled by the high percentage of brands that contain "food starch"—an additive derived from corn. (It thickens and adds body to thin, watery foods.)

Whether your child exhibits signs of allergies or not, if you or other close family members have food allergies, avoid feeding your baby *any* food repeatedly, at every meal—especially those that contain food starch.

Many mothers who have allergies in their families prefer to

make their own baby food. There's very little trick to it. You must add enough water to the cooked vegetables to achieve the desired mushy/liquid consistency. Problems arise with the mess of purée-ing a tiny bit of food, often, for one or two feedings. Besides the constant mess, we must also face the issue of finding the time to do it.

Baby's first food is usually thin rice cereal, followed by strained (or at least puréed/liquefied) vegetables and fruits, thinned with water. If you're processing cooked carrots, for example, just add a little of the cooking water to produce the desired consistency—initially a thin mush. Later, gradually reduce the liquid, to make a medium consistency. "Junior foods" are still mushy, but they retain small bits and pieces of food.

So far, making baby food sounds like a lot of messy work. I know you're asking, "How can I reduce the work, mess and time commitment—and still feed my baby well?" Your secret weapon is an ice-cube tray!

Ice-cube trays average 16 cubes, and each cube holds 2 tablespoons of purée. Two cups of purée will fill one tray. The purée freezes in a few hours or overnight. Remove the cubes from the tray and store them in your freezer in jars, or a canister or bag that closes tightly.

That's it! You've made your own convenient baby food! In one "mess" you've made enough for 16 (or 8) feedings. If you repeat the process a few times, you'll have a varied assortment of prepared foods to offer your baby.

To use a cube of frozen baby food, warm in a small saucepan or "zap" it for a few seconds in a microwave oven. As Baby grows, you simply use two or more cubes to satisfy his growing appetite—with no waste, no messy kitchen, and no more time than it takes to open a jar from the store.

Prepare a quantity of any food you're cooking. Use vegetables from your garden, or take advantage of a good buy on organic pro-duce. Blend turkey or roast leftovers with a bit of broth (*not* the greasy drippings) and freeze them for your baby. Skip the salt. You're only limited by your imagination and freezer space.

Fruits

You can purée fruits and freeze them in cubes, too, but they require special handling. When you purée the fruit, add a pinch of vitamin C crystals (pure ascorbic acid, corn-free) to prevent discoloration. And cover the ice cube tray with foil while the fruit freezes. Store the cubes in a labeled jar with a tight-fitting lid.

In my experiments, I froze the raw purée of bananas and ripe pears separately. I also poured some of the pear purée in a saucepan and simmered it for 5 minutes. Initially, both batches seemed equally acceptable. But in three weeks, the enzymes in the raw fruit caused those cubes to start getting mushy.

Bottom line: If you wish to store fruit for more than 3 weeks, simmer it for 5 minutes to inactivate the enzymes.

Are there any fruits I wouldn't cook? Yes, I think banana, papaya, mango, watermelon, honeydew and cantaloupe lose their identity. I'd just freeze them raw and plan to use them soon. Citrus is another kind of fruit I don't cook. Heat destroys the vitamin C. Citrus is so widely available that you can buy the fruit most any time of year.

What about juices for Baby? John Gerrard, M.D., of Saskatoon, Canada, prefers not to fill Baby's tummy with juices. He suggests waiting until Baby can gnaw on a section of the fresh orange or a wedge of peeled pear, apple, or banana rather than relying heavily on juices. He also says, in effect, "Teach Baby to drink water between feedings. This helps him not to expect something sweet all the time, is better for his teeth and encourages a healthy acceptance of vegetables to satisfy his hunger."

In keeping with Dr. Gerrard's suggestion to skip juices and give Baby the whole, raw fruit, you can feed him scraped raw apple even before he can handle a piece of the fruit.

Just quarter and core a ripe apple (avoid hard, unripe fruit). Draw the edge of a spoon across the cut surface, picking up "scraped" apple. Since you scrape a bite at a time, the fruit doesn't turn brown. When Baby is ready to handle chunky food, offer a small, peeled wedge of apple and other fruits.

❖ SAFETY TIPS ❖

- Ask a physician who knows your child to help you decide *when* to offer chunks of raw fruit.

- *Never* leave an eating or gnawing baby unattended.

❖ EQUIPMENT ❖

Besides standard sizes of food processors, we now find a "second generation" of scaled-down, mini-processors, cloned after Sunbeam's Little Oskar. Powerful, efficient, and easier to clean than the larger models, they're perfect for handling small amounts of food. I prefer my blender or any of the "minis" for making baby food.

> ❖ **NOTE:** You can apply the technique of freezing small amounts ❖ of liquid in an ice-cube tray to other things as well. An example is stock or broth, something many of us have been freezing for years. I've learned to add a couple of those handy cubes of flavor to many dishes—especially oriental stir-fries and sauces. For another application of this idea, see Fruit Sweetener, page 322.

Stevia Tea

To use stevia for an herbal sweetener, combine ⅛–½ teaspoon of stevia powder with the amount of warm water needed for a recipe (¼–2 cups). Set aside to disolve. Use this "tea" with no other sweetener for sweet-tasting pancakes, waffles, muffins, or nut breads.

See Sesame Seed Pancakes, and Nicole Walker's Book, *Sugar-Free Cooking*, in the Recommended Reading Section.

SECTION 3

Other Helpful Information

Meal Planning for the Person Who Isn't Improving

Even though your health problems are yeast-connected, if you aren't improving, you should be carefully reexamined and reevaluated by your physician (see pages 110 of this book and pages 303-304 of *The Yeast Connection*).

Some people who fail to improve are bothered by allergies to many different foods. Although we discuss these allergies in Sections 1 and 2 of this book, we felt that many of our readers needed more complete and comprehensive instructions.

To overcome present food allergies and lessen your chances of developing new ones, you'll need to:

1. Avoid foods you're sensitive to for weeks or months before trying them again.
2. Broaden and diversify your food choices as widely as possible.
3. Follow a four-day rotated diet.

The pages that follow include:

1. General comments and suggestions.
2. A master list of foods to choose from.
3. Menu suggestions for each meal.

General Comments and Suggestions

In rotating your diet, you'll need to remember that foods belong to different "families." For example, the grain family includes wheat, corn, rice and other grains; the legume family includes peanuts, lentils, tofu and many other peas and beans.

To help you plan your four-day rotated diet, we've given you many different choices. For example, for your evening (or main) meal, you can choose a vegetarian, poultry, fish or meat menu. We also provide a number of different breakfasts and lunch ideas.

Rotating your diet may seem complicated until you get the hang of it. And to help you, we've provided a *Master List of Foods* to choose from for each of the four days. Using this list should make your job easier.

As you'll see when you examine it, no food is repeated on any of the four days. Moreover, foods which belong to the same food family aren't listed on consecutive days. For example, green beans and other legumes are listed on Day #1 and lentils on Day #3, with no legumes recommended for Day #2 and Day #4.

Here's another way you can use the food lists. Let's suppose you had planned to have broccoli. But when you shop for Day #2, the only broccoli you find looks wilted and brown. If the kale looks bright and green or the cauliflower looks fresh, firm and heavy, choose one of those vegetables instead of the broccoli. But do not "borrow" from the other days' lists of foods.

You can substitute without breaking your pattern of rotation by running your finger vertically up and down the list for that day and choose another food from the same list. (Of course your choices may be dictated by your available time, the ingredients you have in your house, what you like or dislike, as well as the tastes and desires of your family.)

By planning your menus and shopping for several days, you'll find your meal preparation goes more smoothly. Trouble? Yes. But many people have found it's worthwhile. Diets aren't forever, and as you improve, you may be able to gradually relax.

Comments About the Master List of Foods

1. Because allergies to milk, wheat and corn occur so frequently in people with CRC, we did not include them in our food list or suggested menus. However, if you've tested these foods and they do not cause symptoms, you can rotate them into your diet (Corn on Day #2; Wheat on Day #4). Moreover, some people who react to other milk products, tolerate sugar-free yogurt.

2. Keep a symptom diary during the first several weeks of your rotated diet. If you notice symptoms on a particular day or after a certain meal, you'll need to do further detective work. *Anything you eat can disagree with you,* including grains or grain substitutes, oils, nuts, fish, fowl or vegetables.

3. We did not include alcoholic beverages, because most of them contain sugar and yeast and are derived from grains. Later on, if you aren't potato sensitive, you might be able to tolerate imported vodka. (Domestic vodka is usually made from grains.)

Master List of Foods to Choose From

(See **Notes on Use** that follow the lists)

DAY 1	DAY 2	DAY 3	DAY 4
Proteins/Meat/Fish/Fowl			
pheasant	duck/duck egg	chicken	turkey
Cornish hen	scrod/cod	orange roughy	salmon
sole	monkfish	flounder	grouper
sardines	butterfish	whitefish	black sea bass
tuna	bluefish	halibut	trout
turbot	pike	shrimp	shark
scallops, crab	catfish	lobster	beef/veal
venison	goat milk	pork	milk/yogurt
egg (chicken)	lamb		
rabbit/wild game			
Flours and Cereals			
amaranth	oats, teff, rye, milo	quinoa	barley, millet,
arrowroot	buckwheat	kudzu starch	rice, wild rice
bean flours			tapioca starch
poi, dehydrated			
Nuts and Seeds			
pumpkin seed	almond	sesame seed	Brazil nut
flax & anise seed	pecan	pine nut	walnut
cashews	chia seed	macadamia nut	poppy seed
carob powder	coconut	chestnuts, all	filbert
peanuts	sunflower seed	kinds	
Oils			
olive oil	almond oil	sesame oil	avocado oil
flaxseed oil	sunflower oil	safflower oil	walnut oil
soy oil			canola oil
Sweeteners			
grape juice	puréed nectarine	apple juice,	stevia (herb)
puréed pear	pineapple juice	unsweetened	puréed peach
pear juice	mashed banana	aguamiel	
Vegetables			
carrot	broccoli	fennel	cabbages, all
parsnip	cauliflower	celery/celery root	rutabaga
parsley	bok choy	pea, green/dried	collards
onion, scallion	kale	lentils	brussels sprouts
garlic	mushrooms	shallot/chive	turnip & greens
asparagus	cress	leek	kohlrabi

DAY 1	DAY 2	DAY 3	DAY 4

Vegetables (continued)

DAY 1	DAY 2	DAY 3	DAY 4
hard-shell squash pumpkin, etc.	artichoke, Jerusalem	artichoke, globe	bamboo shoots
cucumber	sweet potato	summer squash	breadfruit
bean, green/dried	radish	zucchini	jicama
sweet bell pepper	okra	eggplant	New Zealand
hot peppers		white potato	spinach
tomato		lettuces, all	boniato
spinach		beets & greens	
		Swiss chard	

Fruit

DAY 1	DAY 2	DAY 3	DAY 4
grape/raisins	pineapple	apple	plantain
currants	nectarine	papaya	plum
canteloupe	cherry	kiwi	peach
honeydew	persimmon	watermelon &	apricot
mango	banana	variety melons	avocado
pear	rhubarb	fresh fig	grapefruit
blackberry	lemon	gooseberry	lime
cranberry	orange	strawberry	ugly fruit
raspberry	tangerine	blueberry	cherimoya
boysenberry		pomegranate	prune

Condiments

DAY 1	DAY 2	DAY 3	DAY 4
dill	turmeric	cumin	mace
lovage	cardamom	coriander	ginger
fennel	clove	caraway	bay leaf
basil	cinnamon	marjoram	mustard
oregano	nutmeg	thyme	horseradish
sage	peppercorns	mint	allspice
savory	black & white	rosemary	
chervil		celery seed	
vanilla		peppermint	
anise		fenugreek	
cream of tartar		cayenne pepper	
gums: guar, acacia		paprika	
parsley		tarragon	
olive		pimiento	

Beverages

DAY 1	DAY 2	DAY 3	DAY 4
rose hips tea	Decopa	chamomile tea	comfrey tea
rasberry leaf tea	almond milk	mint tea	black/green tea
cashew milk		peppermint tea	Brazil nut milk
coffee		macadamia milk	

Please Note: It is best to avoid all alcoholic beverages, at least initially. No beer or other fermented ales are permitted—they're derived from grains and contain sugar and brewer's yeast. For example, whiskey comes from corn, etc. After a while, when your health is stable, perhaps you'd tolerate a little imported vodka, which isn't very sweet and comes from pota-toes. But check with your doctor first.

NOTES ON USING THE MASTER LIST OF FOODS

1. After you've finished your elimination diet you should know some of the foods that bother you. Cross them out of this Master List of Foods—now it's customized to your needs.
2. Start following a rotation diet of your permitted foods.
3. After you've gone through a few rotations, you may notice symptoms following a certain meal. If this happens, eliminate those foods that you suspect and retest yourself. (The problem might be anything—an oil, nut, seed, meat, fish, fowl, vegetable or fruit.)
4. When you're feeling better reintroduce *one* eliminated food. If it now agrees with you, add it to your Master List.
5. Continue monitoring your foods: testing, omitting, adding back.

Breakfast Ideas

Capitalized entries are either recipes in this book or commercially available products.

DAY 1	DAY 2	DAY 3	DAY 4
Breakfast Protein Choices			
hard-boiled eggs	lamb chop	pork chop	Turkey Sausage
Cereal or Breakfast Pudding Choices for Each Day*			
Amaranth Porridge	oatmeal or Oat Porridge	Quinoa Porridge	cooked rice cereals: Quick
Carob Crunch Cereal	Cream of Rye®	Quinoa Breakfast Pudding	'N Creamy®
Alagría	Cream of Buckwheat®	Quinoa Nutri-Ola	Rice & Shine® and others
	Oat Granola		brown rice
	teff cereal		Breakfast Pudding
			Millet-Peach Pudding
Serve Cereals with Appropriate "Milk"			
cashew Nut Milk	goat's milk	macadamia or	cow's milk
grape or pear juice	almond Nut milk	pine Nut milk	Brazil Nut Milk
	Pineapple-Banana Milk		

DAY 1	DAY 2	DAY 3	DAY 4

Pancake or Waffle Choices for Each Day*

DAY 1	DAY 2	DAY 3	DAY 4
Amaranth Pancakes Amaranth Waffles 3-Seed Pancakes	Buckwheat Pancakes Carob-Buckwheat Waffles Oat Waffles oat, or rye pancakes	Quinoa Pancakes Quinoa Waffles	Rice Pancakes Fried Mush (millet) barley pancakes (substitute barley for buckwheat in Buckwheat Pancakes)

Flatbreads or Other Breads for Each Day*

DAY 1	DAY 2	DAY 3	DAY 4
E-Z Tortillas w/amaranth flour Country "Corn" Bread** Amaranth Soda Bread Amaranth Muffin	E-Z Tortillas w/buckwheat, milo, rye or oat flour Buckwheat Banana Bread Buckwheat or Rye Soda Bread Country "Corn" Bread** w/any flour listed above	E-Z Tortillas w/quinoa flour Country "Corn" Bread** Quinoa Apple-sauce Bread Quinoa Sesame Bread	E-Z Tortillas w/barley or millet flour Country "Corn" Bread**

Fruit, Fruit Topping and Jams for Each Day

DAY 1	DAY 2	DAY 3	DAY 4
Topping: purée a ripe pear and mix into berries for "saucey" consistency OR Fresh Fruit Jam w/pears or mix strawberries and pears OR any Day 1 fruit	Topping: puréed pineapple using a little juice OR Fresh Fruit Jam w/mashed banana or pineapple (drained) or nectarine OR any fruit from Day 2 list	Topping: Add applesauce to raspberries or blueberries (hot or cold) OR Fresh Fruit Jam w/blend of fig, kiwi and apple OR any Day 3 fruit	Topping: Fresh Fruit Jam w/plums, peach or apricots OR any fruit from Day 4 list

Nuts for Each Day—To Top Cereal or Fruit

DAY 1	DAY 2	DAY 3	DAY 4
cashews	almonds pecans	pine nuts macadamia nuts	Brazil nuts walnuts filberts

*If you're sensitive to all grains and grain substitutes, choose a lunch selection for breakfast. Or try a chop and sweet potato, meat pattie with vegetables or a fish-vegetable chowder.
**These "corn" breads don't contain corn but are made with other flours, in a pan like cornbread.

Lunch Suggestions

(Keep portions of poultry, meat or fish small to medium. Remember . . . this is a high-vegetable diet!)

DAY 1	DAY 2	DAY 3	DAY 4

Breads

Prepare flatbread, muffins or crackers from a flour for each day. Bake double batches, so you can stock your freezer. Label them clearly.

Salad Ideas for Each Day

(Dress with "oil of the day" and Make-Believe Vinegar)

DAY 1	DAY 2	DAY 3	DAY 4
tomato stuffed w/shredded carrot, onion, tuna fish or boiled egg and minced parsley (if you have leftover cornish hen or pheasant, use bits of that for the protein food)	Spinach Salad w/sliced radishes, broccoli, cauliflower, mushrooms & cold cooked duck, fish or goat cheese	tossed salad of romaine lettuce, zucchini, peas, celery and cold cooked chicken. "C" Salad Dressing (Sauté leeks & let cool, add to salad for oniony taste)	cole slaw of shredded cabbage, and small turnip or kohlrabi. Top w/Avocado-Grapefruit Dressing. Cold turkey or fish, optional

Hearty Soups or Stews for Each Day

(travel well in thermos bottle; eat with raw veggies for a little crunch)

DAY 1	DAY 2	DAY 3	DAY 4
bean soup w/ onion, garlic, bell pepper, spinach, parsley (half of liquid may be tomato juice) raw carrots	lamb stew w/mushrooms, sweet potato and kale leaves raw or steamed broccoli	chicken soup w/stock, celery root, potatoes, leek, chard & zucchini (or split pea soup) raw celery	beef or turkey soup w/stock, barley, cooked rutabaga, and shredded cabbage (for crunch add bamboo shoots)

Hot Plate Ideas for Each Day

DAY 1	DAY 2	DAY 3	DAY 4
broiled bluefish or sole baked butternut squash steamed asparagus tomato & cucumber slices (stuff the squash with sautéed diced onion if you wish)	stir-fry of broccoli & cauliflower, bok choy or kale over baked sweet potato (add a few ounces of cooked duck, fish or lamb if you wish)	broiled halibut potato summer squash (if you wish, sauté celery w/celery leaves & leeks to top the potato)	broiled salmon wedge of lemon brown or wild rice brussels sprouts mashed rutabaga

DAY 1	DAY 2	DAY 3	DAY 4
Pasta of the Day—Top with Stir-fry Veggies of Day			
oriental mung bean thread noodles[1]	buckwheat Soba noodles[1,2]	potato and kudzu starch noodles[1,2]	regular wheat spaghetti, noodles and macaroni Rice Sticks[1]

[1]Shop for these pastas in an oriental market or in the oriental section of your supermarket.
[2]Shop for these pastas in a health food store.

Supper/Dinner

(Remember, easy on the protein and heavy on the veggies)

DAY 1	DAY 2	DAY 3	DAY 4
Fish Meal Suggestions for Each Day			
baked or broiled sole or poached scallops steamed carrots asparagus cucumber sticks	baked butterfish sautéed mushrooms baked sweet potato steamed kale radishes	broiled halibut baked potato steamed beets and greens summer squash, steamed celery sticks	baked black sea bass brown rice steamed nappa cabbage raw kohlrabi sticks
Poultry Meal Suggestions for Each Day			
roast Cornish hen baked acorn squash steamed spinach (optional: sauté a large, sweet onion and serve in the squash) red pepper sticks	roast duck baked sweet potato steamed broccoli Jerusalem artichokes (raw or sautéed)	roast chicken leek, fennel, zucchini & peas (steam or stir-fry) lettuce w/"C" Salad Dressing	roast turkey wild rice and brown rice steamed turnip and greens raw cabbage wedges

DAY 1	DAY 2	DAY 3	DAY 4

Meat Meal Suggestions for Each Day

DAY 1	DAY 2	DAY 3	DAY 4
rabbit (prepare like chicken) mashed parsnip & carrots steamed asparagus tomato & cucumber slices	roast lamb cauliflower & broccoli stir-fry Oat Bran Muffin radishes	roast pork or pork chop Oven French Fries sautéed shallot, celery and zucchini zucchini & celery sticks	beef or veal patty or roast (lean) breadfruit rutabaga, steamed brussel sprouts

Vegetarian Meal Suggestions for Each Day

DAY 1	DAY 2	DAY 3	DAY 4
amaranth tortilla mashed pinto beans sautéed onions and garlic chopped spinach salsa of chopped tomato and a hot pepper (optional: shredded soy cheese on top) carrot sticks scallions	barley-veggie casserole w/sweet potato & bok choy sautéed mushrooms and almonds or sunflower seeds radishes (goat cheese, optional)	lentil/veggie stew w/celery root & leaves, potato, fennel, eggplant, leek & Swiss chard leaves Cooked Quinoa lettuce with "C" Salad Dressing	brown rice & wild rice sautéed New Zealand spinach steamed collards diced peach (plain yogurt over peach, optional) diced avocado

Desserts or Afternoon Snacks

Include these treats in small amounts in your diet only when you've improved and tolerate them.

ALL DAYS—Crackers made with appropriate flour for each day.
Nuts that are listed for each day

DAY 1	DAY 2	DAY 3	DAY 4
amaranth muffin canteloupe or honeydew part of a mango No-Flour Fudge Brownies Squash Pudding	Banana Oat cookies persimmon tangerine cherries Oat Bran Muffin	Raspberry Delight fresh fig pomegranate watermelon & variety melons Quinoa Applesauce Bread	cherimoya plum

NOTE: For maximum variety choose different combinations of foods each time you go through a rotation. In other words, avoid latching onto a few "favorite meals." It's important to try the less familiar options, too.

Shopping Tips

Clean out your cupboards and refrigerator and inventory your freezer. You'll feel better about buying new foods if they have a place to go.

Glance through the chapter "What to Eat and Drink, and What to Avoid" in Section 1, the "Vegetable" chapter in Section 2, and the chapter "Ingredients and Techniques" in this section.

If you want to make a game of introducing new foods, try this idea from Leslie Peickert-Kroker, R.N. Select one new food a week. Prepare it a couple of different ways. Incorporate it into your menus. At the end of a year, you'll have 52 new foods to spark your menus!

Staples—Stock Up and Save Time

Buying in large quantities can save you time and money. But don't do it until you're certain you like a particular food and it doesn't trigger your symptoms.

You'll have to go to a health food store or specialty shop to obtain most of the items on this list. However, you may be able to find a few items in ethnic food markets, specialty sections of a supermarket or at a co-op. Items that you like, but can't find, you may be able to order by mail. (See Foods Sources in this section).

SHOPPING LIST

STAPLES	COMMENTS
Whole Grains rice, rye berries, oats, barley, millet, wild rice	Store in a dry place at room temperature. Store whole grain flours tightly packaged in refrigerator or freezer.
Non-grain alternatives amaranth, quinoa, buckwheat teff	Store whole buckwheat groats at room temperature. Keep amaranth, quinoa, and teff in refrigerator.
Dry vegetables Beans, split peas, peas and lentils	Store at room temperature.

STAPLES (cont'd)	COMMENTS
Pasta	
Soba noodles, bean thread noodles	Soba: only 100% buckwheat kind
Starches	
Arrowroot, tapioca starch flour, potato flour, kudzu	Store in refrigerator.
Oils	
Flaxseed, olive, walnut, safflower, canola, corn, peanut, soy, sunflower, avocado, sesame	Refrigerate after opening. See page 349.
Seeds and Nuts	
Walnut, sunflower, pecan, almond, filbert, pumpkin, cashews, sesame, pine nuts	Buy fresh, raw. Refrigerate or store in freezer. Eat raw or roast lightly at 300° 15–30 minutes.
Canned Goods	
Tuna, water packed	Cans available in supermarkets. Glass jars available in health food stores.
Miscellaneous	
Sea or Kosher Salt, Spices	Purchase items with no additives.

PERISHABLES	COMMENTS
Vegetables	See vegetable chapter for buying and storage tips. Choose a wide variety.
Fish—fresh or frozen	Choose cold-water, ocean fish when possible. Use many different kinds.
Poultry—fresh or frozen	Buy organic, range fed. Cook thoroughly.
Meat—fresh or frozen	Organic, free-range, when available.
Fruits	Buy limited quantities of a wide selection.

Ingredients and Techniques

Aguamiel: A natural sweetener from maguey cactus plants. Thick, dark and with a distinctive flavor. It may remind you of molasses. A concentrated sweet—a tablespoon or two will suffice for a whole recipe. Coming from cactus, it's less apt to cause allergies. Because it's a simple carbohydrate, wait until you feel better to try it.

Amaranth: * A gluten-free grain-like food that isn't a grain. You'll like its grainy, nutty flavor. Nourishing—high in lysine and other proteins, fiber, iron, calcium and other minerals.

Cook whole seeds into hot cereal (see Amaranth Porridge in the Breakfast chapter) or buy the flour for baking. Amaranth seeds are too hard and difficult to grind at home—they dance above the blades of a blender and slide right through the grinding attachment of a Champion juicier. Two exceptions: the Vita Mix and Magic Mill both do a fine job of grinding amaranth flour at home. (There may be others.)

Buy the flour, preferably kept under refrigeration, from a health food store; flour that remains on a shelf too long may become rancid and you'll notice a strong unpleasant odor and flavor. If you can't find a fresh source, order your flour direct from a grower and refrigerate as soon as it arrives.

Amaranth leaves are also edible and nourishing. You can grow amaranth and eat its foliage like spinach. Strip the leaves from the stalk and steam for 10 minutes. In about 2 weeks, these amazing plants will replenish the foliage you remove.

Barley and Barley Flour*: This grain has served as an important source of nourishing food for many thousands of years. It was the chief grain used for bread by the Greeks, Romans and Hebrews and is still an important food source for the Chinese and Japanese.

Whole, hulled barley is more nutritious than "pearled" barley. Plenty of protein and fiber and little fat and sodium. Also, generous amounts of B vitamins and potassium.

---

*For a superb, comprehensive, easy-to-read discussion of grains and grain alternatives, see *Jane Brody's Good Food Book* (Bantam) pages 38–77, 1985, or *The Allergy Self-Help Cookbook* by Marjorie Hurt Jones (Rodale), pages 4–12, 1984.

Whole brown barley and barley flour are available in health food stores. The flour is light in color and texture. Easy to work with—almost like all-purpose white flour. Since barley contains gluten and is related to wheat, it can cause problems in people who react to wheat—especially if consumed every day.

Beans: If you experience difficulty digesting beans, try soaking and cooking dried beans, as detailed on page 234. However, if canned beans don't bother you, read labels carefully and select brands (especially Mexican style) with the fewest additives. They can be rinsed and drained under running water to eliminate excess salt. Organic canned beans available in health food stores.

Blanch: Usually a prerequisite for freezing vegetables. Its purpose is to inactivate enzymes. Plunge raw vegetables into boiling water for 1 to 3 minutes. Immediately place them into icy water to keep them from cooking. After blanching, chill, drain, package and freeze. See also FREEZING.

Buckwheat: Another gluten-free grain-like food that isn't a grain. Related to rhubarb. Contains high quality protein, fiber and minerals. Use the natural unroasted groats to make 100% buckwheat pancakes, waffles, crackers or breads, which yield a mild and pleasant flavor. Using a blender, grind the groats into flour, $1/2$ cup at a time.

You also may be able to find buckwheat Soba noodles in an Oriental market or section of a supermarket. Buckwheat makes a great pasta if you have to avoid wheat or eggs.

Precautions: Read labels carefully, since many commercial Soba noodles include wheat flour. Also, baked goods and "buckwheat pancakes" on restaurant menus usually contain wheat.

Butters, Fruit: Like applebutter, they never contain dairy products. Most commercial fruit butters are sweetened with sugar or honey and should be excluded from a candida diet. For instructions for making your own with fresh fruit juice, see "Fruit Butter," page 316.

Butters, Nut and Seed: You'll find cashew, almond, sunflower and other nut butters in health food stores. Or you can make butters at home from any raw or roasted nuts or seeds. See also Nut and Seed Butters, pages 319.

Eggs: Even unbroken, Grade A eggs can be contaminated with salmonella bacteria. And these bacteria can cause serious illnesses. For this reason we omit homemade mayonnaise made with raw eggs.

According to a report in the October 1988 *Nutrition Action Healthletter,* "Researchers suspect that the salmonella may have contaminated the hens' ovaries which housed the yolks before they were surrounded by the shells.

"*Thorough cooking destroys salmonella,* so until the Contaminated Egg Caper is solved, the CDC (Center for Disease Control) recommends:

"Avoid Caesar salad dressing, hollandaise sauce, egg nog, homemade ice cream or any other food made with raw or undercooked eggs.

"Boil an egg for 7 minutes, poach for 5 minutes or fry on each side for 3 minutes to kill the bacteria.

"Forget 'sunny side up' (not turned) eggs."

Dairy Products: Use in small amounts if you tolerate them. Plain, unflavored, low-fat yogurt with live cultures is best nutritionally. Goat's milk, yogurt and cheese are also good and more digestible than cow's.

Flatbreads: If you must avoid wheat, gluten or yeast, try flatbreads. All ancient civilizations produced their own version, including tortillas, chapatis and "Bible Bread." You can use amaranth, buckwheat, quinoa and all the less common grains. They're easy to prepare. See "E-Z Tortillas" in Bread chapter.

Food Cutting: The way a food is cut will influence your cooking time and the outcome of your recipe. Here are some guidelines:

Slice: to cut across food, producing sizes ranging from paper thin to ½ inch pieces. Sliced carrots look like "pennies."

Dice: after slicing, cut at right angles to produce cubes.

Grate: rubbing a firm food across a grater to produce a powdery or coarse substance, depending on the size desired.

Shred: using a shredder or knife to cut in very thin pieces, such as cabbage, carrots or cheese.

Julienne: to cut in long thin strips, such as meats and cheese atop a Chef's salad.

Purée: to force a food through a strainer, producing a thick, almost liquid, substance. Blenders and food processors accomplish this with ease (without the strainer).

Freezing: Helps you save and preserve many foods, including leftovers, fresh vegetables, fruits and nuts. Here are suggestions:
Leftovers: 1. Store in glass freezer jars. 2. Label and date jars

clearly. 3. Leave empty space in the top for expansion. 4. Leave the lids loose until the food freezes solid. Tighten the lids later.

Fresh Vegetables: 1. Freeze only fresh, top-quality produce (wilted or tough vegetables won't improve in your freezer!) 2. Wash thoroughly and blanch before freezing. 3. Drain to eliminate excessive moisture. 4. Package for the freezer.

Fresh fruits: You'll need frozen fruits for the "All-fruit Sorbet #1" recipes (see Desserts). Put them in the freezer in the morning and use them that evening or in a day or two.

Other suggestions: You can make banana "popsicles" for your children or cut bananas into 1-inch pieces. You can also freeze nectarines, plums, peaches, berries or grapes. Use them within 4 to 6 weeks.

Although many people recommend putting fruits up with sugar, sugar-free fruits will keep for weeks to months without deteriorating much.

Gluten: Wheat, spelt, kamut, and rye contain more gluten than other flours, while oats and barley contain less. Yeast breads require gluten to rise. It makes the dough elastic and spongy and traps tiny air bubbles in the dough. The result is a "leavened" bread. See "Flatbreads" for gluten-free alternatives.

Grind: You can grind nuts and seeds in a blender, 1/3 cup at a time. If a recipe calls for ground nuts and a starch, such as arrowroot, tapioca or kudzu, you can add the starch to the nuts. It will help absorb the oil and produce a finer flour-like nut meal.

Guar Gum: See "Gums."

Gums: Add guar and/or other gums to frozen desserts. They provide fiber, promote a smooth, soft texture and keep ice crystals from forming.

You can also experiment with small amounts of gums when you're making a batch of muffins (no more than 1/4 to 1/2 teaspoon to a cup of flour in the recipe). Gums help non-gluten baked goods rise, hold moisture and promote smoothness.

Although using a little gum in your muffin recipes usually works out okay, putting them in your bread recipes is tricky. The center of the loaf may never get done and may end up looking like pudding. Not recommended without a special recipe.

Herbs: Herbs are derived from aromatic plants. The leaves, stems or blossoms are used fresh, dried, crushed or ground. Initially, you should eat foods plain and ungarnished. Later, your sensitivity can be tested by generously sprinkling a single herb over a food you tolerate. Example: Chopped, fresh basil over cooked zucchini.

Since they are derived from plants, they contain minerals, vitamins and other nutrients. They can also harbor molds and yeasts. Dried herbs are more apt to contain molds. Buying fresh, or raising your own is safer. Typical examples are parsley, mint, chives, dill, bay leaves or thyme.

Jelly Roll Pan: Similar to a cookie sheet, however to prevent spilling, it has four sides and is approximately 1 inch deep.

Meats, Fish and Poultry: Many markets now offer organically grown beef, range-fed and free of antibiotics. Some health food stores sell organic chickens and turkey, possibly fish or meat. Always check labels for additives. If you don't tolerate common foods, look for wild game and check the "Food Sources" in this Section.

Microwave: Excellent for defrosting and reheating. Many recipes can be adapted for microwave cooking by checking the owner's manual.

Millet: A nourishing, ancient grain popular in Asia and Africa. It looks like rounded sesame seeds and contains as much or more protein than rice, corn or oats. It also contains B vitamins, iron, manganese, and other minerals. Tolerated by some people who react to wheat or other grains.

A number of forms of millet are available in health food stores including, millet meal, millet flour, puffed millet and whole hull millet groats. You can use the millet meal and flour in baking, eat the puffed millet like other dry cereals and you can cook the groats like rice. See "Basic Millet" or "Millet Peach Pudding" in the Breakfast Recipes section.

Milo: This grain is the flour of the sorghum plant, used mainly for cattle feed in the United States. Widely used by people of the third world to make pancakes or mush. According to Jane Brody, milo is "comparable to other grains, adequate enough nutritionally to be a dietary staple for more than 300,000,000 people in the world today."

Like millet, milo can add diversity to your diet. Hard to locate but is available in many health food stores. Use up to one third of flour in baking.

Oats: Oat bran and other oat products are currently popular because of their properties which promote good health. Whole grain oats contain lots of vitamins and minerals, superior quality protein and a soluble fiber which helps lower cholesterol. Oat products are available in all food stores.

Oat Flour: Available in health food stores or you can grind rolled oats in your blender and make your own. Commercial varieties may be slightly finer, but both work well.

Oils: During the decade of the '80s, and more especially during 1988 and 1989, we've all learned that high-fat diets, especially animal fats, are harmful. Also, some of the tropical oils aren't good for you. Yet, you'll need oils in preparing some of your recipes. Here are our comments and recommendations:

1. Choose cold-pressed or expeller-pressed vegetable oils. The oil is extracted from seeds and nuts using pressure and not subjected to high heat. Many authorities feel that such oils are better for you.
2. Avoid frying and prolonged heating of oils to high temperatures during cooking. Where possible, add oils to the recipe after cooking is completed, or as a salad dressing.
3. Recommended oils include olive, flaxseed, corn, canola, soy, sunflower, safflower, sesame, walnut, almond, and avocado.
4. Rotate or diversify your oils.
5. Coordinate the oil with other ingredients. Example: If you're using sunflower seeds in your recipe, use sunflower oil. Or use walnuts and walnut oil together.
6. Suggested oils for stir-frying: peanut, sesame and avocado. Their smoke point is higher than most other oils.
7. Olive oil is excellent for sautéing and for salad dressings.
8. Store all opened bottles of oil in your refrigerator.

Oven Temperatures: You'll find most recipes call for a specific temperature. Here are additional guidelines:

Slow oven	300°–325°	Roast nuts and seeds. Bake granolas
Moderate Oven	325°–375°	Most baking: cakes, pies, cookies, most breads. Most roasted meats and casseroles.
Hot Oven	over 375°	Muffins (400–425°). Baked or "oven fried" fish (425–450°)

Poach: Julia Child describes poaching as cooking in "barely shimmering" water—never a rolling boil. Temporarily raise temperature as foods are added. Lower again at the first sign of bubbles.

Cook uncovered, with the water barely moving, until tender.

Best items for poaching include fish, boneless chicken breasts and eggs without shells. (See Poached Fish, page 220.)

Quinoa: A grain-like food that is related to beets, spinach and chard. The National Academy of Sciences called quinoa "the best vegetable source of protein" because it contains an ideal balance of amino acids. Other researchers have called it a "near-perfect food" because of the ideal amounts of protein, complex carbohydrates and natural oils.

Important tip: The outer coating of the seeds contains a naturally bitter substance which fortunately is water soluble. To remove it, wash the whole quinoa seeds thoroughly. Swish them vigorously, changing the water 3 to 5 times, or until the rinse water runs clear without foaming. Cook like rice, for 15 minutes, with twice as much water and a pinch of salt. (See "Cooked Quinoa," page 125.)

Quinoa flour is available in some health food stores. Use it as a grain substitute in tortillas, breads and other baked products. Flour is difficult to make because there is no way to remove the bitter coating.

Rice Flour: Available in health food stores, ground from either white or brown rice. Generally a drier flour than wheat, but very popular with people who have to avoid wheat. Ener-G Foods offers many rice-based products in health food stores. You can also order them by mail. (However, many contain sugar.) Their rice bread or tapioca-rice bread is palatable, especially when you toast it.

Rye Flour: Look for "100% Rye" on the label (some rye flours also contain wheat). You can substitute rye flour in any recipe (except a yeast bread) calling for whole wheat flour. This includes tortillas, cookies, pie crusts and cakes. If you're sensitive to wheat, you may also react to rye because wheat and rye are related. Yet some people tolerate rye very well.

Salt: Sea salt is a pure product available in health food stores and some supermarkets. Kosher salt is also pure, though more coarse. Other salts may contain some corn starch or sugar.

Sauté (as used in this book): To cook a food lightly using very little oil—often olive oil—over medium heat. Meat, fish and fowl can be sautéed. A combination vegetable sauté might include sliced onions, peppers, mushrooms, garlic, celery and carrot (or any of these alone). The food is never breaded, and the oil is never deep. The process is brief, perhaps 10 minutes. If you wish, cover the pan during the last half of cooking to steam and soften vegetables.

If you want to lower the fat content of your diet even more, Burt Wolf suggests that you "sauté" using water and herbs, rather than oil.

Spices: Spices should be avoided initially. Later, a single spice can be tested on a food that you tolerate well.

Spices are generally parts of plants such as berries, bark, seeds or roots. They can be hot, sweet or tangy. Cinnamon, cloves and nutmeg are amazingly potent allergens. To test a spice, sprinkle it on a single food that agrees with you. Example: If adding cinnamon to applesauce causes a reaction, but apples don't, assume cinnamon is the culprit. Other spice examples include caraway, pepper, sesame and ginger.

Starches: These dry, flour-like powders are derived from dehydrated roots. They include potato, poi, arrowroot, tapioca and kudzu. Look for them in health food stores. (See Food Sources.)

Although each of the starches possess slightly different characteristics, any of them can be used to thicken sauces and puddings. Here are suggestions:

1. Use 1 tablespoon of starch per 1 cup of liquid for sauces.
2. Use 2 tablespoons of starch per 1 cup of liquid for puddings.
3. Remove from heat as soon as the liquid reaches a full, rolling boil (or boil 1 minute if the recipe directs it).

The thin liquid mixture thickens more as it cools. Prolonged boiling tends to break down starches so the mixture becomes less thick—even watery.

Steam: To cook quickly over water in a tightly covered pot. Equipment ranges from expensive gourmet cookware to a $5 collapsible "steamer" basket. Boil ½ to ¾ inch of water in a large saucepan. Put the food in the basket and place in a tightly covered pan. Any food can be steamed, including vegetables, meat, fish and poultry.

Stir-fry: To cook chopped, sliced or diced food quickly in a small amount of oil over relatively high heat, generally using a wok. Use large spoons in each hand to constantly lift and turn the food. A typical stir-fry serving 2–4 people takes 10 to 15 minutes to cook tender-crisp. The secret of successful stir-fry cooking is advance food preparation, and cooking quickly.

Vegetables should be washed, thoroughly dried, then sliced, diced or chopped. Wet vegetables may splatter in hot oil, and the addition of water slows cooking and produces a stew.

When all food is prepared, place in bowls arranged with longest-cooking items to be used first. Meat and fowl should be cooked first, removed, and re-added after shorter-cooking vegetables are nearly done.

Preheat wok, or large sauté pan. Add 1–3 teaspoons of oil and swirl to cover entire pan. Quickly add foods and toss. Add 1–2 cups at a time, and allow a few minutes to heat thoroughly. Continue until all is cooked tender-crisp. If using a sauce, add for the last few minutes of cooking.

Teff: A new-to-us non-gluten grain. In a separate tribe, far removed from wheat, it makes a wonderful alternative. High in protein and fiber: fair source of calcium and iron. Absorbs more water than amaranth, quiona or buckwheat—so cook in 4 times the water. (see Cooked Teff, page 125) Available as whole seed or flour.

Teff was brought from Ethiopia by Wayne Carlson, who spent a few years there with the Peace corps in the '70s. He now grows it in the Northwest (1318 Willow, Caldwell, ID 83605), and markets it nationally.

Vitamin C Crystals: Following the lead of Nobel Prize winner Linus Pauling, millions of Americans take vitamin C (ascorbic acid). It is available in health food stores and pharmacies in pills, capsules, powders and crystals. Some powders and crystals are "buffered." This means sodium or calcium has been added to neutralize the acid. Other powders and crystals are "unbuffered."

"Unbuffered" crystals taste sour or "sharp"—like vinegar, and are used in many recipes to provide a tang. They're also used in combination with baking soda as a substitution for baking powder. Some people may not tolerate cream of tartar (made from grapes), corn starch, or potato starch. Others may wish to avoid the aluminum in commercial preparations. For best leavening results, dissolve crystals in a small amount of warm water.

Corn-free vitamin C crystals are available in many health food stores and pharmacies, or can be ordered from Freeda Vitamins and Bronson Pharmaceuticals (see pages 354-359).

Wraps: There are several ways you can wrap and store foods in your refrigerator or freezer. Each method has advantages and disadvantages.

1. *Plastic films and containers:* Plastic containers, sheets and bags are inexpensive and convenient. The sheets seal in the contents and keep out odors. A word of caution: Tiny amounts of petrochemicals can be absorbed by food stored in plastics and can cause symptoms in people who are bothered by chemical sensitivities.*

2. *Cellophane wrap and bags:* Cellophane is derived from wood and is tolerated by individuals with chemical sensitivities. It can be ordered from Erlanders or The Living Source (see pages 354-359).

3. *Aluminum foil:* Convenient and inexpensive. Because of the possible relationship of aluminum to Alzheimer's disease,** some people avoid aluminum pots, pans and wraps. If you use foil, put the shiny side toward the food.

4. *Wax paper:* Convenient and inexpensive. Because it's dusted with corn, wax paper may bother some corn-sensitive people.

---

*If you're sensitive to chemicals, use glass containers and/or cellophane sheets and bags. (For further discussion of chemicals and chemical sensitivities, see *The Yeast Connection,* pages 145–156.)

**See Martyn, C.N., et al, *The Lancet,* January 14, 1989, pages 59–62.

Food and Product Sources

Some of these sources were obtained from the Allergy Products Directory (APD). This directory includes over 1,000 sources for specialty foods. To obtain ordering information, send a SASE to P.O. Box 640, Menlo Park, CA 94026.

Allergy Resources, Inc.
195 Huntington Beach Drive
Colorado Springs, CO 80921
1-800-873-3529

Flaxseed oil. Condiments. Baking goods. Dairy substitutes. Complete line of supplies. Cotton pillows. Air and water purifiers.***

Apple Pie Farm, Inc.
Union Hill Road, RD#1
Malvern, PA 19355
(215) 933-4215

Fresh herbs. Edible flowers. Baby vegetables.*

Arrowhead Mills, Inc.
P.O. Box 2059
Hereford, TX 79045
(806) 364-0730

Cereals, flours, vegetable oils, amaranth, quinoa and teff.**

Bandon Sea-Pack
P.O. Box 5688
Charleston, OR 97420

Silver salmon and tuna packed in glass.*

Briggs Way Company
Ugashilk, Alaska 99683

Glass-canned salmon (shipped by the case).*

Birkett Mills
P.O. Box 440-A
Penn-Yam, NY 14527
(315) 536-3311

Unroasted buckwheat groats or flour.*

Bronson Pharmaceuticals
4526 Rinetti Lane
La Canada, CA 91011–0628

Vitamin C Crystals, sugar-free and corn-free.

Butte Creek Mill
P.O. Box 56 (APD)
Eagle Point, OR 97524
(503) 826-3531

Barley, corn, oat, rice, rye, soy and millet flours.*

Chicago Dietetic Supply, Inc.
405 Shawmut Avenue
P.O. Box 40
LaGrange, IL 60525
(312) 352-6900

Cellu cereals, flours and fruits, vegetables, baking powder, rice cakes.*

Community Mill and Bean
RD 1, Route 89
Savannah, NY 13146
(315) 365-2664

Flour, mixes, beans, grains, cereals.
Minimum 100 pounds.*

Country Pride Meats
P.O. Box 6
Ipswich, SD 57451
(605) 426-6343
(605) 426-6288

Buffalo meat.*

Czimer Food, Inc.
Route 10, Box 285
Lockport, IL 60441
(312) 460-7152
(312) 460-7293

Organic foods, exotic meats, game, game
birds. Come packed in dry ice.*

D'Angelo Brothers Products, Inc.
909 South 9th Street
Philadelphia, PA 19147
(215) 923-5637

Wild game.*

Deer Valley Farm
RD 1, Route 89
Savannah, NY 13146
(315) 365-2664

Meats, produce, grains, baked goods, wide
variety of products.*

Del Farm Food Company
4610 North Clark Street
Chicago, IL 60600

Taro, mountain potato, yucca, boniata,
ginger, aprioroot, fresh fish.*

Diamond K Enterprises
RR1, Box 30
St. Charles, MN 55972
(507) 932-4308
(507) 932-5433

Barley, corn, millet, oat, rice, rye, soy
flours, barley, buckwheat, corn pancake
mixes, sunflower oil, carob chips, nuts and
fruits.*

Diet House
1826 North 2nd Street
Highland Park, IL 60035
(312) 433-4766

Extensive product line, including basmati
rice, guar gum, variety flours including
amaranth and quinoa. Phone orders only.

Dietary Specialties, Inc.
P.O. Box 227
Rochester, NY 14601
(716) 263-2787

Gluten-free, low-protein, milk-free, egg-free
products. Pastas, breads.*

Dixie Nut Company
512 E. Central Avenue
P.O. Box 159
Fitzgerald, GA 31750
1-800-241-3633 (in GA)
1-800-423-1262 (outside GA)

Pecans and other fresh nuts of all kinds.*

Eagle Agricultural Products
Route 4, Box 4-B
Huntsville, AR 72740
(501) 738-2203

Fresh and dried produce, beans and grains.*

Eden Foods, Inc.
701 Tecumseh Road
Clinton, MI 49236
(517) 456-7424
(517) 983-9400

Gelatin, agar and soy products.*

Elam's
2625 Gardner Road
Broadview, IL 60153

Rice, rye, oatmeal, soy flours, mixes, cereals.*

Ener-G Foods, Inc.
P.O. Box 24723
6901 Fox Avenue, South
Seattle, WA 98124

Rice products, soy quik, poi, flours. Baked yeast-free rice bread (many other products too numerous to mention, but many contain sugar).***

Erlanders
P.O. Box 106
Altadena, CA 91001
(818) 797-7004

Cellophane bags for storing foods.

Fearn Natural Foods
Division of Modern Products
P.O. Box 09398
Milwaukee, WI 53209
(414) 352-3209
1-800-241-2360, Ext. 320

Baking mixes, hearty soup mixes, vegetarian burger mixes, rice flour and soy milk or granules. Carob products. Grain cereals. Flours. Gluten-free, milk-free mixes and baked goods.

Flora
7400 Fraser Park Drive
Burnaby, British Columbia
Canada V5J 5B9

Flaxseed oil.*

J. Francis Company
Route 3, Box 54
Atlanta, TX 75551

Pecans. Minimum 5–10 lbs.*

Freeda Vitamins Inc.
36 East 41st. St.
New York, NY 10017
(212) 685-4980
1-800-777-3737

Vita-C Crystals. Product Code 0150. Used in place of vinegar and lemon juice in many recipes in this book.

Giusto's
241 East Harris Avenue
South San Francisco, CA 94080
(415) 873-6566

Various flours.*

Gold Mine Natural Food Co.
1947—30th Street
San Diego, CA 92102
1-800-647-2927 (CA)
1-800-647-2929 (US)

Brown rice, beans, macrobiotic items, wide variety of goods.*

Hain Pure Food, Inc.
13660 South Figueroa
P.O. Box 5481 Terminal Annex
Los Angeles, CA 90054

Soups, tomato sauce, vegetable oils, cashew and almond butter.***

Haypoint Farms
Box 292, Sugar Island
Sault Ste. Marie, MI 49783
(906) 632-1280

Whole grains and products, cereals. Min. 10 lbs.*

Health Valley Natural Foods, Inc.
700 Union Street
Montebello, CA 90640
(213) 724-2211

Wheat-free, milk-free cereals and baked goods. Frozen vegetables. Potato chips.***

Jaffe Brothers
P.O. Box 636
Valley Center, CA 92082
(619) 749-1133

Nuts, grains, beans, assorted goods.*

Krystal Wharf Farms
RD 2, Box 191A
Mansfield, PA 16933
(717) 549-8194

Grains, beans, nuts, dried fruit, fresh produce and other products.*

The Living Source
3500 McArthur Drive
Waco, TX 76708
(817) 756-6341

Cellophane bags and other cellophane products for wrapping and storing foods.

Midwest Nut and Seed Company,
    Inc.
1332 West Grand
Chicago, IL 60622

Nuts and seeds.*

Millstream Marketing
1310A E. Tallmadge Avenue
Akron, Oh 44310
(216) 630-2700

Produce, nuts, grains, cereals.

Mountain Ark Trading Company
120 South East Avenue
Fayetteville, AR 72701

Produce, grains, wide selection of products, macrobiotic items.*

New Dimensions
16548 E. Laser, Suite A7
Fountain Hills, AZ 85268

Flax seed oil.**

Nutritional Food Products
64959 Lincoln
Mecca, CA 92254
(619) 396-2116

Cereals.***

Nu-World Amaranth, Inc.
P.O. Box 2202
Naperville, IL 60566
(312) 369-6819

Amaranth (whole seed, flour, puffed, granola and flour blends). Write or call for a free brochure.*

Olde Fashioned Foods, Inc.
123 North 18th Street
Fort Smith, AR 92901
(501) 782-6183

Various flours.*

Once Again Nut Butter, Inc.
12 South State Street
Nunda, NY 14517
(716) 468-2535

Organic nuts and nut and seed butters.*

Post Rock Natural Grains
Route 1, Box 24
Luray, KS 67649
(913) 648-2382

Amaranth seed and flour.*

J. H. O'Neal
P.O. Box 565
Donalsonville, GA 31745

Nuts, especially pecans.*

Shiloh Farms
Box 97, Highway 59
Sulphur Springs, AR 72768
(501) 298-3297

Bottled water, vegetables, nuts, whole grains, flours.***

Sisu Enterprises
1734 Broadway, Suite 6
Vancouver, British Columbia
Canada V6J 1Y1

Flax seed oil.**

Special Foods
9207 Shotgun Court
Springfield, VA 22153
(703) 644-0991

Wide variety of grain-free pastas. Over 150 products including yeast-, milk-, egg-, grain-free breads, flour, and baked products. Also, nut butters, pancake mixes and mayonnaise.*

Spectrum Marketing, Inc.
133 Copeland Street
Petaluma, CA 94952

Flax seed oil.**

Tropical Nut and Fruit Co.
11517-A Cordage Road
P.O. Box 7507
Charlotte, NC 28217

Unprocessed nuts.*

Weisenberger Flour Mills
P.O. Box 215
Weisenberger Road
Midway, KY 40347
(606) 254-5282

Grains. Flours.*

Ms. Ann Fisk, R.N.
An Ounce of Prevention
3 Twilight Dr.
Denver, CO 80215
303-232-5324.

yeast-free vitamins,
mineral supplements,
flaxseed oil, air and
water purifiers, cellophane bags, cotton
products, hypoallergenic cosmetics and
laundry supplies, dietary consultation

Maskal Teff
1318 Willow
Caldwell, ID 83605
(208) 454-3330

Teff-whole seed and flower

The following distributors require a large minimum order, and are more appropriate for group orders or buying clubs.

Magnolia Warehouse
1036 White Street, SW
Atlanta, GA 30310
(404) 755-2667

North Farm Cooperative Warehouse
204 Regas Road
Madison, WI 53714
(608) 241-3995

North Coast Cooperative
3134 Jacobs Avenue
Eureka, CA 95501
(707) 445-3185

Ozark Cooperative Warehouse
P.O. Box 30
Fayetteville, AR 72702-0030
(501) 521-COOP

Quinoa Corporation
P.O. Box 1039
Torrance, CA 90505
(213) 530-8666

For a more comprehensive list, send a stamped, self-addressed envelope to Americans for Safe Food, 1501—16th Street, NW, Washington, DC 20036.

---

*Foods available by mail order.
**Foods usually found in health food stores.
***Foods available by phone and mail.

Recommended Reading

Adams, R., and Murray, F.: *Improving Your Health With Zinc*, New York, NY, Larchmont, June 1978.

*Bahna, S. L., and Heiner, D. C.: *Allergies to Milk*, Springfield, Illinois, Charles C. Thomas, 1980.

Bassett, B.: *The Healthy Gourmet Cookbook*, Carson City, Nevada, Bestways Magazine, Inc., 1981.

Bland, J.: *Managing the Burnout Syndrome*, Gig Harbor, Washington, HealthCom, Inc., 1989.

*Body, G. P., and Fainstein, V.: *Candidiasis*, Raven Press, New York, 1975.

*Breneman, J. C.: *Handbook of Food Allergies*, New York, Marcel Dekker, Inc., 1987.

*Brostoff, J., and Challacombe, S. J.: *Food Allergy and Intolerance*, Eastbourne, East Sussex, BN21 3UN, England. Balliere Tindall, 33 D Ave., and Philadelphia, Pennsylvania, W. B. Saunders, 1987.

Bryce-Smith D., and Hodgkinson, L.: *The Zinc Solution*, London, Century Arrow, 1985.

Burros, M. F., *Keep It Simple: 30-Minute Meals From Scratch*, New York, William Morrow and Company, Inc., 1981.

Burros, M. F., *You've Got It Made*, New York, William Morrow and Company, 1984.

Cheraskin, E., Ringsdorf, W. M., and Clark, J. W.: *Diet and Disease*, New Canaan, Connecticut, Keats Publishing Co.

Cleave, T. L.: *The Saccharine Disease*, New Canaan, Connecticut, Keats Publishing Company, 1975.

Connolly, P.: *Candida Albicans Yeast-Free Cookbook*, New Canaan, Connecticut, Keats Publishing Company, 1985.

Crook, W. G., and Stevens, L. J.: *Solving the Puzzle of Your Hard-to-Raise Child*, New York, Random House, and Jackson, Tennessee, Professional Books, 1987.

Crook, W. G.: *The Yeast Connection*, 3rd Edition, Jackson, Tennessee, Professional Books, and New York City, Vintage Books Division, Random House, 1986.

Davies, S., and Stewart, A.: *Nutritional Medicine—The Drug Free Guide to Better Family Health*, New York, Avon Books, 1989.

Egan, J. P.: *Healthy High Fiber Cooking*, H. P. Brooks, 1988.

Erasmus, Udo: *The Complete Guide to Fats and Oils in Health and Nutrition*, Vancouver, British Columbia, Canada, Alive Books, 1987.

Faelten, S., and editors of *Prevention Magazine: Allergy Self-Help Book*, Emmaus, Pennsylvania, Rodale Press, 1983.

Galland, L.: *Superimmunity for Kids*, New York, Dutton, 1988.

Gerrard, J. W. (ed.): *Understanding Allergies*, Springfield, Illinois, Charles C. Thomas, 1973.

Gerras, C.: *Feasting on Raw Foods*, Emmaus, Pennsylvania, Rodale Press, 1980.

Gerras, C.: *Rodale's Basic Natural Foods*, Emmaus, Pennsylvania, Rodale Press, 1981, and Simon & Schuster, 1988.

Goldbeck, N. and D.: *The Goldbecks' Guide to Good Food*, New York, New American Library, October, 1987.

Golos, N., and Golbitz, F. G.: *Coping with Your Allergies* (revised paperback edition), New York, Simon and Schuster, 1985.

Golos, N., and Golbitz, F. G.: *If This Is Tuesday, It Must Be Chicken*, New Canaan, Connecticut, Keats Publishing Co., 1981.

*Golos, N., O'Shea, J., and Waickman, F.: *Environmental Medicine*, New Canaan, Connecticut, Keats Publishing Company, 1987.

Gottlieb, I., editor: *Cooking for the Health of It*, Nutrition for Optimal Health Association, P.O. Box 380, Winnetka, Illinois 60093, 1979.

Griffin, G. G., and Castelli, W.: *Good Fat, Bad Fat—How to Lower Your Cholesterol and Beat the Odds of a Heart Attack*, Tucson, Arizona, Fisher Books, 1989.

Hall, R. H., *Food for Nought*, Hagerstown, Maryland, and New York, Harper and Row, 1974.

Hunter, B. T.: *Food Additives and Your Health*, New Canaan, Connecticut, Keats Publishing Company, 1972.

Hunter, B. T.: *Whole Grain Baking Sampler*, New Canaan, Connecticut, Keats Publishing Company, 1972.

Hunter, B. T.: *The Sugar Trap and How to Avoid It*, New York, Houghton Mifflin, 1982.

Hunter, B. T.: *Be Kitchen Wise*, Sydney, Australia, Allen and Unwin, 1986.

Hunter, B. T.: *Yogurt, Kefir and Other Cultured Milk Products*, New Canaan Connecticut, Keats Publishing Company, 1973.

Jacobson, M. F.: *The Complete Eaters Guide and Nutrition Scoreboard*, New York, Doubleday Anchor Books, 1985. (Available from CSPI Publications, 1501–16th St., NW, Washington, DC 20036)

Jones, M.: *The Allergy Self-Help Cookbook*, Emmaus, Pennsylvania, Rodale Press, 1984.

Langer, S. L., and Scheer, J.F.: *Solved The Riddle of Illness*, New Canaan, Connecticut, Keats Publishing Company, 1984.

Lappé, F. M.: *Diet for a Small Planet*, New York, Ballantine, Inc., 1986.

Lee, W. H.: *The Friendly Bacteria*, New Canaan, Connecticut, Keats Publishing Company, 1988.

Levin, A. S., and Dadd, D.L.: *Consumer Guide for the Chemically Sensitive*, 1982. (Available from Alan S. Levin, 450 Sutter, Suite 1138, San Francisco, California 84105)

Levin, A. S., and Zellerback, M.: *Type 1/Type 2 Allergy Relief Program*, Los Angeles, California, Jeremy D. Tarcher, Inc., Distributed by Houghton Mifflin Company, Boston, Massachusetts, 1983.

Lorenzani, S.: *Candida: A Twentieth Century Disease*, New Canaan, Connecticut, Keats Publishing Company, 1984.

Mannerberg, D., and Roth, J.: *Aerobic Nutrition*, New York, Hawthorne/Dutton, 1981.

McGee, C. T.: *How to Survive Modern Technology*, New Canaan, Connecticut, Keats Publishing Co., 1979.

Nugent, N., and the editors of *Prevention Magazine: Food and Nutrition*, Emmaus, Pennsylvania, Rodale Press, 1983.

Null, G.: *The Complete Guide to Health and Nutrition*, New York, Delacorte Press, 1984.

Null, G.: *Complete Guide to Healing Your Body Naturally*, New York, McGraw-Hill, 1988.

Null, G. with Feldman, M.: *Good Food, Good Mood—Treating Your Hidden Allergies*, New York, Dodd Mead and Company, 1988.

Odds, F. C.: *Candida and Candidosis*, Baltimore, University Park Press, 1988 (second edition).

Oski, F.: *Don't Drink Your Milk*, New York, Wyden Books, 1977, and Mollica Press, Ltd., 1914 Teall Ave., Syracuse, New York 13206, 1983.

Passwater, R. A.: *Evening Primrose Oil*, New Canaan, Connecticut, Keats Publishing Company, 1981.

Pfeiffer, C. C.: *Zinc and Other Micronutrients*, New Canaan, Connecticut, Keats Publishing Company, 1978.

Price, W. A.: *Nutrition and Physical Degeneration*, Berkeley, California, Parker House, 1981. (Available from Price-Pottenger Foundation, P.O. Box 2614, La Mesa, California, 92014)

Prince, F., and Prince, H.: *Feed Your Kids Bright*, New York, Simon and Schuster, 1987.

Pritikin, N., with McGrady, Jr., PM: *The Pritikin Program for Diet and Exercise*, New York, Grosset & Dunlap, 1979.

Pritikin, N.: *The Pritikin Permanent Weight Loss Manual*, New York, Bantam Books, 1982.

Randolph, T. G., and Moss, R.: *An Alternative Approach to Allergies*, New York, Harper and Row, 1980.

Rapp, D. J.: *Allergies and Your Family*, Sterling Publishing Company, 1981.

Reading, C. M., and Meillon, R. S.: *Your Family Tree Connection*, New Canaan, Connecticut, Keats Publishing Company, 1987.

Remington, D. W., and Higa, B. W.: *Back to Health: Yeast Control*, Provo, Utah, Vitality Health, 1986.

Remington, R. D., Fisher, G., and Parent, E.: *How to Lower Your Fat Thermostat*, Provo, Utah, Vitality Health, 1983.

Rippere, V.: *The Allergy Problem, Why People Suffer and What Should Be Done*, Wellingborough, Northhamptomshire, England, Thorson Publishing, Ltd., 1983.

*Rippon, J. W.: *Medical Mycology*, (2nd Edition). Philadelphia, Pennsylvania, W. B. Saunders, 1982.

Rogers, S. A.: *The EI Syndrome*, Prestige Publishers, Box 3161, Syracuse, New York, 1986.

Rogers, S.: *You Are What You Ate, A Macrobiotic Way*. Prestige Publishers, Box 3161, Syracuse, New York, 1986.

Rousseau, D., Rea, W., and Enwright, J.: *Your Home, Your Health and Well-Being*, Vancouver, British Columbia, Canada, Hartley and Marks, LTD, 1988, and New Canaan, Connecticut, Keats Publishing Company.

Rudin, D. O., and Felex, C.: *The Omega III Phenomenon*, New York, Rawson Associates, 1987.

Rudoff, C.: *The Allergy Gourmet*, Menlo Park, California, Prologue Publications, 1983.

Schroeder, H. A.: *The Poisons Around Us* (Toxic material in food, air and water), Indiana University Press, Indiana, 1974.

Stanley, M. (editor): *Microwave Vegetables,* a Better Homes and Garden Book, Des Moines, Iowa, Meredith Corporation, 1986.

Stevens, L. J.: *The Complete Book of Allergy Control,* New York, New York, Macmillan Publishing Company, 1983.

Trowbridge, J. P., and Walker, M.: *The Yeast Syndrome,* New York, New York, Bantam Books, 1986.

Truss, C. O.: *The Missing Diagnosis,* 1983. (Available from P.O. Box 26508, Birmingham, Alabama 35226)

Walker, Nicole: *Sugar-Free Cooking, Vol. I and II,* 1341 67 St., Downers Grove, Illinois 60515.

*Werbach, M. R.: *Nutritional Influences on Illness,* New Canaan, Connecticut, Keats Publishing Company, 1988.

Williams, R. J.: *Physicians Handbook of Nutritional Science,* Springfield, Illinois, Charles C. Thomas, 1978.

Wunderlich, R. C., Jr., and Kalita, D.: *Candida Albicans and the Human Condition,* New Canaan, Connecticut, Keats Publishing Company, 1984.

Wunderlich, R. C., Jr.: *Sugar and Your Health,* St. Petersburg, Florida, Johnny Reads, Inc., Good Health Productions, 1982.

*Denotes books of special interest to physicians.

References

Baker, S. M., and Galland, L.: "Whole Person Medicine," Health by Choice Conference, Atlanta, April 1986. (Tapes available from InstaTape, Inc., P.O. Box 1729, Monrovia, CA 91016)

Baker, S. M.: "Notes on the Yeast Problem," Gesell Institute, 310 Prospect St., New Haven, Connecticut 06511.

Blume, E.: "Overdosing on Protein," *Nutrition Action Healthletter,* Volume 14, March, 1987, pp. 1, 4, 6. (Published by CSPI, 1501 16th St., NW, Washington, DC 20036)

Brody, Jane: *Jane Brody's Good Food Book,* New York, Bantam Books Edition, 1987, pages 7–8, 67, 74.

Candida Update Conference, Memphis, Tennessee, September 15–18, 1988 (sponsored by the International Health Foundation, Box 3494, Jackson, Tennessee 38303). Tapes available.

Daniel 1:1–20, Good News Bible: The Bible in Today's English Version. American Bible Society, New York, pp. 954–955, 1976.

Hall, R. H.: *Food for Nought,* New York, Harper and Row, 1974, pp. 7–31.

Hippocrates. As quoted by Bell, I. R.: Clinical Ecology, Bolinas, California, Common Knowledge Press, 1982, page 7.

Iwata, K., and Yamamoto, Y.: Glycoprotein Toxins produced by Candida Albicans, reprinted from the proceedings of the Fourth International Conference on the Mycoses, June, 1977. PAHO, Scientific Publications #356.

Iwata, K.: In *Recent Advances in Medical and Veterinary Mycology,* University of Tokyo Press, Tokyo, 1977.

Iwata, K., and Uchida, K.: Cellular Immunity in Experimental Fungus Infections in Mice, Medical Mycology, Films, January, 1977.

Kroker, G. F.: "Chronic Candidiasis and Allergy," (in Brostoff, J. and Challacombe, S. J.) *Food Allergy and Intolerance,* Balliere Tindall, 33 D Avenue, East Sussex, BN 21 3UN, England, and Saunders, W. B., West Washington Square, Philadelphia, Pennsylvania, pages 850–872.

Lappé, F. M.: Diet for a Small Planet, New York, Ballantine, Inc., 1986.

Oski, F.: *Don't Drink Your Milk*, New York, Wyden Books, 1977 and Mollica Press, Ltd., 1914 Teall Ave., Syracuse, New York, 13206, 1983, pages 8, 9, 85–88.

"Our Bodies, Ourselves," The Boston Women's Health Book Collective, 465 Mount Auburn Street, Watertown, Maine 02172.

Position Statements: "Candidiasis Hypersensitivity Syndrome," approved by the Executive Committee of the American Academy of Allergy and Immunology, The Journal of Allergy and Clinical Immunology, 78:271–273, 1986.

Report I, Part II, of The Allergy Panel, Council on Scientific Affairs, American Medical Association: Invivo Diagnostic Testing and Immunotherapy for Allergy, JAMA, 258:1507 (Sept. 18, 1987).

Rippon, J. W.: As quoted by Crook, W. G., *The Yeast Connection*, 3rd Edition, Jackson, Tennessee, Professional Books, and New York City, Vintage Press, Division of Random House, 1986, pages 71–77.

Rosenberg, E. W., et al: (Letters) Crohn's Disease and Psoriasis, New England Journal of Medicine, 308:101, January 13, 1983.

Rosenberg, E. W., et al and Baker, S.: Archives of Dermatology, 1984. Vol. 120, April, page 436.

Schroeder, H. A.: "The Poisons Around Us: Toxic Metals in Food, Air and Water," Indiana University Press, Bloomington, Indiana, 1974.

Truss, C. O.: "Tissue Injury Induced by C. Albicans: Mental and Neurologic Manifestations." J. of Ortho. Psych., 7:17–37, 1978.

Truss C. O.: "Restoration of Immunologic Competence to C. Albicans." J. of Ortho. Psych., 9:287–301, 1980.

Truss, C. O.: "The Role of Candida Albicans in Human Illness." J. of Ortho. Psych., 10:228–238, 1981.

Truss, C. O.: "Metabolic Abnormalities in Patients with Chronic Candidiasis." J. of Ortho. Psych., 13:66–93, 1984.

Truss, C. O.: *The Missing Diagnosis*, 1983 (Available from P.O. Box 26508, Birmingham, Alabama 35226).

Von Hilsheimer, G. L.: Acidophilus and the Ecology of the Human Gut, J. of Ortho. Psych., 11:3, 204–207, 1982.

Walker, W. A.: "Role of the Mucosal Barrier in Antigen Handling by the Gut," in Brostoff, J., and Challacombe, S. J., *Food and Allergy Intolerance*, London, Balliere Tindall, Philadelphia, Pennsylvania, W. B. Saunders, 1987, pp. 209–222.

Witkin, S. S.: "Defective Immune Responses in Patients with Recurrent Candidiasis," Infections in Medicine, May/June, 1985, p. 129–132.

Wunderlich, R. C.: As quoted by Crook, W. G., *The Yeast Connection*, "A Special Message for the Physician" (Introductory Section), Jackson, Tennessee, Professional Books, and New York, Random House, 3rd Edition, 1986.

Subject Index

Recipe Index

About the Authors

William G. Crook, M.D., received his medical education at the University of Virginia, the Pennsylvania Hospital, Vanderbilt and Johns Hopkins, and has been caring for patients since 1949. He currently specializes in allergy, environmental and preventive medicine.

He is a Fellow of the American Academy of Pediatrics, the American College of Allergy and Immunology, the American Academy of Environmental Medicine and a member of the American Medical Association, the American Academy of Allergy and Alpha Omega Alpha.

Dr. Crook is the author of numerous scientific articles and eight previous books. For 15 years he wrote a nationally syndicated column (General Features and Los Angeles Times Syndicate).

He has addressed professional and lay groups in 38 states, 7 Canadian provinces, Australia, England, Holland, Italy, Malaysia, Mexico, New Zealand and Venezuela. He has served as a Visiting Professor at Ohio State University and the Universities of California (SF) and Saskatchewan.

During the past 15 years, Dr. Crook has presented his observations to physicians at the following medical schools: Georgetown, Johns Hopkins, University of Texas at San Antonio, University of California at San Francisco, University of South Florida at Tampa, University of California at Torrance, Vanderbilt University, Universities of Minnesota and Tennessee, Thomas Jefferson University in Philadelphia, and Stanford University.

Dr. Crook has been referred to as a "preventive medicine crusader" who says, "The road to better health will not be found through more drugs, doctors and hospitals. Instead, it will be discovered through better nutrition and changes in lifestyles."

Dr. Crook lives in Jackson, Tennessee, with his wife Betsy. They have three daughters and four grandchildren. His interests include golf, oil painting and travel.

Marjorie Hurt Jones, R.N., received her bachelor of science in biology from Illinois Wesleyan University, Bloomington, Illinois, and her nursing education at the Northwestern Memorial Hospital, Chicago, Illinois.

She is a member of the American Academy of Environmental Medicine, the International Association of Preventive Medicine, the Nutrition for Optimal Health Association and the Human Ecology Action League.

Because of her own sensitivities to wheat and other grains, Marge conducted original research with the non-grain alternatives, amaranth and quinoa. Subsequently, she established new applications for these foods in allergy-restricted diets. She has also featured tasty, less commonly used vegetables in her own diet and in her recommendations for others—especially those with food sensitivities.

Marge has presented her observations before a number of professional and lay groups, including the American Association of Cereal Chemists, the American Academy of Environmental Medicine, the Rocky Mountain Environmental Health Association, and the Nutrition for Optimal Health Association.

She is the author of *The Allergy Self-Help Cookbook* (Rodale Press) and *Allergy Recipes: Baking with Amaranth.* She serves as a nutritional consultant to professionals and non-professionals and publishes a monthly newsletter, *Mastering Food Allergies.* She also serves as president of MAST Enterprises, Inc.

TIRED—SO TIRED!
AND THE "YEAST CONNECTION"
William G. Crook, MD

Every day, millions of people complain that they are tired. In fact, studies show that fatigue is one of the most common problems for which people seek help from a physician. But tests often fail to provide an explanation of chronic fatigue. *Tired—So Tired!* explains why so many people experience exhaustion and, more important, presents easy-to-follow steps for boosting energy and regaining health.

After years of research, Dr. William G. Crook discovered that sugar and yeast, along with other foods and chemicals to which people can develop sensitivities, are major dietary culprits, and can cause everything from headaches to chronic fatigue syndrome. He also found a connection between fatigue and certain nutrient deficiencies. With this information in mind, the doctor developed a diet and vitamin plan that can eliminate fatigue and related symptoms. *Tired—So Tired!* presents the doctor's treatment program as well as his research on this important subject.

$15.95 • 408 pages • 6 x 9-inch quality paperback • ISBN 978-0-7570-0063-8

THE YEAST CONNECTION HANDBOOK
How Yeasts Can Make You Feel "Sick All Over" and the Steps You Need to Take to Regain Your Health
William G. Crook, MD

Most people don't realize how many health disorders can be caused by yeast. Fatigue, headache, depression, digestive problems, PMS, sexual dysfunction, asthma, ADHD, and autism can all be yeast-related. But once you recognize that yeast is the offender, what can you do to regain your health?

The Yeast Connection Handbook is a great resource for anyone who wants to learn about yeast-related problems. It is comprehensive, not only discussing a wide range of health disorders, but also addressing a wide range of sufferers, including men, women, and children. Most important, this book provides a step-by-step program that effectively relieves health problems through nutritional supplements, dietary changes, medication, and simple lifestyle changes. If you have been looking for a solution to your yeast-related problem, *The Yeast Connection Handbook* provides the information you need to take charge of your health.

$15.95 • 288 pages • 6 x 9-inch quality paperback • ISBN 978-0-7570-0060-7

The Yeast Connection and Women's Health

William G. Crook, MD, with Carolyn Dean, MD, and Elizabeth B. Crook

A growing number of women suffer from chronic health disorders that seem to defy treatment. Their problems, which range from vaginitis to migraines and from multiple sclerosis to depression, interfere with every part of their life. And for too long, there has been no solution.

Finally, hope is at hand in the completely revised and updated *The Yeast Connection and Women's Health.* In this book, Drs. William G. Crook and Carolyn Dean show women who are suffering from a number of debilitating problems how they can take steps to treat existing disorders, and prevent future yeast-related problems. Included is information on diet, both prescription and nonprescription antifungals, lifestyle changes, dietary modifications, and nutritional supplements—all presented in easy-to-understand language and with real-life examples. *The Yeast Connection and Women's Health* is must reading for every woman who wants to restore vibrant health.

$18.95 • 304 pages • 6 x 9-inch quality paperback • ISBN 978-0-7570-0058-4

What You Must Know About Vitamins, Minerals, Herbs & More

Choosing the Nutrients That Are Right for You

Pamela Wartian Smith, MD, MPH

Almost 75 percent of your health and life expectancy is based on lifestyle, environment, and nutrition. Yet even if you follow a healthful diet, you are probably not getting all the nutrients you need to prevent disease. In *What You Must Know About Vitamins, Minerals, Herbs & More,* Dr. Pamela Smith explains how you can restore and maintain health through the wise use of nutrients.

Part One of this easy-to-use guide discusses the individual nutrients necessary for good health. Part Two offers personalized nutritional programs for people with a wide variety of health concerns. People without prior medical problems can look to Part Three for their supplementation plans. Whether you want to maintain good health or you are trying to overcome a medical condition, *What You Must Know About Vitamins, Minerals, Herbs & More* can help you make the best choices for the health and well-being of you and your family.

$15.95 • 448 pages • 6 x 9-inch quality paperback • ISBN 978-0-7570-0233-5

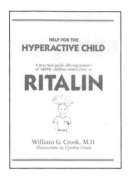

HELP FOR THE HYPERACTIVE CHILD
A Practical Guide Offering Parents of ADHD Children Alternatives to Ritalin
William G. Crook, MD

As hyperactivity in children becomes more and more common, many parents are desperate to find a solution. Although there is no quick fix—prescription medications, for example, can often make the situation worse rather than better—there is an answer that has worked for many families.

Scientific studies have shown that a change in diet—specifically, the restriction of certain foods and the addition of others—can greatly decrease a child's hyperactive tendencies. *Help for the Hyperactive Child* is a user-friendly book that first explains how these dietary modifications can help, and then guides you in pinpointing the foods to which your child may be having adverse reactions. Recipes are included, along with suggestions for making other important lifestyle changes. *Help for the Hyperactive Child* can help *your* hyperactive child.

$16.95 • 272 pages • 8.5 x 11-inch quality paperback • ISBN 978-0-7570-0061-4

SUICIDE BY SUGAR
A Startling Look at Our #1 National Addiction
Nancy Appleton, PhD, and G.N. Jacobs

More than two decades ago, Nancy Appleton's *Lick the Sugar Habit* exposed the health dangers of America's high-sugar diet. Now, in *Suicide by Sugar,* Appleton, along with journalist G.N. Jacobs, presents a broader view of the problems caused by our favorite ingredient. The authors offer startling facts linking a range of disorders—from dementia and hypoglycemia to obesity and cancer—to our growing sugar addiction. Rounding out the book is a sound diet plan along with a number of recipes for sweet, easy-to-prepare, delectable dishes—all made without sugar or fruit.

As children, we fell under the spell of ads that lured us to indulge in all things sweet. Is it any wonder that as adults, so few of us can see the dark side of sugar? *Suicide by Sugar* shines a bright light on our nation's addiction and helps us begin the journey toward health.

$15.95 • 192 pages • 6 x 9-inch quality paperback • ISBN 978-0-7570-0306-6

THE ACID-ALKALINE FOOD GUIDE

A Quick Reference to Foods & Their Effect on pH Levels

Dr. Susan E. Brown and Larry Trivieri, Jr.

In the last few years, researchers around the world have reported the importance of acid-alkaline balance to good health. While thousands of people are trying to balance their body's pH level, until now, they have had to rely on guides containing only a small number of foods. *The Acid-Alkaline Food Guide* is a complete resource for people who want to widen their food choices.

The book begins by explaining how the acid-alkaline environment of the body is influenced by foods. It then presents a list of thousands of foods—single foods, combination foods, and even fast foods—and their acid-alkaline effects. *The Acid-Alkaline Food Guide* will quickly become the resource you turn to at home, in restaurants, and whenever you want to select a food that can help you reach your health and dietary goals.

$7.95 • 208 pages • 4 x 7-inch mass paperback • ISBN 978-0-7570-0280-9

GLYCEMIC INDEX FOOD GUIDE

For Weight Loss, Cardiovascular Health, Diabetic Management, and Maximum Energy

Dr. Shari Lieberman

The glycemic index (GI) is an important nutritional tool. By indicating how quickly a given food triggers a rise in blood sugar, the GI enables you to choose foods that can help you manage a variety of conditions and improve your overall health.

Written by leading nutritionist Dr. Shari Lieberman, this book was designed as an easy-to-use guide to the glycemic index. The book first answers commonly asked questions, ensuring that you truly understand the GI and know how to use it. It then provides both the glycemic index and the glycemic load of hundreds of foods and beverages, including raw foods, cooked foods, and many combination and prepared foods. Whether you are interested in controlling your glucose levels to manage your diabetes, lose weight, increase your heart health, or simply enhance your well-being, *Transitions Lifestyle System Glycemic Index Food Guide* is the best place to start.

$7.95 • 160 pages • 4 x 7-inch mass paperback • ISBN 978-0-7570-0245-8

Eat Smart, Eat Raw
Creative Vegetarian Recipes for a Healthier Life

Kate Wood

As the popularity of raw vegetarian cuisine continues to soar, so does the mounting scientific evidence that uncooked food is amazingly good for you. From healing diseases to detoxifying your body, from lowering cholesterol to eliminating excess weight, the many important health benefits derived from such a diet are too important to ignore. However, now there is another compelling reason to go raw—taste! In her new book *Eat Smart, Eat Raw,* cook and health writer Kate Wood not only explains how to get started, but also provides a wealth of kitchen-tested recipes that are guaranteed to surprise and delight even the fussiest of eaters.

$15.95 • 184 Pages • 7.5 x 9-inch quality paperback • ISBN 978-0-7570-0261-8

Going Wild in the Kitchen
The Fresh & Sassy Tastes of Vegetarian Cooking

Leslie Cerier

Go wild in the kitchen! Be creative! Venture beyond the usual beans, grains, and vegetables to include an exciting variety of organic vegetarian fare in your meals. Step outside the box and prepare dishes with beautiful edible flowers; flavorful wild mushrooms, herbs, and berries; tangy sheep and goat cheeses; tasty sea vegetables; and exotic ancient grains like teff, quinoa, and Chinese "forbidden" black rice. Author and expert chef Leslie Cerier is crazy about the great taste and goodness of organically grown foods. In this exciting cookbook, she shares scores of her favorite recipes that spotlight these fresh, wholesome ingredients.

$16.95 • 240 Pages • 7.5 x 9-inch quality paperback • ISBN 978-0-7570-0091-1